Bodies at Risk

THE SUNY SERIES IN
POSTMODERN CULTURE
Joseph Natoli, Editor

Bodies at Risk

Unsafe Limits
in Romanticism and Postmodernism

Robert Burns Neveldine

State University of New York Press

Published by
State University of New York Press, Albany

©1998 State University of New York

For information, address State University of New York
Press, State University Plaza, Albany, NY, 12246

Production by Diane Ganeles
Marketing by Anne M. Valentine

Library of Congress Cataloging-in-Publication Data

Neveldine, Robert Burns.
    Bodies at risk : unsafe limits in romanticism and postmodernism /
Robert Burns Neveldine.
        p.   cm. — (SUNY series in postmodern culture)
    Includes bibliographical references and index.
    ISBN 0-7914-3649-7 (hardcover:alk. paper).—ISBN 0-7914-3650-0
(pbk. : alk. paper)
    1. Body, Human, in literature. 2. Postmodernism (Literature)
3. Romanticism. 4. Literature, Modern—History and criticism.
I. Title. II. Series.
PN56.B62N48   1998
809'.9336—dc21   97-10555
                                                            CIP

10 9 8 7 6 5 4 3 2 1

For My Parents

Le sexe n'est pas une fatalité: c'est une possibilité de vie créatrice.

Michel Foucault

This is the Stone Age of our desire.

Howard Devoto

Contents

Acknowledgments

I thank my original readers—Hazard Adams, Carolyn Allen, Gerry Baldasty, Katherine Cummings, David McCracken, Steven Shaviro, Gail Stygall, and John Treat—for their support and suggestions while I wrote the various parts of this book. I wish especially to acknowledge Kate, my advisor and first reader of much of this material, for her helpfulness, and kindness through difficulties; and Steve for the inspiration his own work has afforded me. Raimonda Modiano read drafts of chapter 1, and provided invaluable advice. Tim Dean and Jason Friedman helped me shape chapter 5 into a more persuasive argument. And I thank the readers for SUNY Press whose thoughtful reports made the publication of this book possible.

My friends, colleagues, and coffee-drinking partners deserve mention for their encouragement and challenging, stimulating conversation: Paul Bravmann, Andy Brown, Gerald Collier, Neile Graham, Therese Grisham, James Gurley, Rohm Gustafson, Liz Taylor Howard, Tiffany Jones, Mark Kawasaki, Paul Keyes, Rick Levin, Kevin Long, Whipple Neely, Roderick Romero, Jenny Schlieps, Dawn Smithson, Vincent Standley, Wendy Swyt, Brian Thomas, Robert Thomas, Eric Winiecki. To my partner, Charles Cook, go my thanks just for being there, somewhere, nearby, while I wrote, stopped, and wrote more.

I'm grateful as well to the editor of the Postmodern Culture series, Joseph Natoli, for supporting my work over several years now; to past and current general editors at SUNY, Carola Sautter and James Peltz; to Diane Ganeles and Anne M. Valentine in production and marketing; and to the following journals where some of this work originally appeared:

"Wordsworth's 'Nutting' and the Violent End of Reading" (chapter 1). *English Literary History* 63 (1996): 657–680.

"Paradox, Resistance, and the Undead Body of the PWA" (chapter 5). *College Literature* 24 (1997): 263–279.

Preface

Call me critical, but I agree with Todd Levin and Laurie Anderson, but not quite with Donald Morton.

Who am I, who are these eminent gentlemen Levin and Morton, why do I agree with Laurie Anderson, and what's the issue?

I'm an early-middle-aged, white, gay male writer with a taste for romanticism and postmodernism, the two main parts of this book. I like to listen to innovative music like Levin's. He's an American composer, roughly my age, a protégé of Philip Glass, whose first album, *Ride the Planet*, came out in 1992 on Glass's adventurous Point Music label. Now, Deutsche Grammophon, the formerly stodgy old German classical label, has apparently just realized the potential of the youth market (Levin has words with this kind of capitalism), and has recently released his second album, *De Luxe*. The longest track, self-titled and a mix like the other tracks, combines operatic female vocals, the London Symphony Orchestra's playing an abrasive postminimalist disco hoedown, and Levin's answers to his own imaginary interview questions, which are out of numerical order and vary in intelligibility—for a full thirty-four minutes. One of his audible commentaries involves new technologies that evoke from Levin a "hype alert": the Information Superhighway, portable PCs, virtual reality. Levin criticizes them all because they represent a version of the future that is supposedly democratic and accessible but is actually exclusive and expensive, beyond the reach of many people's desires, let alone budgets. But whereas Levin's text takes a strictly sociopolitical approach, *my* response is also aesthetic. I cast a jaundiced eye on these new technologies, fundamentally visual and linguistic in nature, because they operate according to an outmoded paradigm: that of imitation. Although they're powerful and useful tools, they depend on and encourage the mimicking of long-standing activities: *virtual* sex, war *games, interactive* research. Revolutionary ways of thinking, feeling, even being, are claimed for cyberspace, despite its looking, to me and Levin, like the same old thing in brand new drag, come sweeping into view.

Laurie Anderson seems to concur, when in her recent song, "The Puppet Motel" (from *Bright Red/Tightrope*), she sings, "They're havin' virtual sex / They're eatin' virtual food. / No wonder these puppets / Are always in a lousy mood." This from a pioneer in the use of high audio and video technology in performance art, someone of deliberately ambiguous sexuality.

Donald Morton, an openly gay, Marxist professor of English at Syracuse University, suggests a like response. In his recent *PMLA* article, entitled "Birth of the Cyberqueer" (May 1995), Morton says much the same thing as Levin, but goes further to take the "ludic (post)modernism" of cyberspace to task for encouraging the "queer" (that is, neobourgeois) subject to exploit the idealism of pleasure over the materialism of need. Although this isn't the space in which to contend with Morton's argument against nearly every kind of postmodernism I love, suffice it to say that, quite in the postmodern fashion he deplores, he seems to confuse the simple surfaces with the complex interiors. He wants postmodernism's apparent dismissal of conceptuality, meaningfulness, determination, causality, knowing, commonality, and political economics to remain the blunt subtext of every discourse from Gilles Deleuze to Eve Kosofsky Sedgwick, from Michel Foucault to Judith Butler. To make his discussion effective, he oversimplifies—as, perhaps, we all do.

However, what becomes immediately *more* apparent is Morton's misconstrual of the crucial concepts of various theorists. "Oedipal regulation," for example, is not irrelevant to Deleuze and Félix Guattari (Morton 378). On the contrary, Oedipus not only continues to function as a powerful social agent within capitalism, but offers the chaotic potentialities of any desiring-machine considered as merely one out of many. Similarly, Morton identifies "a virtual body of Deleuzean pure intensity" (376) pursuing pleasure in the realm of cybersex—except that Deleuze's virtuality is never reducible to such a pleasure, aside from the fact that Deleuze himself couldn't have been less interested in the sorts of sexcapades enabled and fomented via high technology.

Hence my motto, for the moment: Virtual reality is neither. What, then, might be an even realer virtuality than this dogged realism of virtual reality? Such a concept can indeed be found in the avant-garde philosophy of Deleuze and Guattari, who often get gleefully (mis-)appropriated by the denizens of cyberspace. These collaborators form one of the theoretical b(i)ases for this book. "Schizoanalysis, micro-politics, pragmatics, diagrammatism, rhizomatics, cartography" (Gilles Deleuze and Claire Parnet *Dialogues* 125).

Whatever we call it, their philosophy describes and traces the virtual as "the real without being present, the ideal without being abstract" (Deleuze citing Proust in *Difference and Repetition* 208). For my purposes, in attempting to determine what aesthetic objects really *do*, I've observed that they don't so much merely imitate nature, or some other process itself imitating nature, as create *virtual bodies*. Made by authors, these artifacts in turn make a moment(um) of intense, resonating effects, despite their inertia *as* objects, their becoming actual after virtual, their collapse out of method into style. These bodies will vary from person to person, group to group, moment to moment. They're important and valuable precisely because they cannot be easily grasped, reified, or commodified (despite Morton's insistence otherwise). Nevertheless, virtual bodies are often overwhelming and utterly compelling.

Bodies at Risk demonstrates the operations of virtual and actual dangerous and endangered bodies in romanticism and postmodernism within a broadly queer-theoretical context—bodies created by short poems as much as by loud music and life-threatening illness—and is perhaps the first sustained attempt to do so. If the spirit of Nietzsche seems to be hovering behind all these words, whether Deleuze's or mine, it's no accident, since:

> Nature, artistically considered, is no model. It exaggerates, it distorts, it leaves gaps. Nature is *chance*. To study "from nature" seems to me a bad sign: it betrays subjection, weakness, fatalism—this lying in the dust before *petits faits* is unworthy of a *complete* artist. Seeing *what is*—that pertains to a different species of spirit, the *anti-artistic*, the prosaic. One has to know *who* one is . . . [*Twilight of the Idols* 71]

Overture

The Limits of *Bodies at Risk*

- What could an obscure poem by William Wordsworth teach us about reading texts in a postmodern mode?
- Why does Western culture continue returning to the Frankenstein story so obsessively, and what is there about its protocyberneticism that captivates us?
- How can Lacan, Foucault, and Deleuze and Guattari be made to inhabit a single chapter about limits and risk?
- Why is it that Philip Glass's music used to be more methodical and specialized, but has become more stylized and popular?
- How have theorists of the AIDS pandemic dealt with its multiple paradoxes, and how have Hollywood films and theory both reflected and refused each other?

These are some of the questions that have inspired me to write the following five essays. I say inspired, because I've looked for answers without necessarily finding them. In one sense I'm still looking, and it could be that the strenuous effort in itself will be betrayed by the fun, excessiveness, camp, and experimentation of what follows. These chapters are therefore more like well-posed questions than vigorous assertions or tidy conclusions. I can't think of a more appropriate, more appropriately postmodern, approach.

Much as I love it, though, a certain kind of postmodern frivolity is not the dominant mode here. The subject of this book is a corporeal aesthetics that assumes a subversive politics, both intertextual and interpersonal, in romanticism and postmodernism, but it's not a survey or any kind of comprehensive account, and it doesn't discuss aesthetics in isolation or insist upon yet one more theory of art as imitation. Rather it explores the relationship between two main concepts: 1) the limit—the folding of the extreme experience back into artistic theory as well as into private and social life—inaugurated with the romantic period, then revisited and taken to certain extremes in the postmodern; and 2) conflict, the way that specific antagonisms can produce important, perhaps revolutionary, results without having to establish a winner, lift us to a higher synthesis, or cause permanent harm.

In the famous Preface to *The Picture of Dorian Gray*, Oscar Wilde contends that "*the highest as the lowest form of criticism is a mode of autobiography.*" Since this book is about limits, maybe it pursues such critical extremes; but whereas that judgment is left to the reader, my *intention* is certainly autobiographical, in the sense that my choice of subject matter has been personally and professionally motivated. I've been studying romanticism now for almost twenty years, and postmodernism, whether I knew it, all my life. Certain theorists of postmodernism have looked back over cultural history to find precedents: I've done the same, but have gone back only as far as the turn of the nineteenth century, to the epistemic shift, the creation of "man," that Michel Foucault has identified and discussed, especially in *The Order of Things*, as the one that we're still contending with. Although romanticism isn't typically considered a forerunner of postmodernism, and sometimes even gets shunned as the antithesis, I offer a couple examples, in chapters 1 and 2, of how to read romantic texts in such a way as to locate sources of the postmodern there, and to demonstrate a peculiarly postmodern way of reading. Thus I not only discuss what might be important to us about romanticism, but bring distinctly postmodern ways of thinking to bear upon such figures as William Wordsworth, William Godwin, and Mary Shelley. Either one or the other procedure has often been done before; I hope I've done both in a particular way.

The bulk of this book, however, concerns postmodernism proper, though I hope improperly.

In what is for me the most interestingly subversive and subversively useful French philosophy to the queer discourse around the body—Lacanian psychoanalysis, Foucauldian archaeology, and Deleuze and Guattari's schizoanalysis—we apprehend various discourses about limits that converge and diverge. Returning to the developmental psychology of Freud, Lacan wishes to establish limits for the psychosexual phases through which the human subject passes. He thus wants the imaginary to help secure a dependable identity for us in preparation for the relative stability of the symbolic order, but strangely enough allows for the possibility that the intersubjective strife characteristic of the imaginary will not be resolved and will instead continue to happen throughout personal and social life, ensuring that identification is not only fundamentally homosexual but fundamentally and perpetually unstable, contrary to his Hegelian yearning for resolution.

Deleuze and Guattari, Lacan's most direct antagonists in these pages, pursue other kinds of limits having more to do with the role of the already multiple (schizophrenic) individual in contact with social and textual entities whose interactions are all the more powerful for creating virtual bodies that are hard to define and contain, apart from the actual (arti-)facts that they don't so much represent as foment and serve as the (fragmentary) records for. Hence Deleuze's image of the fold that both embodies and contains the excess of its own movement. Foucault, finally, has theorized the limit in terms of Bataillean transgression:

> The death of God does not restore us to a limited and positivistic world, but to a world exposed by the experience of limits, made and unmade by that excess which transgresses it. ["A Preface to Transgression" 32]

By replacing the contradiction of the dialectic with the transgression of the limit, Foucault offers an alternative to Hegelian political aesthetics. Does transgression overwhelm and erase the limit? Foucault asks. No, transgression establishes the limit by crossing it, just as the virtual body of an aesthetic object in a sense creates that object, validates and valuates it even in its crude existence. Foucault's very language, depending as it so often does upon replacement ("not this . . . but that . . . "), exemplifies the difficult and apparently contradictory nature of his claim, which is nevertheless a provocative, worthy alternative to any kind of simplistic representational criticism.

But all the big words of theory might seem to diminish in the presence of a short acronym, AIDS, a disease syndrome that killed Foucault and has come to subject our body to

brand-new yet strangely familiar stresses, ones that are almost immediately invoked when the words *bodies* and *risk*
are somewhere near each other nowadays. Around the syndrome has developed a reevaluation of risk as a notion and
a practice. Though the once comforting typology of risk groups
has weakened since the earlier days of AIDS (but gets reinforced occasionally, here and there), the assessment of risk
as inherent to human interaction—corporeal and therefore
also intellectual—has become difficult in avoiding. For instance, no one has sex now, at least no one *should* have,
without considering the risk of infection. But this does not
mean that everyone properly understands risk or behaves
accordingly. People negotiate and make choices, or abandon
themselves to chance. Every decision must be respected,
despite consequences. Indeed, the title of this book should
imply that risk is inevitable and even in some cases welcome,
especially if it resists attempts to silence and subdue sex as
well as physical, and textual, interaction in general, whether
two hundred years ago in a musty old poem or tomorrow
after the concert.

Bodies at Risk asks: How has the body, designated as queer
or otherwise, placed itself at risk, such that it has questioned
dominant notions of what it is to be a human subject in Western society, roughly since the time of the romantics? Risk often
implies a kind of conflict, and my plan is to pit this body
against competing forces, whether material or virtual, in the
arenas of artistic endeavor. Similarly, much of my argument
depends upon conflict with other critics—conflict not intended
to decide a winner or solve a problem once and for all, but to
produce new bodies of critical textuality. The battle thus becomes less a sort of dialectic, hoisting itself eventually into a
higher synthesis, Hegelian *Aufhebung* or sublation, than an
experience of limits, a sublime moment from which the body
and text alike fall back, perhaps in Kantian fashion—submit
themselves to the exigencies of surviving thereafter under unforeseen circumstances, but changed for the better. Hence my
second major question: How have certain kinds of artistic
conflicts played themselves out in various texts in the romantic
period and postmodernism, and what have these conflicts produced, corporeally and textually?

For example, in the poetic rivalry between William
Wordsworth and Samuel Taylor Coleridge (chapter 1), we ob-

serve not simply an amicable exchange of ideas, and occasionally hostile parries in print, but a dramatization of sexual tensions extending as far as the human relationship to nature. Charles Altieri claims that in romanticism we discover the founding moment of the modern. I would argue that here occurs also the founding moment of the *post*modern, when I consider the peculiar burden of romantic self-consciousness only magnified by our own period's struggle with the limits of being and knowledge. Hence I conclude this book with a discussion of the strife among dominant and resistant AIDS discourses, epitomized by Hollywood film (chapter 5). When experience is pressed to the extreme by disease, persecution, and death, how do specific forms of rebellion work the ongoing paradoxes of sexual politics?

Cultural history has offered precedents for that struggle: in *Caleb Williams*'s conflict between reciprocally presupposing characters and *Frankenstein*'s contest of creation myths (chapter 2), as well as in the contrasting economies of high modernism and postmodernism (chapter 4). In the midst of this long era, since around 1800, psychoanalysis has emerged as theory as well as artifact, and I certainly adopt a tentatively Freudian/Lacanian approach. The theater in which these rivalries act (primary, pre-Oedipal identification) becomes indeed an imaginary one, not only in the sense of artistic but as a developmental stage. This, I contend, persists beyond any distinct age and compels the mechanisms of recognition into areas of aesthetic and even physical violation, despite the sublimated organization out of chaos, or articulation out of noise, purportedly imposed by the symbolic order (secondary, Oedipal identification). Psychoanalysis remains important because 1) it boasts an illustrious history of usefulness to feminist and queer studies; and 2) insofar as it has influenced the ways we think and feel, it informs many of the texts we use it to talk about, so if a text itself makes use of psychoanalytical ideas, then we're only correct in construing them there. What distinguishes my work from any doctrinaire treatment of its subjects, however, is the introduction of counterpsychoanalytical ideas derived from Bataille (excess and expenditure), Foucauldian archaeology, Deleuze and Guattari (what I designate schizomachy [chapter 3]), and others who examine what Cornel West has termed "the new cultural politics of difference."

A crucial task for anyone writing about the political and libidinal economies of conflicts must reconsider the legacy of Hegel, and thus Lacanian psychoanalysis, which refracts Hegel through Freud—and Kojève and Hippolyte. This way of thinking, based on theories of intersubjective violence as a dialectic of identification, has powerful uses for queer studies, as its presence there (and here) demonstrates. But, 1) given that psychoanalysis can become an insidious technology of normalization and discipline (that is, homosexuality is pathologically narcissistic) as well as an important descriptive, narrative, and analytical tool, especially for queer people (that is, normative heterosexuality can be reached, if at all, only through the defiles of perpetually unstable significations—that is, desires); and 2) since we can't oppose dialectical thinking without in some way recapitulating it and capitulating to it, thus the blackmail to which the dialectic subjects us, as others have noted—the question becomes: How to discuss artistic and corporeal struggles without slavish reference to the Hegelian/Lacanian model?

The response is to theorize alongside or outside the dialectic, to create a virtual body that cannot, by definition, ever be utterly subject to its efforts to resynthesize. And while this response might lie with Foucault and with Deleuze and Guattari most persuasively and usefully, it does not then involve any wholesale adoption of their thinking. *Bodies at Risk* will not become an interpretation of various texts according to some Foucauldian or Deleuzoguattarian orthodoxy. I certainly refer to them when necessary and claim them as significant influences. But their aggressive, affirmative ideas insist in this book more than they dominate here, and cohabit rather uneasily, I hope, with Lacan's guilty and tragic subjects, whom I force to reside in a sort of grand empty frame, like Venturi and Rauch's Franklin Court, where no scene of the family romance can be hidden, no one is safe from the outside, and the sealing tight of the doctrine becomes impossible.

So *Bodies at Risk*, as its name implies, will take a number of chances, from subject matter to style. I've touched on the content of the book; as to the technique, a few words. Just as in writing about imaginative texts we in English studies like, we often struggle to keep liking them even as our writing struggles against them, they in any case usually seem to lie somewhere between, on the one hand, internally coherent complex systems, where disinterest or consensus is supposed to make liking them ultimately irrelevant; and, on the other hand, the overwhelming excesses of libidinal counterculture, where we're supposed to have no choice but to submit to their subjectifications. Intense pleasures, of quite different kinds, can be found at both admittedly exaggerated extremes.

The hypermodernist Pierre Boulez's continually revised scores exemplify the former ("You cannot live on repetition forever" is one of the ways Boulez begs the question of Philip Glass, whom I discuss in chapter 4). The physical limits pushed by the minimalist My Bloody Valentine's all-out assault on the senses typify the latter ("We're . . . controlling everyone's environment by the volume and the lights," as I can attest, from having attended one of their shows, the loudest, and brightest, music I've ever experienced). Pleasures can be found as well as in the in-between where, nonetheless, criticism should register uncertainties and complexities not normally or always allowed in either the political or libidinal economies. And these doubts and appreciations need not get cast in the intricate de Manian weeds of indeterminacy, but in the more fabulous drag we wear to gallop for the surface effects and allow ourselves to succeed or fail, calling each day a good one only because we essayed.

Bodies at Risk, therefore, won't be much of a straight academic text, despite the way it might sound and despite all the appropriate apparatus. As an immanent critique, it wants to take on its own standards precisely by pushing them to occasionally absurd limits, reveling in a libidinal economy that becomes difficult to articulate outside a peculiar strategic homocentrism: a type of intellectual bashing back at the queer-phobic, queer-silent, or queer-appropriating maneuvers, often by straight academicians of whatever gender and ethnicity, we're all too familiar with. Rather than propose one idea and then simply "dotting i's and crossing t's" (McHale xii), this book will try to install its casual gods in its details, and will offer a number of different approaches for your reading. Thus chapter 3 stands on its own as a plane of consistency where Lacan, Foucault, and Deleuze and Guattari find themselves an unlikely foursome, discrete in approach but together in their insistence on the body as a site of protest and possibility. Chapter 1, centering dutifully around one text, demonstrates, in part, how Wordsworth is really *not* to be read, but not in the way(s) we might expect. Chapter 2 deals with two texts, *Frankenstein* and *Caleb Williams*, and in the middle gets bisected by short passages on Blanchot and Sade. This chapter approaches, recoils from, embraces texts, as unruly monsters *themselves*. Chapter 4 begins talking about postmodernism theoretically, then modulates into discussions of Philip Glass, Paul Schrader, Godfrey Reggio, John Barth, Thomas Bernhard, and others, returning to postmodernism as a sort of deadly text, by the end. Rather than always offering yet one more definable and confinable period for our study, postmodernism in some ways can actually discipline the body into unique forms of pleasure and agony whose power we can merely register, somehow, in our discourse. And chapter 5 discusses not only the political unconscious(-ness) created by AIDS but also a trio, a complex, of films that have helped shape our perceptions of the syndrome. The Epilogue reflects back on *Bodies at Risk* by means of a couple of paintings and a diagram, and summarizes the chapters. The preludes to Parts I and II should also helpfully summarize and provide transitions between the major sections.

In the meantime I will be arguing that during romanticism and again in postmodernism, the presence of the body has often caused subject *de*formation. My account of the body's relation to aesthetics observes closely the various ways corporeal and creative experiences have not only proved unique in themselves but have actually spawned unfamiliar, socially resistant forms of life. The artifact thus becomes less a record of loss, as in Percy Shelley, or Freud's followers, than a testimony to the body's ability to resist oppression and create new types of human being.

Part One

Romantic Assemblages

Prelude I

Wordsworth, Godwin, and the Shelleys

Romanticists have become familiar with *two* Wordsworths: the younger, more daring, revolutionary cultural itinerant, lover of and in France; and the older, more conservative, sedentary stamp distributor, government pensioner, and poet laureate. (Coleridge has undergone a similar split.) Criticism has tended, for example, to consider the earlier, rawer versions of *The Prelude* (1799, 1805) to be more inspired and energetic than the revised version (1850) found in collections of Wordsworth's poetry, e.g., the Hutchinson and De Selincourt edition, which I refer to in chapter 1.

Like the more and more accommodating Mary Shelley, Wordsworth reconsidered and rewrote in order to contain previous exuberance and smooth roughness. What results is often more fluid language, tempered by maturity and necessity, though certainly with less boldness. The case of Wordsworth's poem "Nutting" remains important because it stands as a youthful document—a very disturbing one—that was never suppressed or even significantly revised. It has retained its momentum against the inertia of neglect. In fact it has become crucial to any discussion of sexual politics in Wordsworth and in romanticism generally.

In 1798 he writes "Nutting" as part of the incipient "poem on his own life" (posthumously titled *The Prelude*). But he decided to leave it out as an independent work, to be included in the 1800 edition of *Lyrical Ballads*. Thereafter it becomes fairly obscure, virtually buried among his eventual collection, overshadowed by the major lyrics, and ignored by the literature until the beginning of the romantic revival subsequent to the New Criticism's disapprobation of the period—thus Bloom, de Man, Hartman, Hillis Miller, and others help inaugurate the postmodern period in literary studies.

3

Though an artifact of Wordsworth's intense early years, challenging in its subject matter (violent decimation of a hazel tree), sexual suggestiveness, and awkward manner, "Nutting" nevertheless somehow merits inclusion in the elder Wordsworth's self-arranged oeuvre. In Wordsworthian fashion, we've discovered a decisive moment in his work that had existed already for a hundred and fifty years, a moment suddenly charged with a new significance. As I've suggested, that charge is nakedly erotic, whatever sublimations the poem has had to endure—that it's really about the romantic subject's relationship to nature, or simply about masturbation. But obviously it's turned into a poem of powerful critical focus, also, as any survey of the commentary will show (see chapter 1, especially the introduction and the notes).

Once criticism overcomes its need drastically to sublimate the poem's potent eroticism, it tends to gender the decimated bower as female, and thus to make the young male speaker's act one of heterosexual rapine. While I don't dismiss this interpretation, I take issue with an almost relentless insistence on the bower's sex, regardless of poetic tradition. However seemingly unlikely, the bower's possibly male identity must be considered, especially in light of Wordsworth's troubled homoerotic relationship with Coleridge, who by this time had made bowers a central image in his poetry—and become his rival for literary fame.

Nevertheless, the poem remains puzzling. It's finally impossible to know exactly what's going on in "Nutting," beyond the dramatization of a kind of excessive, polysemous, wasteful sexuality that Wordsworth seems to be attributing to his own gender. Because readers of diverse orientations can't ultimately know the poem in itself or agree on a common reading, they're ironically pushed away and left bewildered, after having been so carefully seduced into complicity with its violatory movement. I therefore don't insist that the bower change its apparent sex, so much as argue that "Nutting," despite its ostensibly minor importance to Wordsworth's poetry and to romantic theory, is a text critical to analyses of corporeal and discursive limits and their effects on aesthetics. "Nutting" exploits the body of poetry as well as the body of the reader in such a way as to bespeak a change in our very consciousness of self. How we define subjectivity still does and must contend with romanticism's epistemological and ontological ruptures.

But Wordsworth isn't the only strong example. Romanticism indeed involves a new kind of self-consciousness, and quite in the Foucauldian sense, where the beginning of the nineteenth century marks an irruption in epistemology and "man" gets constituted as the Western subject we're now all too familiar with, and when literature starts to perceive itself as a distinct set of discourses. The self, something new, must now investigate its own origins, as well as the source of its power to create. William Godwin and his daughter, Mary Shelley, take pains to explicate the genesis both of themselves as creative artists and of their works, usually in the form of added or antecedent material to novels (the prefaces, or front matter in the words of the *Chicago Manual*). As they do so, these authors call into question theories of perception and creativity centering on organic wholeness, subjective coherence, and imaginative mastery—all considered concepts central to romanticism. They confront the task of shaping inchoate material into narrative but take the task one step further: they make the act of confrontation an integral part of that narrative.

The text thus becomes a record of the limit faced in the void; it becomes, in Deleuzoguattarian terms, an abstract machine, formed of assembled parts, themselves the superficially desultory or dilatory offcasts of the excesses involved in obsessive rivalry, sexual pursuit, scientific hubris, and death. If the romantic artwork cannot match the sublime, if it cannot occupy the limits it engages, then it pieces together what remains of the extreme experience and places the assemblage into circulation. It makes the machine, rather than the matter, which pursues a line of flight and not only escapes its maker but turns and pursues him or her once again toward the unknowable. In the process, new corporeal and discursive formations are created. Interacting with our bodies, these texts create affects that are both powerful in themselves and powerfully renewing to the task of literary theory. An unforeseen yet strangely familiar body called romanticism arises, then, and compels criticism to answer its challenges: Who was I? What was I? Whence did I come? What was my destination?

1

Wordsworth's "Nutting" and the Violent End of Reading

Prelude

By 1790, Wordsworth is exploring revolutionary France with his friend Robert Jones. That same year, the Bastille having been stormed and his manuscripts' fate uncertain, the Marquis de Sade walks away from Charenton asylum, poor but free, to set his affairs in order.

About Sade's compulsive rewritings of traditional themes, Foucault remarks that it was "not in view of a dialectical reward, but toward a radical exhaustion" ("Language to Infinity" 62). And, belatedly, Bloom has remarked that "the romance-of-trespass, of violating a sacred or daemonic ground, is a central form in modern literature, from Coleridge and Wordsworth to the present" (*A Map of Misreading* 35).

This chapter is not overtly concerned with the relationship between Sade and Wordsworth—contemporaneous and yet ostensibly worlds apart. But the time has been long in coming when Sade and Wordsworth would meet openly on that ground.

Introduction

Wordsworth criticism has been focusing again on "Nutting," the blank-verse allegory he completed in 1799, first published in the second edition of *Lyrical Ballads* (1800), and never assimilated into *The Prelude*, for which he originally intended it.[1] The speaker of the poem, a young man "with a huge wallet o'er [his] shoulders slung, / A nutting crook in hand . . ." (ll. 6–7), leaves home one day in search of hazelnuts. He sounds optimistic enough. When he discovers a worthy tree, he becomes positively playful, but ends up decimating the hazel in a scene of "merciless ravage" (l. 45), and never returns home with his harvest. It is the speaker's startling violence that has most often attracted criticism.

For example, Rachel Crawford, in "The Structure of the Sororal in Wordsworth's 'Nutting,'" reads in this allegory Freudian acts of primary narcissism and castrating vehemence against the phallic mother, complementing similar assertions in Jonathan Arac's "Wordsworth's 'Nutting': Suspension and Decision" with her own concerns for the mechanisms of sisterhood. Crawford seems correct in identifying the sororal as a neglected yet crucial issue here.[2] Charles Altieri, also responding to Arac, takes yet another approach. He suggests, even more powerfully than Arac, that in Wordsworth's short poem occurs the founding moment of modernity. According to Altieri, the hero of the narrative (that is, the poet), frustrated over the inadequacy of the pastoral mode in representing fully the power of the poetic spirit, seeks violence against nature, positioned as object vis-à-vis this newfound source of subjectivity. "Nutting" is thus a "great achievement" (Altieri 190) in establishing the origins of the modern spirit of poetry in the drastic convolutions of the romantic self. All these critics share with their predecessors an assumption about the gender of the hazel's "mutilated bower"[3] (l. 50), as well as emphases on routine psychoanalytical modes, problems of poetic form, and even neo-Hegelian dialectics over issues regarding sexual difference per se, which the poem would seem so meretriciously to advertise.

As far back as the sixties, when "Nutting"—receiving sudden, avid attention—was often implied to be a masturbatory fantasy,[4] these emphases were common, along with the implication that a bower must be female if a male character, in a male heterosexual's poem, assails it. Perhaps it is the rare critic with heterosexual imperatives and prerogatives, feminist or not, who would dare suggest otherwise.

Arac, for instance, in confusing the poem's supposed phallic mother ("dubious fetishism") and feminine lack ("culturally valued sublimation"), seems incapable of conceiving, so to speak, an alternative to conventional readings, when in "Nutting" he finds "something with no natural existence, an act which could not occur" (45): not only because nature is female and therefore always already castrated, but because the poem's representational mode is allegorical—that is, not real.

This is a failure of the imagination, and perhaps lack of experience, that, we should not be surprised to learn,

Wordsworth does not share. Indeed, enough evidence exists in "Nutting" to support the claim that the self-effacing antihero of the poem expends himself, in fact, upon a *male* bower. This idea would challenge not only certain fairly predictable Freudian, Lacanian, structuralist, and deconstructive readings of Wordsworth's troubling different-sex politics, but—even more fundamentally—the troubled relationship of reader to poem. Yet, though "Nutting" has been nothing if not seductive as a subject for criticism, its confusing strategies work rather to discourage than encourage further readings. If "the allegorical work tends to prescribe the direction of its own commentary" (Craig Owens, referring to Northrop Frye, 53),[5] "Nutting," then, tells us to go south.

At first arousing interest, the poem ultimately makes it impossible for different readers of different orientations to respond in ways that would satisfy critical criteria of accountability and universality, to say nothing of the aesthetics of autonomy and sensibility. In Kantian terms, it is hardly a pure object of beauty, and thus judgments about it cannot but be less than perfect. More than a founding, heuristic text, "Nutting" constitutes "that blind confrontation of antithetical meanings which characterizes the allegory of unreadability" (Owens 79)—but not deconstructive indeterminability so much as implosion, foreclosure, expenditure, undoing. In Hegelian terms (but contra Hegel, via Deleuze's *Nietzsche*), "Nutting" dramatizes the all-consuming exertions of the master ("total critique") over the recuperative labor of the slave ("self-consciousness"). In Benthamite terms, to subvert the utilitarian, the poem's narrator makes a "fabulous waste" outside the "moral hygiene" of the behavioral and experiential catalog (see Rajchman 61ff.). In short, he forces an end subsuming the teleology of ends under a peculiarly brutal *telos* of *end*.

Silence to an End

It appears odd when a critic, writing about sexual issues in Wordsworth's poetry, passes over "Nutting." Wayne Koestenbaum is a current example, providing an opportunity to fill in some of the background against which the poem so disturbingly echoes.

"Nutting" is indeed one very erotically charged poem omitted from Koestenbaum's analysis of the erotics of Wordsworth and Coleridge's literary collaboration, *Double Talk.* Koestenbaum focuses on *Lyrical Ballads*, specifically, those poems on which the two poets actually collaborated, such as "The Rime of the Ancient Mariner" and "We Are Seven," and on those in which closet dramas of homoerotic tension are being played out, such as "Simon Lee" and "The Nightingale," along with several poems written before the poets' first encounter. "Nutting" would seem to be more than just a curious omission here. Its openly sexual content, coming across nevertheless as displacement of troubling impulses onto nature through poetry—though veiled by Wordsworth's particular type of decorum—is by now hard to miss.

Koestenbaum's is an inexplicable, seductive omission, and for several reasons. To begin with, it could be argued, and it has been argued, that once Wordsworth and Coleridge met in September 1795 in Bristol, having already maintained a mutual attraction for some time, they lost a sort of double innocence that would never be recovered, even had this been desirable. Indeed, their most individual work kept in circulation a dialog revealing the more neurotic, spiteful, devious, and of course darkly erotic aspects of collaboration, of which *Lyrical Ballads* forms but one record.

Thus, for example, the conspiracy of that revolutionary poetic project later degenerates into Wordsworth's individual piracy in the preface to his own *Poems* (1815) of Coleridge's ideas about the imagination as he expressed them in his lectures on Milton and Shakespeare—followed by Coleridge's unusually swift but carefully damaging response in *Biographia Literaria* (Modiano "The Ethics of Gift Exchange" 243). There, Coleridge holds up the rules of these two most eminent of English poets, along with Bowles, not simply to measure his opponent, but to beat him with them—in his own words "*per argumentum baculinum,*" by the argument from the stick (*Biographia* 93).

Now the *Biographia* is itself a bold piracy, plundering the avant-garde German philosophy of the time to augment its author's weaponry. Both the 1815 preface and the *Biographia* were meant to affirm ascendancy in discourses each writer had long before deferred to the other: in Wordsworth's case philosophy, in Coleridge's poetry, or poetic theory; obviously, however, their roles had long been switched and were only reinforced by these documents.

so it would seem. The narrator or Wordsworth exploits the ballad form while claiming lack of penetration into Martha Ray's case: "More I know not, I wish I did, / And it should all be told to you" (ll. 144–45). Nevertheless, he positions her obsessively next to the phallic tree, perhaps, as Koestenbaum suggests (86), to replace the child she has lost with the thorn's linguistic impregnation.

In "Tintern Abbey," the speaker, who is typically identified with Wordsworth, effects an even more insidious, extraordinary, positively sublime subordination, in the Kantian sense, of the female subject, Dorothy. She is fixed by the poet throughout the narrative yet addressed only toward the end, once he has finished writing "nature and the language of the sense" (l. 108) into his private moral agenda. This "dear, dear Friend," object of condescension, and hyperrationalization, must notwithstanding accept the responsibility of retaining the poet's present feelings for later tranquil recollection—easy access, in other words—as an inviolate vessel, "a mansion for all lovely forms" (l. 140), ones which the speaker alone has articulated and stored within the apostrophized Friend for future exploitation. Her true identity, including sexual, like the speaker's but far less generalized, must remain hidden.

Dorothy's own journals, of course, served a similarly useful purpose. It may be that, the more Wordsworth used them, the more she wrote to be used. The faceless female is made to resemble Wordsworth's image for the poem in his prefaces: the poem's comparable ideality, along with its ability to be reified, makes it the only other such possible cache of emotion. The poem is "the rock of defense of human nature" (preface to the second edition of *Lyrical Ballads*), a site of loss and, more crucially, of recovery of the unfamiliar compelled into familiarity, and just as rigorously protected from the corruption of the "getting and spending" world.

Once matured within a falsely Edenic environment, the Friend will anyhow draw upon these feelings for her own protection and peace of mind. Presumably, she has no original feelings to claim, despite, and not as a result of, her romanticized youth.[10] Memory becoming memorialization, in Wordsworth, becomes language's act of violence upon whatever silence, whatever oblivion, that might have spared these and other female subjects, especially Lucy, from the poet's peculiar forms of romantic importunities.

Wordsworth's much earlier "Lines, Left upon a Seat in a Yew-Tree," completed the year he met Coleridge and the first blank verse to appear in Wordsworth's own arrangement of his poems, contrasts with "Nutting" by preserving instead of ruining its isolated vessel, "this deep vale" (l. 46), in order to house the spirit of its "favoured Being" (l. 6). He, like the hero of "Nutting," goes forth into nature and never comes back, but because the poem is meant to record a useful admonishment, it confidently anticipates the itinerant *reader's* return. Thus, these "Lines" offer another example of unproductive solitude, or self-absorption, though not as radically expensive as, say, the subject's in Shelley's *Alastor*, that critiques Wordsworth. In the yew-tree "Lines," as in "Nutting," the reading figure is apostrophized, as "Traveller" and "Stranger," and admonished to pass by the charged spot in a particular manner.

Of all these narratives, "Nutting" is the most difficult to read, not least because of its overt violence, arresting the reader, almost loud enough to drown out its troubling implications—a destruction so powerful as to incapacitate deconstruction, or a reconfiguration of oppositions. The action in the poem exceeds a rationalized, cathartic sexual economy as described by Freud: "as is well known, temptations are merely increased by constant frustration, whereas an occasional satisfaction of them causes them to diminish, at least for the time being" (73). But "Nutting" hardly achieves the "nonhegemonic (and ultimately homoerotic) economy of desire" of Bataille (Shaviro *Passion and Excess* 95).[11] Like the "Lines" localized to the yew tree and to Tintern Abbey, "Nutting" provides an early example of Wordsworth's mature mode of time-spot blank verse, impossible without the earlier example of Coleridge's conversation poems. Yet the Wordsworth poem seems more willful, staged, artificial, openly deliberate—quite unlike the perfectly natural or effortless poem of the Wordsworthian stereotype.

In a word, "Nutting" is thoroughly allegorical, but in a manner almost polymorphously perverse, which alone describes a range of positive and negative responses.

An Allegory of Reading's End

Indeed, the poem demands an allegorical reading, even though direct correspondences to objects and processes outside the poem remain tenuous, if not evaporative. Put another way, as Crawford remarks, while "the story of 'Nutting' can be simply paraphrased," the ambiguous symbology of the poem impedes both the flow of the poem's narrative and the flow of the narrative of reading—as well as any complete identification with the speaker. The poem attempts to interpellate and inter-polate readers as violators. But it succeeds instead in forcing those readers into metacritical positions that call attention to their subject-formations in terms of sexuality. Voyeurs, seduced into violating, end up reading themselves into and out of the task of "Nutting."

Certainly the poem offers readers plenty of imagery to arouse prurient interest, raising questions about Wordsworth's own sexual, and textual, intentions. The ambiguities of its images, however, prevent us from uncovering any secrets, altering a Coleridgean sublime of indefiniteness (Wlecke 73–94) into a more Burkean sublime of terror and pity that is meant to mask the speaker's own subjectivity. His empathetic pain, occurring upon objectification from his mutilating act, transmutes into the muted pleasure of his realizing his own survival, even if the terms of existence have altered perma-nently. It is as if the violence performed in the poem is so great as to obliterate all traces of the victim's identity, leaving only ruin and the boy's now merely, or absolutely, imperative ("move," "touch") consciousness. "Merciless ravage" thus be-comes more than partaking, more than taking: it is taking away. It is a decimation, one that reaffirms and violates the violator equally. It is a sexual exchange: both parties are af-fected, though the male would prefer to retain his innocence— in both the legal and sexual senses. But the loss is difficult to identify.

Nutting cannot be *merely* a performance, sexually or poeti-cally. In the conflict enacted by the boy, either he or the bower must succeed. Instead, the self he might have sought is perma-nently lost along with his very presence. And the bower is decimated beyond recognition, in the Lacanian as well as the journalistic sense. There shall be no evidence remaining to alert anyone but the solitary reader to the boy's breaking of social taboos.

Beforehand, the phallic images, of course, predominate. The hazel—"tall and erect, with tempting clusters hung" (l. 20)— most closely resembles the thorn in the poem of that name: "it stands erect, and like a stone / With lichens is it overgrown" (ll. 10–11). It also resembles "the woods of autumn, and their hidden bowers / With milk-white clusters hung" in *The Two-Part Prelude of 1799* (ll. 235–36).[12] The overtly masculine shape of the images in "Nutting," which are virtually impossible to mistake for female, renders incomprehensible—except to those sensitive to his (hetero)sexism—Harold Bloom's claim that "the rough analogy is with the human female body" (*The Visionary Company* 129), as well as Margaret Homans's reading of this bower as a woman's (1981 240). Maybe they make the bower female for similar though opposite reasons: Bloom, to ensure that any male protagonist of Wordsworth's will figure nature as the *other* gender, however exploitive the reinscription of heterosexism; Homans, to ensure that the female gender is the one being violated, all the more to indict Wordsworth's motivations as oppressive, however admirably revisionist Homans's feminism might be.[13]

At any rate, phallic imagery abounds in Wordsworth: trees, crags, mountains, eminences, even gibbets (the hanged are said to become erect, even ejaculate)[14]—all of which are usually isolated, privileged symbols of the powerful masculine gender principle as it imposes itself upon the landscape.[15] The dead man in Esthwaite's Lake (*The Prelude*, 1805, V, ll. 450-81)—who "bolt upright / Rose"—represents a clearly Burkean and Freudian moment of terror and guilt repressed by language or the "romance" (l. 477) of the boy's reading that can, so he claims, relieve him of libidinous, parricidal impulses.[16]

This is the very definition of a fetish—poetry taking the place of the violence it describes as absent in its own present.[17] The terrific enjambment here on "Rose" recalls the speaker's powerful movement in "Nutting": there, he says, "Then up I rose" (l. 43, where the word prominently *ends* the line), before he brings down the hazel. In both instances, rising sexual action leads to a fall into a consciousness of death that words can scarcely screen.

What, then, is the nature of the deflowering in "Nutting"? Is it a rape of the male-as-nature (or nature-as-male), with a deeply sadistic component—again, obsessively, "merciless ravage" (l. 45)? The speaker, after all, carries "a huge wallet o'er [his] shoulders slung, / A nutting-crook in hand" (ll. 6–7), a huge endowment, from behind, and proceeds to ravish a phallic symbol plus the nearest virgin opening he can find, that "green and mossy bower, / Deformed and sullied" (ll. 46–47) contrasting with "one of those green stones / That,

fleeced with moss, under the shady trees, / Lay around [him]"
(ll. 35–37), which may conceal some feminine principle to
tempt the boy away from his desired objective: an inexperienced male orifice.

Frances Ferguson suggests that the boy's hesitation to
ravage the bower is meant to allow nature time to seduce
him after a gratification "too easily won" (73). In other words,
he discovers more than he had hoped for: "A virgin scene!"
(l. 21)—three loaded words at the beginning of the line, and
with an exclamation mark prominently positioned. Such an
object itself incites to ravish, according to the terms of the
poem. The "mutilated bower" would typically imply a female
organ, but is it not perhaps a rather male opening, that
"green and mossy bower" instead of "one of those green stones
/ fleeced with moss"? Or do those stones themselves represent a circle of male parts, an audience for the boy's con-
quest?[18] The allegory does not lend itself to an absolute
correspondence of images, yet the drama and its actors cannot, almost helplessly, but suggest this kind of sublimated
fantasy.

Nevertheless, the exact nature of the symbolism remains
mysterious. Does the "figure quaint" leave his "frugal Dame" to
pursue what are to him probably illicit desires? or to satisfy
any desire because this woman—mother, sister, wife? Ann
Tyson?[19]—is inadequate, in which case the "maiden" would
substitute and complete the sexual, allegorical triangle? While
the eroticism is undeniable, the prefix (homo-, hetero-, bi-,
even a-) to the act of sexuality shifts, leaving only speculation
and a reminder of the ultimate emptiness of the oppressive
sexual signifier.[20]

"Nutting," to paraphrase Crawford, is more "ingenious" than
simply to veil a disturbing act. The poem itself pauses many
times. Indeed, the first line begins *in medias res* after a long
dash covering six absent syllables. It includes nine dashes and
liberal caesuras. But then there are as many sudden, startling,
intrusive enjambments, such as "through beds of matted fern,
and tangled thickets, / *Forcing* my way" (ll. 15–16, emphasis
added). "Nutting" textualizes sex, sexualizes language, teases
the reader just as the boy teases the hazel remaining erect
while he dallies on the fleecy stones,[21] finally rearing up and
completing his "service," but savagely. Repetitions echo libidinous yearnings, as in l. 38: "I heard the murmur and the

murmuring sound." The meter, highly syncopated in Wordsworth's experimental fashion, follows the inciting and discouraging rhythms of seduction: "the heart luxuriates with indifferent things, / Wasting its kindliness on stocks and stones, / And on the vacant air" (ll. 41–43).

Alliterations and assonances, plus the magnificent sounds of English onomatopoeia, especially the climactic "crash" (l. 44, line end) of the patient hazel, make the language virtually palpable. But what really happened, despite all the noise, remains unknown, which seduces, too. It is as if the reader were not there, to hear the falling of a hazel in the woods:

> All the categories of language and consciousness, all the struc-
> tures of subjectivity and objectivity, of intuition and compre-
> hension, have collapsed, and yet an indefinable violence, a
> sense of pain or ecstasy, remains. "Something" subsists, even
> when there is no revelation, no truth, nothing to be found.
> [Shaviro *Passion and Excess* 88]

"Nutting" involves recollection versus recalled immediacy ("unless I now / Confound my present feelings with the past" [ll. 48–49]), the most abused Wordsworthian trope. Foucault's fugitive vision of male-to-male sexuality applies here: it inspires the recollection of an act that was performed too quickly for recognition, either of self or of other. An elegiacal, melancholy gazing after the departed object lingers, while all the literary mechanisms of concealment and revelation—that is, diagesis—play through the mind over and over again, offering the promise of the object's continual return ("Sexual Choice, Sexual Act" 223).

Reading/Nutting

Because "Nutting" solicits allegory and an allegorical reader, each reader may take a literarily prurient interest, but not simply because, as Foucault cuttingly remarks, "underneath everything said, we suspect that another thing is being said" ("The Discourse of History" 21). The poem, if read literally, might not merit all the criticism it has recently been offered. Further, certain elements of the poem—manipulations of styles and especially figures—call attention to its allegorical nature. But just as the bower must be portrayed as virgin in order all the more violently to be ravaged, the poem remains indirect, inviting the transgressive act of scanning through its verses, the to-and-fro of earth-breaking (*versus*) and dissemination (semelfaction). And then the force of repeated readings fatigues as well as exhilarates us. The search for the most applicable allegorical reading leads *down*, like the very act of scanning the verses, to disaffection, even disgust, the depression resulting from the most fantastic masturbation, though Wordsworth be the subject and we (critics) the witnesses.

What Allan Stoekl reads in Bataille can perhaps be read in "Nutting": "the terminal subversion of the pseudostable references that had made allegory and its hierarchies seem possible" (xiv). Wordsworth dramatizes and confirms such a headless allegory by having his subject force down the hazel's top and disperse both the subject's and the hazel's self-possession(s), "[w]asting . . . kindliness" (l. 42) in both senses, among all the senses. Similarly, the poem effects a linguistic and sexual perturbation in readers by not allowing them to remain mere observers, much as it seems to ignore them. Seduction, indeed. And abandonment.

Because the poem begs a reading that would substitute external for internal figures—whether that of the mind/nature dichotomy (Ferguson 73), guilt over literary indolence (Magnuson 180), justifiable destruction of the phallic mother's threat (Arac 45), or demonstration of poetical authority (Galperin 140)—it also begs the reader to adopt the subject-position of ravisher, importunate, as to meaning. Hence, Galperin's contention that the reader finds it difficult to identify with the speaker (95) is apparent to the point of impracticability, even though his interpretation of the reader's being marginalized is thoroughly practical, in terms of apostrophization—that is, the reader cannot be the maiden. "Nutting" interpellates the reader as a violator, interpolating him or her into the poem, which itself had for some time existed as an undiscovered bower whose discovery has pleased Wordsworthians and anti-Wordsworthians alike.

Galperin, an example of the former, reads "Nutting" as yet one more early demonstration of the undermining of genius's authority that would only develop, rather than fail, during Wordsworth's decline. "Nutting" has thus become an allegory of reading, a poem about writing and getting re(a)d, ruining its symbols just as surely as the boy brings down the hazel tree "deformed and sullied" (l. 47), an accurate description of the act of reading the act of nutting. It bloodies the bloodier.

In the meantime, the speaker of the poem remains disguised as a romantic "figure" and then perhaps as a "spirit in the woods": the *I* is concealed while the reader's *eye* is brought out into the open, forced to look, like Anthony Burgess's intrusive criminal, at the very acts he has performed over and over again, for the sake of some perverse discipline. Readers or subjects cannot remain disguised; every reading discovers them, shocks them into the recognition of their own complicity. Revealed in this way, readers are obliged to adopt a metapoetic stance in order to call attention to their own subject-positions vis-à-vis the poem, and to maintain *defensive* positions as well. Admittance to the violating act therefore *must* identify readers with the speaker critically, in both senses, forcing them to read, react, and respond from subjectivities that can no longer remain subconscious. Yet these responses remain defensive because they rely on sexualities that readers declare and live, not necessarily the multiple possibilities to which they themselves might be subject. The consciousness of the poem thinks it knows its readers, but knows only as much as any embodied come-on. "Nutting" backs them into a corner, rendering their defenses untenable by delimiting the terms of their reading.

Here is where Ferguson's interpretation comes across as the most believable: the imagination in this poem figures negatively, as absence, and, because nature "[deludes the speaker] into writing himself into his own text" (75), the reader has to do the same. Imagination sleeps while apprehension importunes. It is therefore possible, contra Galperin, that it is the reader who gets figured as the "maiden" (Magnuson, conventionally, reads her as Dorothy [182]),[22] who should not tread too harshly on this fragile concatenation of speaker, poem, and narrative. "Nutting" can indeed inspire a variety of speculations—a strong poem to the extent that it manipulates responses (wholly disturbs), a weak one to the extent that the message remains linguistic and overconfident (remains wholly *and* merely literary).

At any rate, its effectiveness must be measured on the outside, in a manner of speaking, by how successfully it can embody itself apart not only from Wordsworth's gothic church of a life's work, never completed, to which it would seem only tangential, but apart from the very page on which he allowed the poem to appear and represent him.

"Nutting" as Con-catenation

This lyrical ballad, or antiballad, as Mary Jacobus might say, intersects with other genres that disturb it. "Nutting" is narrative but not stanzaical or rhymed; it moves in the manner of "Tintern Abbey," with its "fluctuating, overflowing blank verse . . . its restless enjambments and its disdain for borders" (Koestenbaum 82). The speaker's "sense of pain" (l. 52) suggests elegy, while the quaintness of the boy's appearance—indeed, the quaintness of his very self-consciousness, the very Spenserian diction in which his narrative is couched (that of the knight errant: "a Figure quaint / Tricked out in proud disguise of cast-off weeds / Which for that service had been husbanded . . . Motley accoutrement" [ll. 8-10,12])—is deliberate archaism, as had been Spenser's, along with the image of the feminized bower. Ferguson observes "an artful character stepping from the pages of romance narrative" (73).[23]

But the poem hardly resolves—so unlike Wordsworth, or so critics have tended to think. Like Spenser's extended epic-allegory, it never quite finishes. And this is due partly to a complex of forms that is not perfectly synthesized.[24]

"Nutting," as it leads us into the silence of the "far-distant wood" (l. 8), stays disquiet, admonitory, as if the hazel continues to vibrate along with the language, discouraging further action.[25] Is the poem responding, in a sexual and textual sense, to Coleridge's own bowers?[26] Does the poet want to ravage the rival's bower of poetry, of whom, as the boy, he claims to be "fearless" (l. 24)? Does "rival" here refer to what the "banquet" (l. 25) of the hazel, then, is not? And does the recognition of pain bespeak guilt over having deprived this adversary of some innocence, naturalness, perfection? We must acknowledge the pain in intercourse for the inexperienced, but here it is the penetrator who accepts the pain, or considers, quite openly, only his own, perhaps because it can only ever be referred to one's own, and is never completely displeasing.

Adela Pinch, wishing to deemphasize the notion that "engagement with literary suffering is like a form of personal violence," claims that ". . . meter and the invocation of sexual difference provide partial solutions" to the "pain" of reading (837). (Wordsworth hopes, in his prose prefaces, that meter will help restrain passion.)

Yet it is Elaine Scarry who, linking pain to the turning in upon oneself and the precluding of imagination, has perhaps the most to say to the convolution of the "Nutting" reading experience:

> The less the object accommodates and expresses the inner requirements of the hunger, desire, or fear, the less there is an object for the state and only the state itself, the more it will approach the condition of pain. [169][27]

In other words, readers respond with their own sexual and damaged subjectivities, making it obvious that the poem has violated *them* through an act of consciousness-making. The seduction of "Nutting," as well as nutting, succeeds only in turning actors—whether inside or outside the text—back painfully upon themselves, rendering the poem far less interesting to look at than, as Coleridge might advise, to reimagine: a process of becoming self-aware yet necessarily disinterested sexually, since, admittedly, the artificiality of the style chills potential eroticism. "Nutting" rehearses, over and over again, this type of Kantian (virginal) sublime.

Finally, does the importunity of poetry gloat or feel, itself, guilty? To Galperin, the poem, purportedly a confession, by pushing aside the reader-as-confessor and then the reader-as-auditor, becomes dramatic monolog, pleased with its own speaker's perfect reception (96). This monolog, yet another form, contains possibilities for pride as well as shame—adolescent but also ideologically repressive sexual affects. And if the sexual politics of the poem are as convoluted as they seem, the male reader indeed must be positioned differently from the female ("maiden"). However, the male reader becomes somewhat of a problem if he is actually feminized—that is, figured allegorically as female for the purposes of concealing a male-to-male sexual act. Because readership was largely female in Wordsworth's day, the society of male writers—and Coleridge and Wordsworth can certainly be read as their own homoerotic society—thus trafficked homosexually (à la Irigaray [193]) in these women, whether inside or outside their poems (Koestenbaum also makes a point of this).

Remember that the boy remains apart from his "dame," acting out a conflict between recollection and expenditure without her, reproducing a typical domestic arrangement. The boy must waste to collect, an ambiguity conveyed by the poem's very title. He must wreck to become rich, pull down to gather, destroy to enjoy. Though he seeks the utility of accumulation, he produces instead a futility of expenditure: an increasingly startling problem in the early years of the Industrial Revolution and corporate capitalism. This problem would, in part, goad the English romantics into reconstructing crucial myths: Cain, the fratricide, who kills to gain autonomy and is exiled; Prometheus, the rebel, who must recall the curse that was meant to bring down the despotic head; Pygmalion, the artist, chipping away the cold, excess stone to achieve the living ideal; Ahasuerus, the wanderer, condemned to homelessness, bearing his own forms of destruction.

The boy of "Nutting" is, perhaps, the capitalist who, despairing in his inability to decode all the partial flows of wealth (as in Deleuze and Guattari), withdraws from life after the crash of his resources. He invests far too much.

Language is violence upon nature, but does nature have to be figured as innocent? Perhaps the speaker must do so in order to make the act that much more appealing, and appalling. A female principle may be "both pivotal and underplayed" (Webster 57) in Wordsworth, and is perhaps ultimately "picturesque" (58), but this does not mean that *any* human principle has been emptied out of that bower, which the speaker of "Nutting" is, at the same time, careful to keep allegorized, and anxious to possess. The poem's self-awareness, disguising itself, like the speaker, thereby as a kind of innocence—a deceptive maneuver, of course—seduces. That the hazel, it seems, has never before been touched does not render it "virgin" unless the boy loads the rift beforehand with as much dispossessable meaning as possible.

Nutting Readers

The boy seems, for his own purposes, rather successful in doing so, yet he is bound not to persuade the silent companions he has brought along on his expedition—his imagined readers. One reason for his failure in establishing a community of violators is that his own subject is decisively split: into the I of the narration, that of past events, and of the intermediary existing, though hardly thriving, in the interstices of allegory and metaphor, the reader's solicitors. And if the speaker can be said to carry within himself and deliver to the hazel the Oedipal triangle (frugal mother, absent father, castrating and castrated self), his companions may not be sure who is leading them into criminal complicity. And against whom—the father to be seduced and preemptively castrated? The speaker cannot force his way into the reader as a unified self, and this somewhat vitiates his potential.

Furthermore, where does he end up? Does he return to his "dame"? (One psychoanalytical reading, figuring her as mother, would likely disallow him from returning, except linguistically: to rehearse and rehearse his expectable act on the mossy couch of anamnesis.) He has become "rich beyond the wealth of kings" (l. 51) but is also deprived painfully of—what, precisely? His real life, which he can only recall from the shadowy position of a spirit? But if he never really had such a life, his is the most dastardly of crimes. Ferguson's reading of an unstable message in the poem (70) is therefore understatement. The message *is* wholly literary, and wholly disturbing, one that can leave the reader as much dismayed and displaced as the nutting, nutted boy.

Though readers realize the multiplication of the speaking subject, and resist "Nutting" with their own histories,[28] they nevertheless may exploit the potentialities that its "merciless ravage" has afforded, drawing from the experience of revolutionized sensibilities the power to eventuate subversive, liberating, and motivating actions that are "voluptuous" (l. 24), like the speaker's while he observes the "unvisited" hazel "with wise restraint" (l. 23). ("Voluptuous," appropriately, marks another erotic enjambment.)

Here is the allegory of one possible reading: the poet, expecting to be read, pens the confession; and so readers, bringing the poem into consciousness, mobilizing the mechanisms of seduction and violation, seduce the poet into leaving behind tracings of the pen(is) to be followed—not so much back to their originator as to his narrator, upon whom he has apparently displaced his motivations. Readers, then, hearing from the woods the speaker's admonishments to the maiden, themselves become that shadowy, feminized, allegorical figure vanishing into the poem by participating with the "spirit" that has been left there, and may experience, upon *reentering* "Nutting," a "sudden happiness beyond all hope" (l. 29). This will not be some unpersuasive instance of the imitational fallacy,[29] but a repetition of the literal silence of reading prior to consciousness of the poem's success-in-failure.

But to conclude might be to render "Nutting" metaphorically, myself, and cease for a moment the flow of narrative it has initiated and reiterated, to silence this brief supplement ("Wordsworth's 'Nutting' and the Violent End of Reading") to the brief supplement ("Nutting") to the Wordsworthian project (*The Recluse*). I offer a tripartite reply to the subjection fostered by the threesome, the "grotesque triangle,"[30] that is the seductive voice of Wordsworth's poem. "Nutting" is a misericord: a suspension of obligations (the boy's), a side chapel to the greater edifice of poetry (Wordsworth's), and a phallic, chivalrous weapon for delivering the coup-de-grâce to its fatally wounded subject—reading.

2

Romantic Fiction Double Feature:
Caleb Williams, *The Homotextual Adventure Begins*,
and
Frankenstein *Meets Pygmalion*

1.

William Godwin refers to *Caleb Williams* as his "mighty trifle."[1]
Frankenstein Mary Shelley describes as a "hideous progeny."[2]
What animates the famous daughter of this novelist and politi-
cal thinker to characterize her book in parthenogenetic terms?
And why Godwin's oxymoronic modesty?

Criticism has tended to answer the first question with what
has by now become a monstrous collection of commentary,
recently emphasizing the parallels between composition and
gestation. The second question might be dismissed as idle,
until we examine the ways in which Godwin himself came to
regard the writing of his most renowned book as a
Frankensteinian act.

2.

Caleb Williams, a book by a reasonable author, is one that
critiques, among other things, the pursuit of truth—with the
aid of the tongue—by means of reasoning. Were it a detective
novel, and it almost is, I would substitute the word *ratiocination*, or *argumentation, observation, generalization*, all of
which energize the courtroom while (em)powering the species
of justice typical of Anti-/Jacobin England, so brutally and
depressingly portrayed in its pages. The courtroom, the dissatisfying *telos* toward which most of the action tends, is
thus where the truth can be told but not found. This truism
about the book hardly requires annotation, and, meanwhile,
it gains little force through frequent repetition, yet begs for,

even demands, attention to the style of whatever commentary we might bring to bear.

In my estimation, not enough of such attention has been given. Though it is not my project to survey the literature exhaustively, to categorize it as to camp or position, I want to release a reading of the novel that slithers among the structures, like the artificial snake belonging to the replicant Zhora, in Ridley Scott's film, *Blade Runner*, flicking its tongue among both *Caleb Williams* and the burgeoning studies, my own included, whose titles are fitted with colons in such a way as to fix positions, to establish ratios, as it were, which I suspect will continually be disturbed by its force: an artificial organism from which, I hope, the reader, like Zhora, can take pleasure.[3]

3.

Now the idea of *Frankenstein* as critique of scientific—and, by implication, rational—arrogance[4] has become as wearisome as that of *Caleb Williams*'s indictment of justice, but should be reinscribed, and therefore revaluated, as a caution against self-satisfied explications. *Frankenstein*'s escape into the public domain should be enough to silence them decisively, whereas the often delightful abuse the novel receives at the hands of playwrights, filmmakers, and other novelists should make us careful enough about utter neglect of the original.

4.

We should thus pursue three areas of inquiry: the 1832 preface to *Fleetwood*, the subject of subjection and its ambiguous politics, and the use of vocabulary itself as an erotic texture. These are merely three of countless daguerreotypes, arrestations of observation for convenience, pictures taken to improve memory, documentations of moments under motion, in which questions are carefully posed only to be allowed to relax afterward. What we shall *not* do is any of the following: offer explications, either of Godwin, the Shelleys or their work; unfold an exposition or formulate a fastidiously reasoned argument; establish correspondences between Godwin's political thought and his fiction (indeed, in the case of *Caleb Williams*, I would speculate that this particular text, for himself and his characters, constitutes a disruption of or swerving away from his politics) or between, say, Percy Shelley's social thinking and Mary's text, which hardly mirror each other; pass judgment on the characters; or try to read a moral, despite the moralizing that often appears. Though these attempts are frequently helpful, even occasionally interesting, we should rather avoid them—in writing certainly; in reading, with more difficulty—in order to further a project that I would like to believe dances more in step with the spirit, the energy (a word so often reiterated, and so important to that prophetic contemporary already mentioned, especially vis-à-vis reason) of these texts.

5.

I will offer a theory that both Godwin and Mary Shelley suffered from creation anxiety based in the subjection of the flesh, both metaphor and recalcitrant substance, both for a sexual pleasure and the pain of (re)production, hindering as well as mobilizing their narratives. While Mary's is the more convincing—I dare submit: being a woman, she was the more physically subjected and could speak more intimately about parturition—and powerful (her anxiety was added to, and aggravated by, her father's own expectations), Godwin's anxiety is no less important for all that in suggesting an erotics of composition in which the page becomes the site of a conflict determining much more than any disembodied identity.

6.

In addition, a number of English and continental sources come to bear upon themes in *Frankenstein*, specifically the Pygmalion/Galatea myth—as retold by Dryden, Rousseau, Madame de Genlis, and others—as it applies to Mary Shelley's figuration of the creative process. For her, this process involves pains and torments like those associated with childbirth and childrearing. In the retrospective of both her (and Percy's) prefatory narratives and Frankenstein's own narrative, memory shapes creativity as (does) a Pygmalion evoking warm flesh from inchoate lifelessness. But it also resembles Prometheus's primal acts of creation, which involve the molding of man from the mud and the bestowal of the forbidden fire.[5]

In the Shelleys' narratives, a contrast is established between two central paradigms: the Promethean (additive) creative process and Pygmalion's subtractive method. "The Modern Prometheus" himself describes his procedures in terms of the peculiar anguishes of an additive process that cannot quite attain the powerfully shaping force of his mythical namesake. Victor's labors miscarry, in part because he must resort to the mere *bricolage* of decaying materials not easily acquired, instead of evoking life from shapeless, inert matter readily available. Mary, recalling how she was "collecting her materials" (that is, reading and researching) for *Frankenstein*, seems to identify with her protagonist in lamenting over her inabilities both as a writer and as a mother, looking back to the crucial period of 1818-19. In fact, the Pygmalion/Galatea myth becomes especially compelling for Mary, whose difficulties with childbearing at this time, ironically, help her form an artistic autonomy apart from those (mostly male) figures who inspire her nightmare.

Finally, though, Mary's authority as a mother, her personal experiences with, and memories of the pains of, creativity, enable her to bear *herself* into the world as a writer, and declare herself as a fellow, rather than a fallow, romantic, with her first major work.

7.

For my discussion of the *Fleetwood* preface, I will read (it) through the famous preface to the 1831 edition of *Frankenstein*—another Standard Novels edition by another increasingly quietist and retrospective author—whose compositional issues are not only similar but influential. Since *Frankenstein* is usually read and studied first, and since its stature in our culture as a (however inaccurate) catchword and paradigm continues yet to grow, it could be said that the later novel influences the earlier, in Harold Bloom's convoluted sense, no matter how shaped by her own father's *Caleb Williams* and her husband's early poems was Mary Shelley's narrative of two central figures, posed in reciprocal presupposition, engaged in the politics of subjection. Meanwhile, I will trace the dynamics of this very action, looking to the paradigmatic example of Godwin's contemporary, Sade, through the eyes of Blanchot, to see more clearly how it is operating: that is, how the maintenance of Caleb and Falkland within the arena of the seduction tale—and this is what, it seems to me, Caleb's narrative resolves itself into—serves both as a way to explore the theme and to power the narrative, during the three requisite volumes of the longer romance or sentimental novel, to a conclusion that is not merely one of narrative thematics.

And at the same time, I will reread the very words of Godwin's and Mary Shelley's novels in such a way as to imply that, for example, rather than being simply clumsy or dilatory writing (Rothstein 209), their prose operates through a controlled use of limited vocabulary, a drama of substantives, that sextualizes their novels beyond any hope for recaptured innocence through objective discourse. When I conclude, and I hope to be even less conclusive than *Caleb Williams* or *Frankenstein*, I should try to lead the discussion out and away, extroduce, toward a theory that might piece together the shots—of the author in the act of looking back on the text (by this time well independent), with which s/he dances the pas de deux of subjection, and incarnating in the language itself the flesh as it is taking pleasure, filling with life, and feeling pain—in order to limn the interaction of writer and book, and suggest further investigations toward a theory.

8.

Anatomy, whose etymology means cutting up, and which has come to mean the study of animal or plant structure, the structure itself, dissection, the body dissected, skeleton, the human body, and any minute examination (*RHD* 75), all of which come to bear on *Frankenstein* and *Caleb Williams*, is twice alluded to in the 1832 preface to Godwin's *Fleetwood*. Godwin remarks:

> The thing in which my imagination revelled the most freely, was the analysis of the private and internal operations of the mind, employing my metaphysical dissecting knife in tracing and laying bare the involutions of motive, and recording the gradually accumulating impulses, which led the personages I had to describe primarily to adopt the particular way of proceeding in which they afterwards embarked. [*Caleb Williams* 339]

Turning, secondly, away from the private procedure to the public relation with the body, Godwin says, rather vividly, that he and his fellow authors "were all of us engaged in exploring the entrails of mind and motive, and in tracing the various rencontres and clashes that may occur between man and man in the diversified scene of human life" (*Caleb Williams* 340).[6]

In the first instance, he emphasizes instrument, process, and personal motive; in the second, community, flesh, and social motivation. The vocabularies are similar. He repeats the words *mind* and *tracing,* the stress points of the novel's genesis, consciousness and writing. The vocabularies are also dissimilar: particular becomes various and diversified, for example, an inductive motion that itself traces the movement of the action. In both cases Godwin speaks as if mind and motive are somehow already present—like the organs and vessels and nerves of a corpse, to be traced and recorded, written down from the dictation of observation—also, heaped up beside and outside that body's territory—in the bodies of his characters.

9.

This is Godwin's desire as he writes: that the project he has undertaken will in a sense write *itself.* He seems anxious that, for one thing, the story will be substantial enough to tell ("Here were ample materials for a first volume," he says [*Caleb Williams* 337], relieved, after outlining the third and second volumes); and, for another thing, that such a substantial story, a *responsibility* having started as a "vocation" (*Caleb Williams* 335), will actually get written: "I wrote only when the afflatus was upon me" (338). He makes a remark that excuses him from any "idleness," to which he submits in silence[7]—at the same time that it validates the end product. The fleshly metaphor is throughout this preface clothed, consciously or not, as double entendres: dead-born, elevation, conceive, conception, excitement, energy, labor, imaging the fifteen-month composition of the book as *re*production as well as production.[8]

The first and last words of the list above, carrying with them all the anxiety of a successful childbirth, in a period of many unsuccessful ones, which, as texts, Godwin was "rather inclined to suppress" (*Caleb Williams* 335), curiously figure the author as mother, like Godwin's wife Mary, dying as a result of bearing another Mary, who herself would bear a sickly child and participate in the anxiety both of the birth of children and the birth of books.

10.

By now, the 1831 introduction to *Frankenstein,* which Mary resisted writing, has become as infamous among commentators on romanticism as the novel-as-myth among most people. Perhaps Mary feared the great variety of sometimes monstrous biographical and bibliogenetical analyses with which her "account of the origin of the story" (*Frankenstein* 222) would be ravished.

The following discussion will attempt one more such violation, but only to reaffirm what Mary herself brings forward: her sense of despair in the work, a novel that clearly she viewed as a memory and remnant and artifact of a fleeting inspiration, "the offspring of happy days" (*Frankenstein* 229) with a life of its own, much as her husband viewed *his* work—because *Frankenstein* turned out to be the wretched assemblage of a modern Prometheus rather than another Galatea, organically shaped and brought to life by some ideal Pygmalion.

11.

Mary describes a familiar romantic creative process: an inspiration filling the mind in a dream state, "a spontaneous overflow of powerful feelings," as Wordsworth would say, or trauma, which gets recorded afterward in such a way as to provide a memorial to the event (or loss) of the inspiration itself, "[recollection] in tranquillity" or self-conscious literary discourse. Thus, just as Prometheus does not create the clay from which he molds his man, the writer does not conger the inspiration, the raw materials:

> When I placed my head on my pillow, I did not sleep, nor could I be said to think. My imagination, unbidden, possessed and guided me, gifting the successive images that arose in my mind with a vividness far beyond the usual bounds of reverie. I saw—with shut eyes, but acute mental vision,—I saw the pale student of unhallowed arts kneeling beside the thing he had put together. I saw the hideous phantasm of a man stretched out, and then, on the working of some powerful engine, show signs of life, and stir with an uneasy, half vital motion. [*Frankenstein* 227-28]

The writer remains passive throughout the event. Upon waking, she begins to act, to write, thankful for being given the desired materials:

> I opened [my eyes] in terror. . . . I recurred to my ghost story,—my tiresome unlucky ghost story! . . . On the morrow I announced that I had *thought of a story*. I began that day with the words, *It was on a dreary night of November*, making only a transcript of the grim terrors of my waking dream. [228, Mary's italics]

Frankenstein has therefore been born. But it might not live long, Percy reasons, unless the transcript grows and develops under Mary's close attention. So she starts immediately expanding her short tale into a novel roughly the size of its Gothic predecessors, and with an intent similar to that behind those other works: "O! if I could only contrive [a story] which would frighten my reader as I myself had been frightened that night!" (228).

12.

But Mary has already shown that the process is somewhat more complicated. Her nightmare is predated not only by that terrifying evening at Byron's, nearly as infamous itself as the novel it helped inspire, but by an imaginative childhood, one of "indulging in waking dreams" (*Frankenstein* 222) as much as of scribbling. Indeed, Mary says, "my dreams were at once more fantastic and agreeable than my writings" (222), admitting that her imagination, as well as her recollection, works proleptically, in classically romantic fashion. "[As] the daughter of two persons of distinguished literary celebrity" (222), she has been favorably inclined by nature for the nurture of marriage with Percy Bysshe Shelley and her friendship with other literary celebrities. When she encounters the ghost stories, and is called upon to create one herself, she sees the challenge as a demonstration of ability, certainly, but also as the fulfillment of a terrible responsibility. And her introduction suggests that the fulfillment was not quite complete.

13.

The *Edinburgh Magazine* of March 1818 wondered "why [*Frankenstein*] should have been written."[9] The purpose of exorcising the terror and thrill of fear that awakened Mary (Rieger xxxiv) does not seem a likely explanation. It is not just that Mary explicitly wanted to *reawaken* those feelings, which invalidates this answer, but that the act of writing the novel was much more powerfully determined by her desire to create something that would be worthy of the inspiration, of her father, of her husband, and of her colleagues. During that galvanizing conversation between Byron, Polidori, and Percy, Mary found "not only . . . a striking subject, but . . . a description of her own situation as she was trying to 'think of a story'" (Small 35).

Critics have suggested that Mary's imagination operated in large part on the level of the literal or real, and that this limitation explains the highly autobiographical nature of her output (Small 28). "[Mary] could not help putting into her writing a large share not only of what she thought but also of what she experienced. Not gifted in invention, she turned to actuality for character and incident" (Nitchie xiii–xiv).[10] But it is much more helpful, and fair to Mary's obvious talent for invention—she wrote much more fiction after Percy's death—to think of the situation in the following terms:

> . . . [Mary's] developing sense of herself as a literary creature and/or creator seems to have been inseparable from her emerging self-definition as daughter, mistress, wife, and mother. . . [*Frankenstein*] is . . . a female fantasy of sex and reading [and] a gothic psychodrama reflecting Mary Shelley's own sense of what we might call bibliogenesis. [Gilbert and Gubar 230]

Further, "in her alienated attic workshop of filthy creation she has given birth to a deformed book, a literary abortion or miscarriage" (Gilbert and Gubar 233). The birth analogy is helpful (again, perhaps only women are authorized to speak intimately of the experience) and logical, because it derives from Mary's sense of herself as a failed mother: in February 1815 she gives birth to a daughter, conceived out of wedlock, who, dying a few days later, never gets named (Frankenstein's creation remains nameless, also). Sometimes the analogy is expressed with shifting emphasis:

> Making a transcript of a dream—that is, turning an idea into the 'machinery of a story'—a dream that is about the transformation of a 'phantasm' into a real body, is equivalent here to conceiving a child.
>
> Writing a transcript of a dream that was in turn merely the transcript of a conversation is also giving birth to a hideous progeny conceived in the night. [Homans 117]

But the comparison remains compelling, and will guide the remainder of this investigation. It is certainly true, at any rate, that "*Frankenstein* must have had something of the quality of a declaration, to the world in general, and to some persons in particular . . . [as] her first serious literary undertaking" (Small 72), and that

> The narrative that Mary Shelley wrote between that 'eventful
> summer' and the following April was less a wholehearted cel-
> ebration of the imaginative enterprise she had undertaken in
> order to prove her worth to Percy than a troubled, veiled
> exploration of the price she had already begun to fear such
> egotistical self-assertion might exact. [Poovey 121]

A "wholehearted celebration," no, a "troubled, veiled exploration," yes, as the following pages would like to claim.

14.

The scene of the conflict whose antagonists lend their names to
the facetious title *Pygmalion Meets Prometheus*, my imaginary
matinee, is Mary Shelley herself: she sits enlarging her "short
tale" (*Frankenstein* 228), on Percy's wish, into a novel-size
narrative, suturing the gathering pages into her first work "of
a gigantic stature" (49).

15.

The character Lionel Verney's last work in Mary Shelley's huge
novel, *The Last Man*—his last act, geste, gesture, gesticulation,
as well as gestation—comes forth eight years later, when Mary
looks back to eight years earlier, the year *Frankenstein* was
published, the year she and her companion, visiting and exploring Naples and surroundings, find the Sibylline leaves upon
which Verney's last words lie strewn:

> The translucent and shining waters of the calm sea covered
> fragments of old Roman villas, which were interlaced with sea-
> weed, and received diamond tints from the chequering of the
> sun-beams; the blue and pellucid element was such as Galatea
> might have skimmed in her car of mother of pearl; or Cleopatra,
> more fitly than the Nile, have chosen as the path of her magic
> ship.[11]

One of the myths of Galatea tells of her love for Acis, and the
jealousy of Polyphemus, who attacks the couple while they sit
in the woods. Galatea jumps in the water; Acis runs, calling for
Galatea's help, and gets killed by the rock that Polyphemus
hurls. Acis becomes the river Acis upon which Galatea floats.

16.

The maiden recounts the story to Scylla from her grotto, a cave
similar to the one Mary and friend insist on investigating only

to come across the prophecies that Mary feels compelled to transmute for readers:

> I have been employed in deciphering these sacred remains. Their meaning, wondrous and eloquent, has often repaid my toil, soothing me in sorrow, and exciting my imagination to daring flights, through the immensity of nature and the mind of man. . . . I present the public with my latest discoveries in the slight Sibylline pages. Scattered and unconnected as they were, I have been obliged to add links, and model the work into a consistent form. [*The Last Man* 3–4]

Once again, Mary distances herself from her work—only this time she does not wait for the additional distance of eight years to erode her memory and heighten her self-consciousness (the 1831 introduction to *Frankenstein* was yet another male wish for Mary to fulfill).

17.

But it is not the Galatea story above that suggests this working method (editing prophecy), as well as her consciousness while engaged. It is, rather, the story of Galatea's creation at the hands of Pygmalion (and the heart of Venus), references to which come later, in the body of the novel, when Lionel Verney is speaking—perhaps for, perhaps as, Mary:

> The perfect moulding brought with it the idea of colour and motion; often, half in bitter mockery, half in self-delusion, I clasped [the statues'] icy proportions, and, coming between Cupid and his Psyche's lips, pressed the unconceiving marble. [338]

18.

Mary was probably familiar with the story of Pygmalion and the statue from several significant versions. One is Dryden's translation of the Tenth Book of Ovid's *Metamorphoses* (1700). There, a sculptor, turned misogynist by the lascivious behavior of the Propoetides whom Venus has turned into stone, carves a maid out of ivory (also, apparently, out of fear from what Blake would call his Spectre, a malevolent power that stifles creativity). Pygmalion becomes enamored with this image of female perfection, and embraces the statue, although with some dread of despoiling "his idol" with marks of the human touch which might reveal the "art, hid with art" and offend his sensibilities—indeed which does "[catch] the carver with his own deceit" (Dryden 293 ll. 17–18). He adorns her with rich and "pow'rful bribes of love" (l. 36) and, in effect, makes the statue his bride.

Pygmalion prays to Venus to make the image come alive, and returns to his workshop to find her flesh "like pliant wax, when chafing hands reduce / The former mass to form, and frame for use" (ll. 85–86). Their union produces Paphos, the "lovely boy" (l. 99) who eventually gives his name to the city.

19.

Another version of the myth is Rousseau's *Pygmalion. Scène lyrique* (the most recent French edition was printed in Geneva, 1782), a libretto. This particular sculptor's Spectre is *preventing* the "happy skill" of Dryden's carver: *O mon génie, où est tu? Mon talent qu'es-tu devenu? Tout mon feu s'est éteint, mon imagination s'est glacée, le marbre sort froid de mes mains* ("Oh my genius, where are you? My talent, what have you become? All my fire has gone out, my imagination has frozen, the marble goes cold from my hands") (1224).

Convinced that his inspiration has died, he sees his statue both as monument to his becalmed creativity and as consolation for the ensuing ennui:

> *Quand mon esprit éteint ne produira plus rien de grand, de beau, de digne de moi, je montrerai ma Galathée, et je dirai: Voilà mon ouvrage! O ma Galathée! quand j'aurai tout perdu, tu me resteras, et je serai consolé* (When my extinguished spirit produces nothing more from me of the great, the beautiful, and the worthy, I will show my Galatea, and I will say: Behold my work! Oh my Galatea! when I have lost all, you will remain with me, and I will be consoled). [1225]

Not quite convinced, however, of the statue's perfection, Pygmalion approaches to make the finishing touch, and finds *la chair palpitante repousser le ciseau!* ("the palpitating flesh spurning the chisel!") (1227). He prays ardently to heaven, where Venus—not at all offended, apparently, by Pygmalion's claim that even she is less beautiful than his "goddess"—is sufficiently moved to animate the statue, even at the cost of the sculptor's "life": *je t'ai donné tout mon être* ("I have given you my entire being"). He tells his rather laconic Galatea, *je ne vivrai plus que par toi* ("I shall live no longer but through you") (1231).

20.

Caroline-Stéphanie du Crest Comtesse de Genlis Marquise de Sillery's *Pygmalion et Galatée; ou La Statue animée depuis vingt-quatre heures* (*Pygmalion and Galatea; or The Statue Given Life for Twenty-four Hours* [1802]) provides the last example. "Mme de Genlis' prefatory note [to *Pygmalion et Galatée*] indicated that [it] was written to be played after the 'scène lyrique' on the same theme by Rousseau" (Polin 101). A prolific, independent, and didactic writer in the revolutionary period of France, who critiqued Rousseau and whose counsel was sought by Napoleon, Madame de Genlis bears an obscure name to most English-language readers;[12] but she was well known to the Shelleys. "I assume that Mary read [*Pygmalion et Galatée*] before the evening of her inspirational 'nightmare,' described in her preface of 1831" (Polin 100). Unfortunately, despite the increased attention that Madame de Genlis should gain, for the purposes of this investigation, she is a presence only in that Mary added the comtesse to her reading list of 1816, when she was "collecting her materials" for *Frankenstein*.

21.

Percy alludes to Galatea in at least two places: *Prometheus Unbound* and *A Defence of Poetry*. Both references associate motherhood with artistic creation, but only after Mary has already done so (as several critics demonstrate) in crafting *The Modern Prometheus*. Asia, while offering her own version of Greek creation myth, speaks in Percy's play (II.iv.80–84) about the birth (and fall) of sculpture:

> And human hands first mimicked and then mocked
> With moulded limbs more lovely than its own
> The human form, till marble grew divine,
> And mothers, gazing, drank the love men see
> Reflected in their race, behold, and perish.[13]

The marble here is not only that of sculptures depicting gods and goddesses but of those that are eternal, like Galatea, in their own right: those that cause mothers despair in creating anything so beautiful. This despair—manifest when Frankenstein flees from his recently animated creature, and when Pygmalion prays for the life of the ivory goddess of his creation—operating in Mary Shelley while her "hideous progeny"

(*Frankenstein* 229) grows in that dark womb/winter of 1816–
17, is aggravated by Percy's idealizing defense of poetry:

> Milton conceived the Paradise Lost as a whole before he ex-
> ecuted it in portions. We have his own authority also for the
> Muse having "dictated" to him the "unpremeditated song," and
> let this be an answer to those who would allege the fifty-six
> various readings of the first line of the Orlando Furioso. Com-
> positions so produced are to poetry what mosaic is to paint-
> ing. This instinct and intuition of the poetical faculty is still
> more observable in the plastic and pictorial arts: a great statue
> or picture grows under the power of the artist as a child in the
> mother's womb, and the very mind which directs the hands in
> formation is incapable of accounting to itself the origin, the
> gradations, or the media of the process. [*Shelley's Poetry and
> Prose* 504]

Mary wants to "conceive" before she "executes"; wants to take
from divine dictation rather than merely "develope [an] idea at
greater length" (*Frankenstein* 229); wants the picture whole,
and not the assembled mosaic; desires a progeny that will *live*
(unlike her first child). And, though she may not seem fully to
understand "the origins, the gradations, or the media of the
process" that animates *Frankenstein* by means of the modern
Prometheus as distinct from that which animated Galatea by
means of the timeless Pygmalion, she shares Percy's conception of art, bearing the sickly and sickening results in that
"offspring" of desk work.

22.

The following is a statement typically misleading in masculinist
discussions of Frankenstein *cum* Prometheus:

> As the novel proceeds and Frankenstein carries out the tradi-
> tional achievement of Prometheus by forming and giving life to
> man, he clearly transcends his merely Promethean aspect and
> becomes, in the texture of the novel, a version of the "Creator"—
> of God Himself. [Walling 42]

In discussing the subtitle of *Frankenstein*, critics seem to ignore the importance of the adjective *modern* and its meaning
for Mary Shelley's and—by extension, Victor Frankenstein's—
acts of creation. But this deceptively simple attributive, which
tempts the reader to scan over it and register "the Prometheus
of the modern age" or "Prometheus in the guise of the protago-

nist," means much more. It indicates how Mary felt about "those muscles and joints" (*Frankenstein* 53) as well as her own "several pages" (229). For the modern Mary, Prometheus has become something far less than he once was.

23.

But what *was* he?

> The idea of Prometheus as the creator of mankind in general crops up in various Latin authors . . . often with the accompanying notion that the work was ill done: or at least that man's imperfections, and especially his "animal nature," are to be blamed on him. [Small 48–49]

In Greek myth, the Titan Prometheus, like the God of the Old Testament, forms humans out of the clay, after "[Jove] and Nature at last [interpose], and put an end to [Chaos]" (Bulfinch 15), separating the intermingled elements. Unlike the God of the Old Testament, then, Prometheus does not form the clay itself. He only mimics the Platonic (and Shelleyan) demiurge, who also does not create the clay itself. But Prometheus has the advantage of being provided with his materials before beginning work on his organically whole creature, whom he will endow with the fire of intelligence and ingenuity that will raise the human above the level of all other animals, however "ill done" the work.

Prometheus plasticator, as he is often called, therefore uses an additive process in sculpting this work, building it up from a mixture of the two earthly elements—soil and water—before infusing it with that most agitated of elements, fire, so that it can walk upright in the air, and look at the stars.

24.

Pygmalion, conversely, like any sculptor with hammer and chisel, is confronted with a block of material, itself a chunk of earth, which must be chipped away in order to achieve the sculpture. His will be a subtractive process: the chaos, the shapeless dross, of the stone will be reduced to the order, the balanced lineaments, of the figure. The cold marble falls from his hands to the floor, while the warm marble lives on the pedestal. Pygmalion manages results as organically perfect as the classical Prometheus's, through a process described by Asia in the passage from the *Unbound* above: not only does his sculpture live, it reproduces, like Prometheus's first man.

25.

So remarks such as "Frankenstein . . . is Promethean first and foremost as a maker of man" (Small 48) and "Frankenstein 'is' . . . *Prometheus plasticator*, the creator of mankind" (Oates 244) become misleading, qualified as they are, unless qualified as follows:

> Woman must be the work of God. There is a difference to be seen here between the act of Prometheus and that of Pygmalion, where overwhelming desire for the woman he has made as a work of art brings her to life (or causes Aphrodite [Venus] to do so in pity for him).
>
> It is not so much that Prometheus is to be thought of as the original teacher of anatomy, and that Mary Shelley knew as much, as that analytical reason necessarily acts in this way: the human form in dissection is an emblem of analysis in general as readily available to the modern as to the ancient imagination. [Small 50]
>
> Since Frankenstein's creature is made up of parts collected from charnel-houses and graves, and his creator acknowledges that he "disturbed, with profane fingers, the tremendous secrets of the human frame," it is inevitable that he be a *profane* thing. He cannot be blessed or loved: he springs not from a natural union, but has been forged in what Frankenstein calls a "workshop of filthy creation." [Oates 249]

Mary saw herself, saw Frankenstein, as such a corrupted, imperfect, probably immoral—as a *modern*—version of Prometheus. She desired, like Victor, to be a type of Pygmalion, an ideal romantic creator, disposing of the chaos and excess and filth to achieve the whole, living art rather than assembling parts and attempting to animate them in the manner of her contemporaneous industrial manufacturers. And yet the book *Frankenstein*, as well as its namesake's creature, results from the latter procedure, and becomes a dramatization of Mary's creation anxiety and fear of failure:

> The sudden flash of inspiration must be supported by the meticulous gathering of heterogeneous, ready-made materials: Frankenstein collects bones and organs; Mary records overheard discussions of scientific questions that lead her to her sudden vision of monstrous creation. [Johnson 7]

And two more feminist critics refer to "the Miltonic skeleton around which Mary Shelley's hideous progeny took shape" (Gilbert and Gubar 230). In Mary's day, "anatomy" could mean "skeleton." Though a student of "natural philosophy ... in the most comprehensive sense of the term" [*Frankenstein* 45], Frankenstein will have to resort to such an armature, which the ideal Prometheus does not. And his creature will end up a see-through, an anatomical model, analytical as well as synthetic, one whose "yellow skin scarcely [covers] the work of muscles and arteries beneath" (*Frankenstein* 52). Not only does Mary "abundantly ['identify'] with Victor Frankenstein" (Spivak 259): she "was always encouraged to live up to the Romantic ideal of the creative artist, to prove herself by means of her pen and her imagination" (Poovey 115).

26.

As the conflict continues, Percy proofreads, and subtracts, adds, and alters the growing tale himself: "[Percy's] assistance at every point in the book's manufacture was so extensive that one hardly knows whether to regard him as editor or minor collaborator" (Rieger xviii). At first the book is assumed to be his, and thirteen years later, nine years after his death, Mary admits that the preface is wholly his. Like Sir Timothy, who wouldn't die, and let go of Mary and Percy Jr., who tried to annihilate his rebellious son from wide public knowledge, this book would be the one Shelley that would seem never to release its hold.

27.

Despite Victor Frankenstein's astounding success in animating his corporeal assemblage, he fails. And his failure is not simply one of ethics—that he will not take responsibility for what he has done—but one of aesthetics: he, like other characters, is horrified by what he *witnesses* (the creature has not yet actually done anything), and flees: "Oh! no mortal could support the horror of that countenance" (*Frankenstein* 53). Also, like other characters, he is intent on its destruction— but *he*, at least initially, only to assuage his fear and loathing. Perhaps Frankenstein's sense of beauty explains his extreme repulsion *upon completion and motivation of his creature* and not before. "I had gazed on him while unfinished; he was ugly then; but when those muscles and joints were rendered capable of motion, it became a thing such as even Dante could not have conceived" (53).

Frankenstein, of course, uses a word deeply embedded in the body of the novel that bears his name—a word, like dilate, labor, animation, fatigue, consummation, impulse, and many others, relevant to Mary's several roles. The creature possesses a terrible beauty, a living death, that is homoerotically powerful, even alluring, like a "vampyre," as Homans (106) and Spivak (230) suggest, as well as romantic in the demonic sense: a beauty that lies beyond Frankenstein and yet controls him even when he has escaped it. "Frankenstein thinks he wants to create the demon, but when he has succeeded, he discovers that what he really enjoyed was the process leading up to the creation" (Homans 107). Falkland's pursuit of Caleb Williams takes on similar contours: only when he has destroyed him does he see that the other, though malignant, was necessary for self-presence: "Alas!" exclaims Caleb. "I am the same Caleb Williams that, so short a time ago, boasted, that, however great were the calamities I endured, I was still innocent" (*Caleb Williams* 325).

28.

Above all, Frankenstein's first reaction to the live creature resembles Mary's reaction to her nightmare, and her life, closely enough to necessitate her identification with him (*Frankenstein* 52–53 [Frankenstein narrating the creature's awakening], 228 [Mary remembering the dream that sketched the scene]). While Victor's narrative suggests a literary act ("toils," "anxiety," "agony," "instruments," "candle . . . nearly burnt out"), Mary speaks of the creature as if it were a text.[14]

Her scientist, an "artist," "communicates" the spark of life through a creator's "mechanism" (the biblical creator's first creative act is to *speak*), and then hopes for its oblivion through "silence." Moreover, she refers to the creature's life as "imperfect." Later she calls the novel her "hideous progeny" and recalls its writing elegiacally: "the offspring of happy days" (*Frankenstein* 239), while feeling grateful that she need only "describe the spectre" of her "waking dream" in order to fulfill her promise to write a ghost story.

29.

One of Caleb Williams's "paroxysms," outbursts of despair within his generally controlled narrative, sounds much like one of the creature's: "Accursed world! that hates without a cause, that overwhelms innocence with calamities which ought to be spared even to guilt! Accursed world! dead to every manly sympathy; with eyes of horn, and hearts of steel!" (*Caleb Williams* 252). It could be that Caleb is describing a machine, an assemblage, created by, and standing, through synecdoche, for, all people. Caleb eventually prowls unseen around the Denisons, much as the creature does around the DeLaceys (*Caleb Williams* 298); and, when importuning himself upon Laura, gets called a "monster" (300). Collins refers to Caleb as a "machine" (310), much as Frankenstein calls his creature a "vile insect"[15] (Rieger ed. 94). Yet Falkland ends up resembling Frankenstein's creature more than does Caleb: "His whole figure was thin to a degree that suggested the idea rather of a skeleton than a person actually alive" (*Caleb Williams* 281).

Similarly, Caleb gets figured as a type of Christ (224, 235, 236, 323, 324), but also as a sort of Satan "turned out loose in the world to do [his] worst" (285; Thomas's words). In the final courtroom scene, first Caleb cries "Do with me as you please!" (323) and then Falkland says the same (324) in reply. Who is the victor, and who the vanquished? Who is the creator, and who the made?

30.

Is this ambiguous subject the one, finally, that begs, please, for no additional discourse? And, if so, is this because the subject is continually rehearsing its own elimination? I say rehearsing, because, if performed, this removal threatens to be, though without ever succeeding to be, conclusive. Even if it cannot believe in its own finality, the alternative becomes the subject's death. Maurice Blanchot's discourse, at least, seems simultaneously self-eliminating and self-perpetuating. Similarly, Godwin's contemporary Sade's macabre dance of seduction must preserve not so much the object of undoing as the ever-self-negating subject, though incarcerated: to kill him would be to provide the ultimate justification ("Sade" 52), the "unnameable jouissance" (Kristeva 1986 473), which is always untenable according to the terms of the social contract. Blanchot's dialectic—vibrating between alienation and intimacy; between, for instance, the typical neglect shown Sade and Blanchot's own atypical respect that seems only its obverse, locus as well as focus for scandal and infamy and debauchery—achieves abnegation.

This is no mere inversion of scriptorial selfhood, no martyrdom in writing's name, no effeminizing of the roué. Blanchot
may partake of the sadism that must revert to masochism
once isolated. He writes, "When I am alone, I am not alone,
but, in this present, I am already returning to myself in the
form of Someone" ("The Essential Solitude" 31). Also, had the
sadist no object, his imprisonment would be harder to bear
than death, being a triumph of technology over nature. Yet
Blanchot's dismissal of the writer is indeed convincing, since
it is willed by an inescapable reason at the same time as it is
surrendered to fascination, the gaze of the debauchee as it is
held by its victim.

31.

Only the perpetrator has meaning, yet only so long as the
innocent possess an overabundance. This is no real contradiction. It doesn't alter practice; in fact, it confirms it. Blanchot
avers that the power principle "assigns man a future without
saddling him with any feeling of indebtedness to any transcendental concept" ("Sade" 65). Once a transcendental, perhaps
humanistic and teleological concept has been negated, all that's
left is negation itself, magnifying itself to infinity to match the
seemingly overwhelming meaningfulness of the object.

32.

Thus Blanchot reverses the power structure: "a transcendent
power of negation" must first see others as nothing before it
can destroy them. It "does not even presuppose their previous
existence" ("Sade" 58). To achieve this power, the destroyer
turns himself absolutely into God-on-earth. From this position
he can assail nature the most effectively. Yet he finds that
"Nature eludes his negation, and . . . the more he insults and
defiles it the better he serves it" (62). What results is the tor-
turing bliss and the blissful torture of peripeteic role reversal
in the sexual drama.

33.

Of course Blanchot's own project of exposing as marginal, if not
unnecessary, the self-centered author believing (traditionally)
himself to be master over the domain of his text resonates with
this rewriting of Sade's life and work, and echoes with echoes

of self-reflexivity. For instance, in Blanchot's discussion of the mirror image in "Two Versions of the Imaginary" (in _The Gaze of Orpheus_), he wishes to unseat the idea that the object is somehow more real than its reflection. He asks: Isn't the reflection "more spiritual than the object reflected?" (81). This image, being an ideal of the object of which it is supposedly a mere representation, Blanchot suggests, seems to precede, like the cadaver preceding any idea of its having a soul, that very object, thereby menacing its ascendance.

The spirituality of the mirror image and the resemblance of "mortal remains" to the imaginary both come as a surprise _and_ seem antithetical. Then, they come as no surprise, and seem a supplanting truth. Blanchot is turning his own discourse in upon itself, subverting orthodoxy as to categorical oppositions (real vs. ideal, spiritual vs. material) as he goes:

> The apparent spirituality, the pure formal virginity of the image is fundamentally linked to the elemental strangeness and to the shapeless heaviness of the being that is present in absence. [_The Gaze of Orpheus_ 83][16]

34.

Turning to Sade, and playing on the word adamant, Blanchot remarks, "in order to convert passion into energy, it must be compressed and mediatized by passing through a necessary moment of insensibility, after which it will attain its apogee" ("Sade" 67).[17] Just as the seemingly ethereal image possesses heft, so the impulsive force of energy increases through inertia. And it is not simply that, whether Sade's or Blanchot's, paradox undoes the subject through this mass and velocity, but that the undoing gets, itself, perpetually undone. Sade's pro-/ antagonist discovers, in "Sade," to his dismay, that "there is no crime possible," by means of Blanchot's vicious syllogism—the thesis and antithesis having first established that, one, crime is the spirit of nature, and, two, that there is no crime against nature (63). Conversely, Blanchot's subject finds that "the ungraspable is what one does not escape" (_The Gaze of Orpheus_ 84) through an analogous perversion of ratiocination.

35.

Blanchot, judiciously delighted, can thus uncover affinities, even in matters of style, praising Sade's "rich but precise and firm" language. Barthes remarks of Sade that "pornographic messages are embodied in sentences so pure they might be used as grammatical models" (*The Pleasure of the Text* 6). Blanchot also *dis*-covers in Sade a logic driven "to its ultimate limits," a "psychoanalysis" that explores within its own "text" limits of reasoning and coherence (39, 62, 70, respectively). He boasts that Sade's philosophy can "modify the bases of all comprehension" (72), after dislodging the marquis from his position as an unapproachable "masterpiece of infamy and debauchery" (38). Sade becomes that shadow of Blanchot going before and behind, reassuring and terrorizing at once. Both writers can be seen as haunting the anarchism of an implosive movement such as romanticism.

36.

In a prosaic sense, Blanchot can speak of the unspeakable because he lies at two removes, at least—he produces a text upon Sade's text—from the sphere of Sade's action and influence. But also because he has conspired with the marquis in formulating a workable absolute in which the reader, as object, gets alienated—that is, shunned—following noncompliance, or made intimate, compelled, regardless of the same.

    Blanchot writes beyond Sade, finally, into a more essential solitude than self-abuse, whether physical or psychological, practiced either alone or in the presence of an object. Sade remains locked in conflict with nature, by necessity, even though he gets removed to the Bastille, which gets removed, and his books get removed from shelves, while Blanchot removes himself from the inside, from the imagined debauchery spilling onto the page, by an ultimately more powerful debauchery, leaving the abuse to his expositors. Possibly, then, when the subject undergoes this calamity, it achieves the *extasis* possible in vulnerability, succeeding without fail. "A transformation such as this, involving a labor of self-destruction, is not accomplished without the most extreme difficulty" ("Sade" 68).

37.

What has led Falkland and Caleb to a kind of sudden reversal (Graham 48–49) Caleb summarizes apostrophically, using the archaic second-person singular, on the last page of his "mangled tale":

> Year after year didst thou spend in this miserable project of imposture; and only at last continuedst to live long enough to see, by my misjudging and abhorred intervention, thy closing hope disappointed, and thy death accompanied with the foulest disgrace! [*Caleb Williams* 326]

Caleb closes by admitting that his own project of self-vindication has shown itself empty, suggesting that, without Falkland to constitute that self through pursuit, there is no longer a "character... to vindicate" (326). Hence, there is no reason to continue the narrative (Walton 61). If Caleb is his text, or other texts within the one he himself constitutes (see 79, 263, 265), one that depends on Falkland's and others' importunity, then there is little point in extrapolating from what Caleb offers as "truths" that will only slip off the margins (Scheiber 255–56). We have to dispose or impose.

38.

Perhaps Falkland accepts this dilemma as a modus operandi on the example of Barnabas Tyrrel, who is a Sadist, fulfilling the paradigm above, in the grip of some power beyond him.[18] For example, after noticing the young Hawkins's "agility and sagacity" (*Caleb Williams* 69), Tyrrel begins to court the boy. When the rival in the person of the elder Hawkins declines to let the boy go, Tyrrel becomes single-minded: "the only effect of opposition was to make him eager and inflexible in pursuit of that to which he had before been indifferent" (69). He is "provoked beyond bearing" (71), his rage "ungovernable and fierce" (79), to the extent that he comes to embody the force that no one seems capable of controlling: "Of this malice he was beyond all other human beings the object" (80). This power has succeeded in seducing Tyrrel, for one.

Earlier, Tyrrel's characteristics have been described as heroic (17), with a truly sexual influence over those in his immediate circle (18) and a peculiar violence of expression (27). To Emily Melvile, pawn in the game of chivalry between Tyrrel and Falkland, he remarks, "When did you ever know any body resist my will without being made to repent?" (57). As a result of his failure in defeating Tyrrel (though dead, he still "served eventually to consummate the ruin of a man he hated" [104]), Falkland becomes not just hopelessly melancholy (see Collins's observations on 103) but vindictive, with a need to turn his hatred to the consummation of the ruining another object.[19]

39.

Falkland will himself come to adopt the qualities of the godlike Sadean persecutor. Shortly before the trial scene in which Falkland indicts Caleb for burglary, Caleb muses on "the super-human power Mr. Falkland seemed to possess of bringing back the object of his persecution within the sphere of his authority" (163). Like Tyrrel, Falkland has an "insatiable vengeance" (133) as well as an "all-dreadful name" (293). Not seldom does Caleb express his experiences as to the squire in near-sexual terms (Graham 51).

For instance, when Caleb decides to be Falkland's observer, he speaks as one approaching a love object:

> I remembered the stern reprimand I had received, and his terrible looks; and the recollection gave a kind of tingling sensation, not altogether unallied to enjoyment. The farther I advanced, the more the sensation was irresistible. I seemed to myself perpetually upon the brink of being countermined, and perpetually roused to guard my designs. The more impenetrable Mr. Falkland was determined to be, the more uncontrollable was my curiosity. [*Caleb Williams* 107-08][20]

Afterward, involved in litigation over the deaths of Tyrrel and the Hawkinses, Caleb "[seems] to enjoy the most soul-ravishing calm" (130), possessed of the knowledge that, his curiosity somewhat satisfied, he can inform on him at any time. And, pursued, Caleb allows paranoia to "[tingle] through every fibre of [his] frame" (238).

40.

It is clear enough, by the peroration, that the two parties in this exchange are as essential to each other as sexual partners. "There was something in the temper of [Falkland's] mind," writes Caleb, "that impressed him with aversion to the idea of violently putting an end to my existence; at the same time that unfortunately he could never deem himself sufficiently secured against my recrimination, so long as I remained alive" (304). On the next page, Caleb makes much the same maneuver on behalf of himself:

> [Being followed] was like what has been described of the eye
> of omniscience pursuing the guilty sinner, and darting a ray
> that awakens him to new sensibility, at the very moment that,
> otherwise, exhausted nature would lull him into a temporary
> oblivion of the reproaches of his conscience.

Caleb never can be alone. Interestingly, he combines one sort
of science and another: that of the all-seeing eye, and that of
the inward-looking ego. It is just that, even by this point, Caleb
does not seem to realize the permanence this "oblivion" can
have for the dependent. No longer content to pass by in disguise (305), he must face himself and see that, without
Falkland's "eye of omniscience" overhead, there is little to be
found within.

41.

Frankenstein mentions "infinite pains and care" and "ardour":
the effects and affects of creation. He prepares for "the accomplishment of [his] toils" through, among other activities, reading. Mary has done the same, before starting *Frankenstein.*
Reading lists certainly become subtexts of this novel: Frankenstein reads Cornelius Agrippa, Paracelsus, and Albertus Magnus,
as well as some books recommended by Krempe and Waldman.
The creature reads Plutarch's *Lives,* Milton's *Paradise Lost,* and
Goethe's *The Sorrows of Young Werther.* Mary's reading includes
the scientific, the speculative, and the literary: works ranging
from Erasmus Darwin's and Humphrey Davy's empirical investigations, through those of renaissance and enlightenment
philosophy, to epistolary and gothic novels.[21] Preparing to write
a life of Percy Shelley, Mary remarks in her journal, "I must
collect my materials"[22]—a method reminiscent of Frankenstein's
grave robbing.

42.

Godwin is also busy reading before starting work on his first
large novel. His own (short) list consists of *The Adventures of
Mademoiselle de St. Phale, God's Revenge against Murder,* and
the *Newgate Calendar,* a sort of police blotter of the time, as
well as the story of Bluebeard, and the fiction of his contem-
poraries (*Caleb Williams* 340), with whom he feels an affinity.
And he has made Caleb a reader in the service of Falkland,
who himself loves "the heroic poets of Italy" (*Caleb Williams* 10)

and takes his cue, tragically, from their sentiments. Godwin fills his pages with references to documents of various kinds: letters, overheard narratives, speeches, allusions to books and mythology. Caleb becomes a poet, though he privileges prose, and is constantly discussing his composition processes in ways that must have resembled Godwin's own struggle. For instance, attempting to imitate the model of Addison, Caleb notes, "I often threw down my pen in an extacy of despair. Sometimes, for whole days together I was incapable of action, and sunk into a sort of partial stupor too wretched to be described" (259).

Language speaks about its failure to describe its very production, while veiling the sexual suggestiveness with the sheerest of drapery: a *jouissance* of incapacitation. Caleb allows his narrative to penetrate the consciousnesses of the other characters, sometimes recounting action that he himself never witnessed *as if he did in fact witness it*, in that "theatre" to which he so often refers, calling into question the reality of those characters and that action, implying that he is *building* as much as reporting. And it could be said that the overall movement of the book is a hot Freitagian curve, a protracted, ten-year-long intercourse, compressed into three large acts, with Caleb's final courtroom speech the "extacy" for which the entire novel has been preparing, his friction with Falkland eventually leaving him with a sort of postemissive depression in the form of a thematic denouement.[23]

43.

For each—Frankenstein, the creature, Mary, Caleb, Falkland, Godwin—reading and writing thus direct the course of the rest of the individual's life, forming the inventions that may indeed get extracted from his or her body of labor. One way to see how this effect is operating is to contrast the two sculptural paradigms mentioned above: that of Prometheus with that of Pygmalion, the additive versus the subtractive process, both of which Mary was familiar with. Any further investigations would have to take account of this comparison. In Godwin's case, we should make closer studies of Caleb's narrative strategies and maneuvers, of the physical demands of writing in Godwin's time, and of the difficult politics inherent in authorship in terms of one's concepts of self-presence as a sexual animal.

Part Two

Postmodern Virtualities

Prelude II

French Theorists, Minimalism, AIDS

As I write, the latest filmic version of *Frankenstein* has appeared on video, directed by Kenneth Branagh. I avoided the theatrical release, but I remember that accompanying the film were the usual commodities: a soundtrack album and a companion book ready for gift giving. There was even a novelization, by one Leonore Fleischer. Her last name happens to mean butcher or sawbones, colloquial German terms for surgeon. Also, her first name resonates with Beethoven's tragic operatic heroine: she's Shelley's Elizabeth to Branagh's Fidelio, perhaps, or this new monstrosity's bride?

The confusion inherent between maker and made in Fleischer's name somehow reproduces the same confusion that *Frankenstein* has experienced since publication in 1819, the title seemingly referring to the monster instead of Victor. Fleischer offers a book "based on the screenplay by Steph Lady and Frank Darabont from the Mary Shelley novel," including an afterword by the director discussing the "epic struggle" of making this movie (310). This palimpsestual novel, from the very title, explicitly links Shelley's labor of writing to the labor of childbirth. Her book is her creator/monster, therefore the monster is Victor's child. Branagh admits having drawn this idea from literary criticism. Here the child is indeed father to the man, this particular father having become even more difficult to identify with the addition of all these disparate parts, figurative or literal.

Because I bought my copy in Tower Records, the book comes with attachments: a bar-coded, magnetic prosthesis meant to discourage shoplifting, which covers yet another magnetic strip, with a serrated sale tag hanging sideways. I picked a copy without a bent spine—no mean feat, since pages 158–59 are interrupted by a series of color stills with captions, the only excuse, to many shoppers, no doubt, even to peruse this book, if not pursue it, and then put it back. Foucault's six-sided document now has added dimensions. *Mary Shelley's Frankenstein* was displayed in the store next to the original novel—that is, the revised, 1831 edition—Americanized in spelling and typography, with an afterword by the ubiquitous Harold Bloom. I wonder how many editions of *Frankenstein* these two consumer goods now constitute, how many plays, movies, operas, and other treatments have multiplied the Shelleyan body? I once began a list, but gave up on the assemblage.

Branagh's film, in any event, would seem to represent the postmodern as a kind of neoromanticism. The flouncy, open-necked shirts cast off, in finest Morrissey style, to reveal a buff, sweaty torso; the wavy hairdos; the focus on the love affair; the grandiose mises-en-scène; the tender moments—all filmed in a swooping, stylized, self-conscious manner, with set designs drawn straight from Caspar David Friedrich. Such spectacle reminds me of a movement in British pop music from the new wave period called New Romanticism, which defiantly brought colorful style to punk's blank antistyle: very early Depeche Mode, Duran Duran, Fashion, Japan, Spandau Ballet, Ultravox, Visage, all bands I still listen to for their Bowie-influenced sense of dance, artifice, camp, sexual ambiguity—in short, their insistence on the enthralling vagaries of romance.

Branagh, along with other filmmakers, such as Roger Corman *(Frankenstein Unbound)*, realizes that, like *Frankenstein* itself, romanticism has copied itself into Western culture like a virus. It's an entrenched, proliferating text. I don't discount the interventions of Victorianism, fin-de-siècle, modernism, and even postmodernism in its parasitical form. But romanticism, although banalized and commodified, capitalizing (on) postmodernism, continues to confront us with questions about the status of the human body (Robert DeNiro's sutured aspect?) and the imaginative text—still being assembled from previous texts, belying an additive construction. In fact the romantic might even be able to revive the postmodern, now usually considered an exhausted period and a dead issue, as far as criticism is concerned. (It's been domesticated, oriented toward commodities, and given a smaller p.) Once again the body is the site of contest and possibility.

Actually, in certain forms of postmodernism, the body, with its chaotic autonomic and motor nervous systems, its memory, its complex responses to pleasure and pain, its resistance to power, has become as forceful, innovative, and challenging as the mind, perhaps more so. Using the body in this way has characterized some of the most important theories based on queer and feminist studies, psychoanalysis, Foucault, Deleuze and Guattari, and others. I'd like to contribute to the discussion in the latter part of this book, by construing the postmodern as a corpus in itself needing a new life and self-definition (maybe as a sort of body without organs), and then by demonstrating the postmodern's work upon the body itself: in minimalist music, film, and fiction; and during the AIDS pandemic.

We've seen how reading and writing are bodily as well as discursive and interpretive activities; how criticism has confronted its own corporeality, even while responding to canonical British literature. Now that we've moved into our own period, it might seem hard *not* to see these activities as having anything to do with the human body, in one way or another, no matter what the focus. AIDS, for example, has been causing worldwide suffering, but it has also revolutionized sex, reproduction, family life, drug use, and literary theory. It has taken us to the furthest limits of the good and bad in art as well as personal experience and public policy. The bad has, unfortunately, been the more visible extreme, for example in terms of efforts to contain the syndrome by rendering it negligible with statistics about risk groups and demonizing those considered to be their dedicated members. These haven't been very subtle responses to the crisis, but neither have they been very effective.

In chapter 5 I attempt to construe some of the more complex instances of AIDS writing and film, examining the various ways they represent the bodies of PWAs (persons with AIDS) as compliant, resistant, or both. This chapter, entitled "Skeletons in the Closet," interprets writing about AIDS from the late eighties, along with three films dealing with the subject, *Longtime Companion, Parting Glances,* and *The Living End.* I suggest that both AIDS discourses and AIDS activism should benefit from careful management of irony and paradox as to sexual practice and character portrayal, rather than from a paranoid effort to control representations of the syndrome and human behavior. Writers on AIDS allow themselves ambivalence about the crisis as well as moral indignation over social neglect and hostility, thus remaining hopeful and even affirmative in the midst of a dire health emergency. At the same time, obstreperous characters, filmic PWAs with bad attitudes, fly in the face of homophobia and create new forms of life for themselves—forms that will survive and persist well into the future. For example, *The Living End* draws consciously on romantic tropes, such as wander-lust, rejection of social conventions, disease, experimentation with sex and drugs, the extreme power of love-unto-death, that have lost none of their force since romanticism—indeed, that have only become all the more relevant to our own experience.

As far as I know, Philip Glass hasn't written any piece bearing directly on AIDS—a possibility is the String Quartet No. 4 ("Buczak"), written in remembrance of Brian Buczak, the artist who died of AIDS in 1988. However, many of the operas, musical theater works, and accompaniments (*Mishima, Akhnaten, The Fall of the House of Usher, The Juniper Tree, The Mysteries and What's So Funny?*) involve issues of personal identity and erotic behavior relevant to the syndrome. In any case I've always strongly suspected that Glass's song "Light-ning," one of the *Songs from Liquid Days*, which was even per-formed in 1986 (subsequent to the death of Rock Hudson) on *Saturday Night Live*, normally host to rock acts, somehow was about AIDS. Suzanne Vega's lyrics, set to the runaway train of Glass's music, evoke a traumatic experience out of control: lightning has struck, and has left the speaker "shaken . . . laughing and undone." She continues, "Now I feel it in my blood/All hot and sharp and white." She wonders who will be left "when the fire finally dies."

Typically for Glass, the song ends abruptly, leaving the listener also shaken and undone, and maybe laughing ner-vously, especially because of the ways in which the music has hurled him or her into a headlong rush of rolling arpeggios, blaring horns, and clattering percussion. And because of the almost instantaneous transition into the next song. I can't help imagining being trapped aboard an unstoppable locomotive, the engineers and conductors dead or helpless, the passengers panicking, someone, anyone, striving to slow the momentum before the inevitable disaster.

First encounters. At about the same time as I was driving truck in the mornings and spending afternoons trying to write, and this particular disaster was just getting under way, I de-cided, finally, to buy a couple of CDs by the two most famous of the so-called minimalist composers, Philip Glass's *Glass-works* and Steve Reich's *The Desert Music*, two of the first digitally recorded albums to appear on CD. I don't remember the exact date; perhaps it was 1985, when Glass was named musician of the year by *Musical America*. The recent availability of Glass's and Reich's music on compact disc probably piqued my interest. I'd just bought my first CD player, a Sony D-5 portable, now a collector's item sought after even by the company itself. Their music wasn't really familiar, but later I realized I'd either been exposed to it unwittingly or had been reading about it for years.

When I lived in Missoula, Montana, from 1982 to 1984, I participated as backstage help, the go-fer, at the local gay and lesbian organization's annual talent show. One year, a young woman performed a dance, to her own choreography, of the a cappella Knee Play from *Einstein on the Beach*. I reacted at the time, as did my fellows, with amusement and disbelief to this otherworldly chorus repeating numbers—onetwothree onetwothree onetwothree—over and over, very rapidly, even more rapidly than you can scan them. In the meantime I was reading John Rockwell's *All American Music*, which includes a chapter on Glass and Reich, sitting on a balcony, feeling the chugging of the washing machines in the laundromat below. I'd heard almost none of the music Rockwell was discussing—or so I thought. When I found out that I *had* heard Glass, at the Wilma Theater in Missoula for that young woman's dance, it became harder for me to say that Glass exerted no influence over my imagination or my work, and was only a confirmation of my thinking about postmodernism. He'd actually influenced me, almost as unconsciously as had life itself. But Glass and Reich did more than to confirm the validity of my ideas: they gave me a whole new kind of music to love.

Another early exposure I just remembered. I was home in Manlius, New York, watching TV one afternoon. A show, whose name I can't recall now, came on. It was meant for young people: a straight-looking, blond-haired man would interview in front of a live audience one person from the arts, education, or politics, each day. Glass was the guest, along with the band he was producing at the time, Polyrock, long since defunct. Glass mentioned that he should have had his own bin for his records in the store, because he wasn't easy to categorize. Polyrock played a song or two. That's all I can picture after all these years, that and the bemused looks on the young audience members' faces.

And one more such memory. It was the middle of summer, long ago, between school years. My parents and I were enjoying a weekend afternoon at our cottage on DeRuyter Lake in central New York. The radio inside was tuned to the classical station in Syracuse. We could pick up the signal clearly because we were at a much higher elevation than the city. The station played what I now know as Gregory Fulkerson's recording, recently reissued on CD, of the Knee Plays from *Einstein*, arranged for solo violin. I distinctly remember reacting with interest. What strange and exciting music! It called to mind any number of vivid images, not the least of which was that of Einstein himself, sitting in a chair on the beach, playing the violin to the sound of the surf. It was another unconscious assimilation: I'd already seen this picture on the cover of the original Tomato edition of the opera, a set of four LPs with Milton Glaser's watercolor painting positioned against a stark, black background.

My response to the music, convulsing my muscles and energizing my visual imagination, exemplifies the Philip Glass effect for which he's become famous, or infamous, depending on your point of view. I surrender. Others can't stand more than a few minutes of the repetition; messages posted to newsgroups on the Internet, for example, will ridicule Glass by translating his music into long strings of repeated keyboard characters, or dismiss him cursorily, as the tiresome knock-knock joke, which the reader can easily reconstruct for him- or herself. Few are indifferent. Glass himself allows for any response, never the authoritarian master. "Lightning" really cooks, in part because, like all of Glass's mature music, it represents a folding of style into method. The earlier, more rarefied, longer stretches of repetitive figures—seminal experiments in American music from the seventies—give way to the tighter, more compressed, more swiftly, even vertiginously modulating pieces of the eighties and nineties. His music has shifted with the increasing pace of life, becoming more popular, salable, and imitable in the process. In any case his music has effected a vigorous music of the body in contrast to the often cerebral complications of high-modern integral serialism. Not that Glass can't be closely analyzed musicologically (he was trained in mathematics, after all) but that, like rock, his work risks subjecting the body more than the mind to intense forces. These forces alter our conception of the nature and operations of the text called serious music, and of postmodernism.

In the case of Glass's music, for instance, it sometimes seems as though the musicians are playing in a state of intense ecstacy. The booklet for the CD reissue of *Music in Similar Motion* shows a young Glass at the keyboard in an orgasmic posture, his eyes closed, mouth agape, head thrown back. But actually the musicans are concentrating all the harder—in Peter Moore's photograph, Glass is in reality about to snap his head back down to signal the other musicians to shift into the next section of the score—in order to allow the listener all the more ecstatic convulsion from the repetitions. So although the performance is carefully orchestrated, the effect is wrenching and explosive. The music passes from the performer to the listener in a virtually physical way, as might an infection, or blow, or shock, or sexual thrill.

The subject, as we've come to define it since the Enlightenment, has been transformed, but then so has the text as we've defined it since poststructuralism. The death of the author has been endured, and I think the death of the text as a tissue of signs or a matrix of unintelligible codes must be given a decent burial, too, here at the close of the millennium. Postmodern fiction, as I interpret it toward the end of chapter 4, evidences such a transformation. John Barth turns the text into a Möbius band to be sliced from his book, while Thomas Bernhard establishes plateaus of intensity, much the way Glass does. This makes reading about serious physical and mental illness an act not only of endurance but of renewal.

First of all, however, I offer a reading of four French theorists who have strongly influenced my thinking, Jacques Lacan, Michel Foucault, and Gilles Deleuze and Félix Guattari. I must admit immediately that chapter 3, located in the middle of this book not to make it central but to make it seem not overmastering, is more of a close reading of some of their most important work than an attempt to synthesize the ideas of these often contentious thinkers into a new theoretical framework, much less a tool, presuming any kind of universal applicability.

If, as Oscar Wilde claimed, it is the spectator, and not life, that art really mirrors, then one could read this obviously personal interpretation of all this rigorous poststructural, postmodern theory as an autobiographical account. I've shared with many other people a fairly recent exposure to what in academia is now called theory, a particularly iconoclastic way of thinking about culture that has given many applicants jobs

and publications, and many old-fashioned professors a profound resentment and fear of retiring. In any case the chapter
should serve both to provide some theoretical background to
the arguments I'm making and to offer those interested my own
perspective on these four philosophers.

Briefly stated, my argument is that, despite their strong
differences, these three philosophical sets—the Freudian/
Lacanian, Foucauldian, and Deleuzoguattarian—can be thought
of as overlapping in several significant ways that are helpful in
thinking about postmodern and even romantic culture. Indeed
romanticism has prepared us, in a sense, by embodying the
corporeal nature of textuality, and by form(ulat)ing new models
for aesthetics. Now that we've examined a poem and a couple
of novels by the lights of contemporary criticism, itself become
a virtual body in promiscuous contact with its subjects, we can
trace some of the influences of post-Enlightenment thought on
the artifacts of our own time, which include the theories that
have become so popular to apply to various kinds of artworks.
In *What Is Philosophy?* Deleuze and Guattari are at pains to
keep philosophy and aesthetics distinct; philosophy is conceptual, while art is more affectual. I'm not a professional philosopher, but by definition a professional aesthete. That's why I
read Lacan, Foucault, and Deleuze and Guattari for the lus-
tres, as Emerson would say, rather than for their profound
philosophical implications, which are the purview of other
philosophers. I watch closely as they *perform* through their
writings. I detect not only important ideas about the body and
textuality but artworks in themselves that teach me as much
by example as by argument.

The histrionic Lacan, like Freud, argues for, and even from,
a series of developmental stages through which each human
being passes toward or away, as the case may be, from some
kind of stable, mature identity. Lacan complicates Freud's theory
by introducing three registers—the imaginary, or mirror stage;
the symbolic, or order of language; and the real—the bizarre,
utterly alien, seemingly *un*real, the terrible and sublime—which
don't have timetables even as definite and dependable as do
Freud's shifting psychodynamic stages.

Lacan observes us departing from the imaginary, with its
apparently decisive yet deeply ambiguous processes of
identification, into the symbolic order, much as Freud sees a
progression from the orality and anality of childhood and youth
to the genitally oriented sexuality of adulthood. But just as

Freud spends more time analyzing those whose development has been somehow stymied or diverted, Lacan suggests ways in which, say, the ambiguities of imaginary intersubjective violence continue to haunt its rivalries, such that a truly counter-Hegelian conflict makes any kind of higher resolution impossible. The result is that identification is always already an ongoing struggle, one that occurs not only between bodies but as a virtual body in itself with all the freight of psychosexual anguish as well as the force of conscious resistance.

Resistance becomes the later Foucault's theme, as he develops a model of the power structure inherent to a socius that is no longer a simple object of an implacable authority, but one that is involved in a more horizontal network of interrelations of which resistance is a necessary component. Whether Foucault is to be psychoanalyzed—or dismissed because of psychoanalysis, as some would have it—remains a secondary consideration to the rich counterpoint he brings to the Lacanian theory.

Foucault has become virtually infamous by now because of several posthumous biographies that have detailed his once very private sex life, wherein he apparently indulged a taste for sadism/masochism, drugs, and danger. These revelations, rather than posing Foucault as the object of our paranoid defensiveness or bourgeois disgust, have actually helped us to draw connections between the subtle discursive strategies Foucault had always made quite public and the dangerous experiments he made with his own body, whose eventual reports are nothing less than *The History of Sexuality*, which he didn't live to complete. Thus the resistance that Foucault had once interpreted in Bataille as a folding of limits back over the trangressions that cross them ("A Preface to Transgression") seems to circle near to the Freudian or Lacanian dialectic obtaining between the garrulous impotence of prohibitions and the ostensibly silent power of misbehavior, or, as Freud himself puts it, "the suppressed impulse and the impulse that suppresses it find simultaneous and commmon satisfaction" (*Totem and Taboo* 64).

It is precisely this kind of seemingly endless agony between power and resistance from which Deleuze and Guattari wish to pursue lines of flight, which nevertheless must remain ambiguously successful. Deleuze, for his part, hewed more closely to psychology in his earlier work, later placing its mechanisms within a broader philosophical framework, much as Foucault had tended to write more about vertical structures of power and then shift his focus onto the bases of resistance, declaring (sometimes questionable) allegiances without becoming partisan. Deleuze often gets praised for his resistance to capitulation to the neoconservatism that swept the Western powers in the 1980s. Indeed, his work appeared to become all the more staunchly radical right up until his leap into death. His stubbornness, his being difficult to reign in and master, his refusal to be captured, parallel a tendency in Deleuze and Guattari's work to engage in discussions about conflict that grow less polemical and more exemplarily elusive over time. They pose, for example, a nomadic, indecisive, accelerated form of warfare over the deliberate exertions of national governments, partly in order to provide a model for the operations of virtual bodies.

If Lacanian identification is a continual struggle over representation, and Foucauldian resistance overloads the circuits of power networks, then Deleuzoguattarian nomadics—complex, ambiguous, chaotic, compelling—offer an alternative to the age-old imitative theory of aesthetics. D & G aren't easy to read, and virtuality, outside the rigors of philosophy, is hard to picture apart from the effort and failure to be real. These actions suggest imitation, or the phenomenon of virtual reality, a computer-generated simulation whose virtuality is philosophically unsound, and practically dull. Deleuze instead insists that "the virtual is opposed not to the real but to the actual. *The virtual is fully real in so far as it is virtual*" (*Difference and Repetition* 208, italics Deleuze's). Like the particles and antiparticles on the event horizon of a black hole that appear and annihilate each other, nonetheless giving off a definite radiation, the virtual and the actual come into brief, explosive contact, and leave residual traces whose effects we attempt to describe in aesthetic terms. "Indeed, the virtual must be defined as strictly a part of the real object—as though the object had one part of itself in the virtual into which it plunged as though into an objective dimension" (*Difference* 208–9).

Formation, explosion, annihilation, reformation elsewhere and differently . . . how better to delineate the aesthetic object with a new form of life, whose worth's unknown apart from the affects we allow it to activate in us each time it touches? It is an actual, physical body, appearing as alive and dead at once, with a virtual emanation.

3

On Lacan, Foucault, and Deleuze and Guattari

A Theoretical Introduction

I should really like to have provided an introduction to these difficult theorists, whose ideas have already been impinging on this book and who, certainly, deserve some explanation. The custom in such a chapter is to provide an introduction *in theory*. That is, there are three possibilities: an introduction provided theoretically, with just enough jargon to make it intelligible to some and baffling to others; a basic introduction to the theories used in this book, which this chapter doesn't provide; and an introduction to these theories generally—lying beyond the scope of this project, as the saying goes. But there's a fourth possibility. Not Bataille's "Theoretical Introduction" (in *The Accursed Share*, volume 1) that introduces a whole new theory, demonstrated in the successive chapters, but an introduction in name only, rendered back to its etymology: a bringing or leading in, an "apparatus of capture" in Deleuze and Guattari's terms.

Since I'm syncretizing ideas from three sets of discourses—Lacanian, Foucauldian, and Deleuzoguattarian—I can't claim utter originality. But I do claim some personal insights and a way of compelling the three sets to overlap, creating a fourth set that remains in excess of all three, that pushes the overlap to an uncomfortable limit, but which might afford a means of rethinking aesthetics not depending on Marxism or psychoanalysis, but also not seeking a firm orthodoxy to replace them with.

Making the three discourses of my chapter title coexist here, making them confront each other, is a way to avoid such dogmatism. They're going to have to settle some differences, and at least acknowledge others that are insurmountable.

Schizomachy, my term for a type of conflict that isn't ego-centered or dialectically productive, is a coinage become a token, good only for a limited time and for specific purposes. Fortunately, the discourses purchased by this term will never form a system among themselves. Foucault and Deleuze and Guattari, for example, take serious issue with psychoanalysis, especially in its Lacanian guise, since Lacan returns to Freud with a vengeance fueled by structural linguistics and a disaffection for ego psychology, making himself a master of Western cultural discourse. Foucault shares that disaffection without relying on linguistics to oppose the oppressive ego. On the contrary, he locates psychoanalysis in a history of Western technocracy, evoking a domestic horror in calling it "another round of whispering on a bed" meant to channel eroticism and normalize behavior (*The History of Sexuality*, volume 1, 5).

Deleuze and Guattari, of course, following on the earlier Foucault but also anticipating the later Foucault, make themselves famous by attacking psychoanalysis with *Anti-Oedipus* (trans. 1977). They want to "shatter the iron collar of Oedipus and rediscover everywhere the force of desiring-production" (53). They will do this primarily by identifying "the real in itself" within a productive rather than deterministic unconscious, one that doesn't keep it all in the family but runs through the entire social body. This very notion of the real, however, is derived from Lacan, even if it operates for Deleuze and Guattari in a more positive, less impossible, partial, corporeal manner than Lacan's elusive register. I, too, should like to retain this notion, but to trace its eruption within the imaginary, that presymbolic register involving the formation of self-image through an ambiguous process of identification, narcissism, and intersubjective rivalry. When the real disturbs the imaginary, it transforms its conflicts from passive and insidious into open, daring, even creative. It makes of the familial self an orphan again, taking it to the limit of collective being, inciting while endangering its ability to operate intensively. As Deleuze and Guattari remark about one of these orphaned existences, the BwO (Body without Organs):

> If you free it with too violent an action, if you blow apart the strata without taking precautions, then instead of drawing the plane [of consistency] you will be killed, plunged into a black hole, or even dragged toward catastrophe. [*A Thousand Plateaus* 161]

Thus they emphasize sobriety and care. Deleuze's own lifestyle bore out such an ethic—a happily married man, a retired professor, who hated to travel, who carefully cultivated friendships and also allowed them to cool, who could stand the ministrations of Western medicine no longer and chose his own fate, in part, no doubt, to relieve the burden of his illness on others.

By the time Foucault begins seriously to explore his sexuality in the late seventies and early eighties, his friendship with Deleuze becomes more distant. He, a globetrotter unlike Deleuze, travels more, primarily around the United States. Here he investigates "laboratories of sexual experimentation" that would profoundly affect his thinking and behaving and, in turn, affect our own. James Miller's biography (1993, discussed below) makes Foucault's experimenting with extreme sex a central theme.

Sex becomes a platform from which to launch new archaeologies of human being. Regardless of the merits of Miller's account or Foucault's alleged behavior, it's clear that Foucault was pursuing limits of physical experience; thresholds of endurance; domains of impersonality, speed, and uncertainty— perhaps with foreknowledge of possible consequences that only drew him further. He was engaging the real as one of Deleuze and Guattari's "schizos" and returning to build theory atop the ruins of the strife, the "mache," that, in a sense, he survived only until June 1984. He saw himself, possibly, as having risked his life for the love of boys.[1]

What links Lacan, Foucault, and Deleuze and Guattari, then, are the following characteristics: an emphasis on the power/ resistance of the human body; openness to sexual differentiation that is not merely linguistic; anarchistic politics, whether spoken or implied; examination of personal and aesthetic conflicts as productive and positive, though in divergent ways; and a pursuit of limits, whether in the real within the imaginary, the body-as-discourse and the body-as-flesh, or in a becoming-nomad of collectivities. This list is a reterritorialization of three discrete and unruly discursive sets that I call schizomachy.

The Term

The word *schizomachy* (skit-só-ma-key) is my queer original, but combines elements from two existing discourses, one by honorary queers and another by an honorable one. The "schizo" derives from Gilles Deleuze and Félix Guattari's schizoanalysis, that counterpsychoanalytical horde of concepts already under way in their *Anti-Oedipe* (1972) and moving out rhizomatically with *Mille plateaux* (1980), the two volumes of their monumental collaboration *Capitalisme et schizophrénie.*

The earlier book engages Freud and Lacan directly, while the later shirks win-or-lose dialectics with these imposing figures, as I myself am trying to do. It moves nomadically across many subjects and disciplines, making guerrilla raids on culture and always avoiding capture, often utterly undoing what it encounters. The schizo is D & G's replacement for the Oedipal self. Instead of a castrated, guilty, tragic subject, they posit "an orphan . . . an anarchist and an atheist" (*Anti-Oedipus* 311). Already multiple, speaking a number of languages, forming machines to couple and uncouple with others, producing the unconscious rather than representing it or being completely determined by it, s/he evades the family romance with its alienating contentions. S/he joyfully reconstructs the world along more practical lines, ready to move at any moment, skirting or subsuming whatever stands in the way. S/he isn't necessarily a pacifist, and certainly not submissive: s/he'd rather "deterritorialize the enemy by shattering his territory from within" (*A Thousand Plateaus* 353).

A molecule in the war machine and, as such, not an officer or state representative content with compromise and the drafting of treaties perpetuating political economies, s/he's member in "a band of pillage, of piracy" (*A Thousand Plateaus* 360). S/he might break and run; you might wake up tomorrow morning to find s/he's already left. Just when you think you know what s/he believes, s/he's already devised another strategy and has gained a day on you. S/he doesn't fight the war to win, but to capture or destroy.

"Let difference surreptitiously replace conflict," says a voice in Roland Barthes's *Pleasure of the Text* (15): an excellent description of the schizo's subterfuge. S/he sneaks into the camp under cover of darkness and says, "Let's get started right here and now. Why wait for the field of dawn?" Barthes continues, in his own voice:

> Difference is not what makes or sweetens conflict: it is achieved over and above conflict, it is *beyond and alongside* conflict. Conflict is nothing but the moral state of difference; whenever (and this is becoming frequent) conflict is not tactical (aimed

at transforming a real situation), one can distinguish in it the failure-to-attain-bliss, the debacle of a perversion crushed by its own code and no longer able to invent itself: conflict is always coded, aggression is merely the most worn-out of languages. . . . I love the text because for me it is that rare locus of language from which any "scene" (in the household, conjugal sense of the term), any logomachy is absent. [15–16]

Hence the "machy" in my invented term. Etymologically it goes back to the Greek, meaning battle. The *Random House Dictionary of the English Language* (2nd ed.) even uses Barthes's word as an example (1152). "Logomachy" is a struggle over signifiers. However, when you read "schizomachy," please do not only read "molecules' warfare" but "schizoanalytical war of words," as in schizo(phrenicalogo)machy. Retain a sense of what my invented word has dropped out, but flatten it in the crush between the schizo and the struggle s/he makes of life, since the struggle is more than simply linguistic. Schizo | machy. Notice, as well, Barthes's disdain for the psychoanalytical stage, with its institutionalized divisions of labor, gender, sexual practice, and *jouissance*—and its inherent violence. Barthes realizes, and the schizo realizes, that family values are always already identical to our aggressive and exploitive culture's in general. The drama must be a tragedy, ending when someone dies, but no one's holding their breath.

Instead, imagine a routine written by the players themselves, maybe partly improvised: something about the body, with a device for opening it up to the audience's desires. Skit, soma, key. Soma: one's corporeal entity without the germ cells. You don't need to reproduce, just produce pleasure. But you might get bloody.

How, then, to talk about risk and conflict without inciting a war of vested interests, of battling representations divided across ideological lines? Three propositions involving three nominated discourses (tensors) will suffice for a place to start.

1) *Lacan* identifies in the imaginary a prohibition against contention with the object of identification. Imaginary rivalry persists even during the civilized structurations of the symbolic order, disrupting it precisely by worrying this prohibition into a wound, a breach in the social body, that will not heal. 2) *Foucault* in his work and life places his unruly body at risk. He derives an aesthetic and ethics that poses the belief in *mens sana in corpore sano* against the ruptures of history and the

raptures of dangerous physical interactions, offering powerful resistances to the technologies of subjective discipline. 3) *Deleuze and Guattari* molecularize this unsafe body, banding it together with others equally reckless and unpredictable. They identify and encourage becomings-nomad that contend openly with Oedipally restrained forces, predicting an end to their cathartic tragedies with a philosophy of immanent difference, unrestrained movement, and positive affect.

1) Lacan

We know from "The Mirror Stage as Formative of the Function of the I" that it mounts:

> A drama whose internal thrust is precipitated from insufficiency to anticipation—and which manufactures for the subject, caught up in the lure of spatial identification, the succession of phantasies that extends from a fragmented body-image to a form of its totality that I shall call orthopaedic—and, lastly, to the assumption of the armour of an alienating identity, which will mark with its rigid structure the subject's entire mental development. [*Écrits* 4]

During the mirror stage or imaginary, the child (mis-)recognizes itself in the image of its mother, or father, or itself-in-the-mirror. This troubled recognition becomes a sort of foundational event, in which the newborn yet premature self both pleases it-self and displeases it-self. The self-identified image is one that the nascent ego is content to cite as proof of its imaginary plenitude, knowing meanwhile that that self-same image rivals that same self as a kind of alternate sibling, reminding him or her that, in fact, plenitude is fictitious, fantasmatic, spec(tac)ular, all-too-familiar. The image thus becomes bifurcated, an object to be loved as well as destroyed. And this bifurcation causes a similar split in the subject, where, despite his or her upright jubilation over self-discovery, almost immediate acts of repression make the self all too aware that it exists in parts rather than in some organic wholeness.

Subsequent actions serve, for instance, to destroy the imago in such a way that the destroyer's self will be made to feel that much more plenitudinous, self-justified, perhaps immortal in a way; however, these actions never succeed. Imaginary movements thus last *beyond* a certain stage in the drama as well as the development, *beyond recognition*, as it were.[2]

For me as a gay man, part of whose work involves investigating representations of the queer body, this (quite oversimplified) theory of ego (de-)formation is useful. It not only enables me to theorize the intersections of supposedly discrete discourses—gay/straight, male/female, normative/rebellious—but helps deconstruct these oppositions with an eye toward new theories, new configurations, and, of course, hopefully, a new episteme. Therein oppressive notions of the humanistic, normative subject have been so obscured as to become illegible. This is my own act of sibling rivalry. Subject to the symbolic order, I return to the imaginary for sources of queer indiscipline.

Identification is itself homosexual, in any case. But homosexuality (queerness) resists identification purely. How is this so? The infant perceives the imago as a reflection of itself, but it may not even at this point apprehend sexual differentiation. When it sees its own image, the child construes it not as different in the sense of utterly alien but different in the sense of not-quite-itself: a difference it (supposedly) attempts to fold back into the plenum of the *same*, since it perceives this imago as a picture of the selfsame self of which it has abruptly been made aware. Efforts to contend with the image, once it has been perceived as some kind of rival, disclose the subject's need to efface the agent of difference, the originating self-consciousness.

Homophobia, for example, results when the subject perceives in the queer image a (segmented and incomplete) rival for its own fantasmatic sense of fullness, self-satisfaction. The image bifurcates into friend and foe: the friend is *I*, the foe is the *other*, even though they are two faces of the same image. So whether the subject apprehends the friend as the foe, it presumably apprehends primarily an image of sameness, including sexual sameness, that oscillates between registers of pleasure and displeasure as it does between sameness-as-identical and sameness-as-identifiee. It is the object with which to ally oneself, according to gender prerogatives. Friend need only take a turn, and there appears the foe.

The imaginary remains, therefore, prior to the symbolic (order), which imposes yet another sense of difference—this time clearly sexual: the subject feels *compelled* to identify with the image of its own gender rather than *contend* with that image. It is thus in the contention with one's own image, which is inevitable, that makes identification homoerotic. So homophobia, ironically, reveals the homosexual nature of the process of identification even more clearly than does tolerance, just as repression reveals the unconscious precisely through failure utterly to repress (dis-)content. And this is no more obvious than in the phenomenon of introjection of the father's homophobia in homophobic queers. The subject must not only identify with the father's image but with the father's law, which includes the prohibition against incest with the mother. Yet this prohibition remains anterior to *a primary prohibition against contention with the object of identification*, since it is the *contention* that reveals difference, not the satisfaction.

Jane Gallop remarks, "Lacan's writings contain an implicit ethical imperative to break the mirror, an imperative to disrupt the imaginary in order to reach 'the symbolic'" (59). Yet we see that the imaginary has already caused enough disruption, and continues to do so. The father's law is homophobic even before it is directed outside the family scene, because it disallows rivalry with that image the subject was presumed simply to adopt. When the anterior homophobia directs itself *outside* the family, at the queer body alien to its romantic realm, it disavows the previous homophobia, which would in actuality impose adequation between the subject and his or her selfsame image. The father's law then directs contention outward rather than inward, onto fantasmatically unitary images, in a projection of its own sense or desire for unitariness. Thus one mode of homoeroticism supplements the other. The exteriorized conflict replaces, supplants, masks the introjected identification, when really that détente is in itself a form of homoeroticism. Contrary to psychoanalytical doctrine, it is the heterosexual mirroring Narcissus, rather than the homosexual (queer), who perpetually refuses to comply with the imperatives of identification.

Heterosexuality, then, becomes the perversion, the swerving away from, the original and persistent homosexuality. It embodies a representational violence in which one image-effacement serves to disavow another image-effacement, which the nascent subject has all along been attempting to complete but has at some point been prohibited from doing. But that more primary contention is locked into a dialectic without sublation, since the contention does not seek utterly to erase the imago in the symbolic order—in fact, it must *pose* that image as a limit-point of identification that should not be transgressed. The anterior/exterior disidentification seeks, for its part, to efface and rewrite the fantasmatic image of unitary queerness in order to establish a false sense of identification as utter sameness, coextension, simultaneity, adequation. The earlier contention, conversely, maintains difference primally by refusing to let the dialectic collapse into rationalized coexistence or sublate into some higher order of plenitude. Rivalry substantiates partiality, both in the sense of incompletion, lying about in parts, and of subjectivity, always remaining the part-object of one's own consciousness. It drives the ego continually back into a realm of imaginary strife.

Hence the queer is not what s/he seems to be. Not (really) not queer but also really not the same as itself. Queerness means difference itself, in the Deleuzean sense—inadequation, diachrony, heterotaneity—standing forever for imaginary differentiation that the supposedly not queer wishes to disclaim: "Yes, but . . ."—where the affirmative supplements the qualification, rather than the other way around, thereby continually supplanting it.

Culture, rather than sublimating and in some sense thereby diffusing conflict, actually helps perpetuate contentiousness, if we think of artifaction as the manufacture of images meant to be applied to the world. Since the sublimation, resulting in the artifact, necessarily fails, it must be reproduced endlessly, but it must also, like the primal rivalry, maintain what it would contend with—just as the queer body must be maintained as such by the homophobe as an object of disavowal, and maintained by the queer him- or herself as a material resistance to effacement and reinscription, as well as persistent scandal to the homophobic representation which it does, in part, participate in. The queer subject is the monster in a box, contained yet beyond control and in some way under its *own* control: a caged monstrosity we keep nearby to see and refuse, a docile body nevertheless uncanny and unyielding. "Box": sexual parts confined to a discrete and discreet location—a sessile body—so that they won't detach and circulate very far beyond their socially expected limits. "Box," a predicament: What shall we do with an abnormality that, clearly, won't stay locked up for long, won't stay put? This monster of the closet?

Three revealing anecdotes follow.

a) I see photographs of Arthur Ashe. He holds his head, appears to grieve. The media construct a news story out of the news itself (e.g., *USA Today*). One story discloses the other.

We're burning Ashe by focusing our hot lenses on his person. Paranoia multiplies. We have to be told what the transmission route was (blood transfusion) so we (think we) can establish Ashe's sexuality publicly. The media distract us from themselves. In the course of a news story about a news story about Arthur Ashe, the first story disavows the voyeurism and invasiveness of the second(ary) story, which is actually prior. *See how we are*, they seem to say. *Honorable enough to catch ourselves in the act of staring* (but not enough to stop). *Don't read (into) our motivations for writing the original story. Pay attention to that man behind the curtain*, so that you'll ignore his raison d'être.

b) I stand in the garden beside my partner. Summertime. The straight couple from downstairs, weeding, and their children playing nearby, see us together for the first time. Double (multiple) or nothing. Because the queer doesn't always signify him- or herself as such, or you can't tell just by looking. The husband never thought of my partner as gay, until he saw me standing there. He looks back and forth between us; eyes won't settle on one or the other, not seeing what they recognize as whole in one (queer) person. So the common assumption goes: the queer is concealing him- or herself behind a mask of invisibility s/he's fashioned (for) him- or herself; without it s/he's only an absence, like the signifier that *is* only by being not everything (or something) else.

My partner, and I, are assumed to be straight, until our proximity reveals what they assume we've been hiding.[3] We become an empty set, defined by functions but lacking the one member differing itself from all others, and therefore making all others possible: 0. The presumption of heterosexuality confers a plenitudinous identity upon the ordinary person denied to the queer, a vessel that hasn't properly been filled with consciousness of different (hetero-) defining behavior (-sexuality). *You're still acting like the straight people who raised you! Identify yourselves!* We've realized the duplicity of identification, and enjoy performing whatever roles we choose. *What is the name of that hybrid?* he seems to ask, turning back to his roses and tomatoes.

c) "Germans." I grew up in a small suburban town in central New York state where there were few blacks, so they were noteworthy to an outspoken young boy. If I saw them at the ice cream stand, I would exclaim, "Look, Mom—Negroes!" My family couldn't, or wouldn't, silence me, so they taught me that these people were "Germans." Subsequently, whenever I saw blacks in public, I would exclaim, "Look, Mom—Germans!" which would nevertheless attract the blacks' confused attention.

How did calling them "Germans" function? It applied an incoherent signifier to blacks, which anyway allowed my family members to disguise themselves as non-racist, thereby allowing them to perpetuate their racism and to emphasize the difference between me or us and them. I suppose it also allowed them to perpetuate notions of racial difference ("German") in general. But why would they choose this particular nationality? As it turns out, the signifier wasn't as incoherent as I thought at first. It was not just an expedient alternative to Negro, it was a culturally determined choice. If you think of the European as always already different from the American, you think of the most threatening of Europeans—the Germans, whose culture, language, and behavior seem alien but not as bizarre as Eastern, which is far less scrutable. It's a way to maintain our difference from those nasty Germans: "We're white but not racist or aggressive or alien or obscure." So we apply this negation to the most immediate objects of difference, blacks. We project our racism onto these objects in a maneuver of disavowal: not only are they different (read: mad, bad, and dangerous to know), but they're apt to maintain this difference deliberately by inciting our racism.

Our alibi is, of course, racist in itself. Their incitement is racist, we claim, but so is our reading of it, which is only a misreading of lacking intent. My calling attention to their difference interpellates the blacks as other but also interpellates my family as racist, causing the defiant black gaze to return our probing white gaze. The child functions as the conduit, the innocent interpellator calling attention to what should have remained implicit, unarticulated, and therefore perpetual. I'm actually silenced by having my signifier shifted from openly though harmlessly quaint to the supposedly quaintly harmless. In reality, I'm being disciplined. It's not that my family cared about what the blacks thought, but that they cared whether other whites saw them as outspokenly racist. We gaze at the blacks; meanwhile, other whites watch us gazing; finally, the blacks return our gaze, drawing the other whites' attention back to *us*. And all this occurs in the absence of the working father.

My interpellation addresses itself to my mother, who is called upon to look, as if she's not already (not) looking. At this moment, the mother represents the head of the white family who must also represent its racism. What she does or doesn't do, says or doesn't say, will determine how the family is considered. We don't want to *ask* to be judged racist, when this would contest the entire racist milieu where this phantasmagoria operates. Mom must train her family members to respond to difference in ways which will not call attention to it and thus keep it other-than-us: not to engage it but to keep it discursively and corporeally separate. Two levels are operating: *difference ↔ disavowal of recognition of difference.*

One of the mechanisms of the second level is liberal humanist universalism. We're taught to recognize difference only if it serves the purpose of maintaining that difference beneath the sign of universal brotherhood: "We're all really alike, so we shouldn't hate each other." Again, the symbolic order attempts to prohibit contestation with one's own image. It misrecognizes sameness in difference and fails to acknowledge history, cultural contingencies, and expedient strategy. It's ourselves we care about, not the blacks. We negate them with our gentility.

2) Foucault

Michel Foucault, in the so-called "Discourse on Language,"[4] invites interruption into his performance, as if it would defer, but then only protract, the time when he had to begin. "I would really like to have slipped imperceptibly into this lecture," he begins (215/148). In his very first paragraph, written in such a way as to familiarize himself to his audience (I'm taking his paragraphs seriatim, as only makes sense), he strikes a pose difficult to maintain: he wishes to become a listener, surrendering himself to a voice already speaking—the lecturer or speaker— upon entering late; but he *is* that speaker, speaking about the difficulty of speaking—that is, of beginning: he begins by speaking about the difficulty of initiating the act, about the gathering of strength against a truly material resistance called language (216/149).

So, bent into a tenuous contrapposto, he's glancing into and across the audience, making people turn and look while he prepares to begin again, imagining if he could slip *away* imperceptibly. But no one is coming in, and the speaker is there yet, readying to start over, when heads turn back around. Foucault asks to be "enveloped" and "lodged" in words (215/148), letting out an almost imperceptible sigh, as if he isn't already *in*. Actually, he sees himself as a hindrance, a *mere* snag in the flow of language, possibly strong enough to stanch it.[5]

In the second paragraph, he figures himself as a speaker with a voice coming from behind, *before* he begins to speak. Foucault will circle back to this figure at the end, desiring a certain stage management that the solemnity of the institution to which he speaks, by way of introduction, won't allow. He wants the occasion to be a sort of Beckett play already in progress, and his role as discourse cum masked truth (217/150) to be a mad one: a scene he can enter and disrupt, sweeping up attention. How to be inside and outside, how to be this beast and maintain control, the actor's dilemma, at the same time—this question guides the third paragraph. In the fourth, he adopts a sailing metaphor: speech is a treacherous ocean, and, by metonymy, the monster, that the institution would have the speaker negotiate. It's their own arena and brute, after all, shaped by their need for entertainment. The voice of inclination expresses misgiving, and that of the institution answers with rather ominous encouragement (215–16/149), like voices calling and echoing at sea; the speaker would rather just be a "happy wreck" of their power[6]—force, region, current, desart. This metaphor continues in the next paragraph, where Foucault imagines himself as a type of Odysseus contending physically against oblivion (216/149). Finally, in the seventh and last paragraph of his Introduction/introduction, he reemphasizes the virtual impossibility of his task, "to fix the terrain—or perhaps the very provisional theatre" where he'll work, while advancing his hypothesis concerning the production and exploitation of discourse. The terrain shifted endlessly, and the theater was never allowed to remain beyond a few performances. This, the first six paragraphs imply. Here, the beginning ends, and starts over, or starts at last, his hypothesis the transition between introducings.

And by the time it's begun, Foucault has offered several poses for his role, all of which charm but which cannot be simultaneous, and for good reason. In essence he has already begun an infinite number of times.

Moreover, a survey, though attempted, surrendered to Foucault's temptation, can't begin to treat of them all. From the very title—listed, perhaps, on programs in listeners' hands and on posters, words that possibly would themselves be lodged in some complete introductory sentence starting "The title of my lecture is . . . ," itself another starting over—"a terrifying form of monstrosity" (Derrida "Structure" 92) has been prowling. *L'ordre du discours* is *The Order of Discourse*, but what could this mean? Rather, *how* does it mean? *Discours* can also be used idiomatically to signify *twaddle*, while *ordre*, resonating as it does with *ordure* (excrement, filth, slime—Foucault will refer to Bataille before long), can mean agenda, class, command, method, nature, order[7] (221/153), order for, orderliness, peacefulness, sequence, working order. This particular play of signifying might be ranged on the side of inclination, which is going to speak soon. It wants discourse to remain "infinitely open" (215/149).

What, on the other hand, can "The Discourse on Language" suggest? a) the only discourse; b) Foucault's (only) such discourse; c) a survey of the subject; d) any such discourse. What else? Not much, and nothing of much interest. So it could be said that this peculiar translation of the French title takes the side of the institution, which would have the speaking/attending distinction remain fixed (226/156), with Foucault in the role of some rhapsodist singing to the sea, answering with the modulating rote of procedure.

Less than a year after Foucault gave the speech, Swyer's translation was offered to the world in *Social Science Information* (April 1971). The speech had long become a publication for institutions to acquire, but with its audience reduced to individuals reading separately. The drama, the charisma, are gone, the speaker is no longer present (see 221/153). "Silent attention" and "attentive silence" (215/149, 217/150) alike are now consigned to the printed word. The journal has the virtue, at least, of reproducing the text in its entirety, as does the Pantheon edition. What's omitted from the Adams and Searle anthology, in which it partially appears, "the last few pages," is quite important. It recapitulates helpfully; it reiterates the notion of recommencement as a trope for philosophy, whether inside or outside Hegel via Hippolyte (235–36; see how the other text runs out) at any moment. It is a speech act in itself, taking the form of a tribute and dedication to Foucault's mentor. It is, at least and at last, a beginning, the one implicit at the beginning. Most important, however, is that it contextualizes the event: the speech is being given upon invitation to teach at the Collège de France. It thereby has the qualities of a project, of work to be done, whose outlines Foucault clearly and consistently provides.

Second, these last few pages return to the beginning and give Hippolyte that voice Foucault wanted to hear speaking from behind as he walked to the podium; it's a presence that, sadly, is not present to hear Foucault, except that Hyppolite acts as that latecomer slipping in to listen to a lecture already under way, the one voice Foucault wishes to lodge in his *own* speech (237). Arrested at his refutation of structuralism, the Adams and Searle edition may therefore sound more open-ended, but in fact neglects the thematical conclusion of the complete text while enacting its own sort of metaphysical closure, which would no doubt have perturbed the author, who cares who's speaking, after all.

Foucault has had some rather significant antecedents in the practice of speech contextualization. For example, in *Five Lectures on Psycho-Analysis*, Freud posits a disorderly listener, and his lasting though troublesome banishment from the lecture, as an analog to the operation of repression. He says, speaking hypothetically, "I have to announce that I cannot proceed with my lecture; and thereupon three or four of you who are strong men stand up and, after a short struggle, put the interrupter outside the door" (25). Freud would then put up resistance to his reentering, perhaps failing, using this fable as a demonstration of the operations of repression. Resistance, especially failed resistance, to that which is not or no longer immediately apparent suggests an outside or other, against which I am pushing, and that is the unconscious trying to return and disrupt the ego's orderliness.

But Foucault has already pursued a line of flight away from such strife, becoming himself a transition into nomadic thought. Gilles Deleuze and Félix Guattari remark:

> A line of becoming is not defined by points that it connects, or by points that compose it; on the contrary, it passes *between* points, it comes up through the middle, it runs perpendicular to the points first perceived, transversally to the localizable relation to distant or contiguous points. A point is always a point of origin. But a line of becoming has neither beginning nor end, departure nor arrival, origin nor destination; to speak

> of the absence of an origin, to make the absence of an origin
> the origin, is a bad play on words. A line of becoming has only
> a middle. The middle is not an average; it is fast motion, it is
> the absolute speed of movement. [*A Thousand Plateaus* 293]

This "absolute speed" had been Foucault's wish from the start:
that line of becoming not only already in the middle but the
very middle itself, where a person's discourse might lodge and
get lodged into. But also where it might effect, through the
irruptive event, not only the end of the human as traditionally
and oppressively constructed and circulated, but an end to
the rhetorical discourse that made the undoing possible. Foucault says, "the mark of the writer is reduced to nothing more
than the singularity of his absence; he must assume the role
of the dead man in the game of writing" ("What Is an Author?"
102–3).

He laments the ongoing resistance mustered against an
event that has been occurring at least "since Mallarmé" (105),
but also refuses to stop at the "empty affirmation that the
author has disappeared" (105) without further investigation into
that death, its causes, and its implications—Freud's, Blanchot's,
Barthes's, Derrida's precedents notwithstanding. This project is
therefore hardly a trivial or flippant one, though the means be
ludic. When Foucault remarks, "One ought to read everything,
study everything" (*Foucault Live* 3), he means it. "In other words,
one must have at one's disposal the general archive of a period
at a given moment. And archaeology is, in a strict sense, the
science of this archive."

Foucault's precise, conscious, painstaking scholarly devo-
tion and drive (Said 291) are enough to consternate the most
devoted and driven critics, but also to make evident how much
research, thinking, and writing will be necessary for the decisive elusion of the "hyperrepressive desublimation," the flows of
power through oppressively constructed bodies and minds, of
which Foucault speaks. In terms Foucault would appreciate,
namely Nietzsche's, it is a superhuman act of will—a will *through*
power and knowledge—that might thus reorient the human,
one who is willing "to begin and begin again, to attempt and be
mistaken."

* * *

For Foucault, this act of daring did not limit itself to discourse,
but played itself out—that is, attempted, and pursued extremes—

in the drama he staged with his own body. It is a drama that
has made Foucauldians uncomfortable, and given the
Francophobes of cultural reaction one more excuse to be scared
of Foucault's ideas. I'd like to discuss a conflict among academicians and biographers that has arisen since Foucault's death
in 1984. It focuses on the ways in which the writing of the
philosopher's life, and responses to that writing, have become
a logomachy involving the deployment of Foucault's body, a
body, of work as well as flesh, that has caused controversy as
a result of its reputed irresponsibility in its *jouissance* of sa-
dism/masochism.

To begin I shall dust off that old interview of Foucault's
again—"Sexual Choice, Sexual Act"—and search for an archaeology of the gay man's body's experience during the AIDS
emergency. Leo Bersani, in "Is the Rectum a Grave?," is the
antagonist here, setting up a homosexual exchange that I shall
try to regulate and maybe partially resolve. Afterward, I shall
briefly argue that accounts of Foucault's life/work, most notably James Miller's *The Passion of Michel Foucault*, have elicited
a predictable neoconservative reaction against Foucault and,
by extension, contemporary French theory, homosexuality, and
resistance—but that it's a reaction that nevertheless should
simply strengthen the resolve of Foucauldians, despite their
differences.

Early in "Sexual Choice," Foucault wants to deconstruct
the opposition between desire and the law. It's not as simple,
he says, as posing instincts against permissions and restric-
tions. Modes of living, in which subjects ascribe meanings to
their practices and practices ascribe meanings to subjects,
complicate the dialectic. Thus, in Foucault's thought, resistance doesn't merely throw itself up against power but helps
constitute it. The dialectics of presence/absence, and admis-
sion/denial, operate similarly. One isn't separable from the other.
With the late John Boswell, Foucault prefers the term *gay* to
homosexual because *gay* can refer to any number of these
modes of life, whereas *homosexual* retains a peculiar medicalized
and disciplinary history. "Even on the level of nature," says
Foucault, "the term homosexuality doesn't have much meaning" (217). In the history of AIDS, we've seen instances where
the victim, the diseased, the other has been posed against
efforts to contain, banish, and void him or her. AIDS is allowed
to reveal the queer insofar as that queer body can then become

an object of discipline. On the other hand, we've seen counterexamples of the queer's, the PWA's, choosing his or her own mode of life along with the meanings to ascribe to that life. This, to Foucault, is the true scandal of being gay. "It is the prospect that gays will create as yet unforeseen kinds of relationships that many people can not tolerate," according to him (229).

Bersani takes issue with Foucault at just the point where he sees Foucault privileging a potentially normalizable form of life over a model of sexual experience that is "anticommunal, antiegalitarian, antinurturing, antiloving" (Bersani 215).[8] Bersani goes so far as to find use value in the antipornography feminism of Andrea Dworkin and Catherine MacKinnon, because they don't try to redeem sex of its brutality, its primarily violatory nature. He also appears to value the masculine potency of the leatherclad master over the flaccid parody of camp, despite his irony toward both, despite his disaffection toward the antipersonal politics of the bathhouse, a politics that is indeed capable, contra Bersani, of producing "a . . . radical disintegration and humiliation of the self" (217). Now it is true that in the Foucault, "unforeseen kinds of relationships" are still relations between social equals, presumably, and therefore normalizable, unlike certain limit experiences caused by sexual disequilibriums. Conversely, if these kinds of relationships become more common and visible, perhaps the normalization of the acts might also, and oppression ease a little. After all, it seems that at least during the earlier years of the AIDS epidemic, the focus remained almost obsessively on the sex practices of gay men rather than on their relationships, which remained almost totally inscrutable mysteries. That the Supreme Court upheld the states' rights to impose antisodomy laws (Bowers v. Hardwick 1986) tells us much about what hegemonic culture would just as soon keep unseen, or limit to such luxurious spectacles as fist-fucking parlors in nightclubs.

It seems right for Bersani to react to Foucault's valorization of a kind of medieval courtship as quaint, until we realize that Foucault has no illusions about the quick and impersonal nature of much gay sex in an age when "laboratories of sexual experimentation" ("Sexual Choice" 225) spring up in response to the lack of acceptable forms of interpersonal expression among queers. For Foucault the gay man concentrates on the memory of the act, which is essentially its future, because social interdictions have prohibited the knowledge of a past leading up to it and the visibility of the present of that sexual act. Foucault is, in a sense, a pragmatist, in that his best moment of love and hope, when the lover departs in the taxi, grows from trust in the lover's, or some lover's, return and the repetition of the act, perhaps a better one.[9]

Foucault remembers to remember the lover's body, but Bersani forgets Foucault—the body of the PWA, a scandalous omission from Bersani's text—even though he could be said, finally, to agree with Foucault. "Male homosexuality," says Bersani at the end of his article, "advertises the risk of the sexual itself as the risk of self-dismissal, of *losing sight* of the self, and in so doing it proposes and dangerously represents *jouissance* as a mode of ascesis" (222). Through sex one abdicates power—therapeutically, as it were, repeatedly—only to gain increasing resistance to the notion of the body being "read as a language," as language continues covering the body with its scripts, Bersani's included.

Yet another kind of script has been the biography. Three major accounts of Foucault's life have so far appeared: Didier Eribon's *Michel Foucault (1926-1984)* (Paris: Flammarion, 1989); James Miller's *The Passion of Michel Foucault* (New York: Simon & Schuster, 1993); and David Macey's *The Lives of Michel Foucault* (London: Hutchinson, 1993). Of the three, Miller's has generated the most controversy. Whatever the title of John Guillory's review of Miller's biography might really mean to Guillory ("The Americanization of Michel Foucault", *LGSN*, summer 1993), I'll coopt it for critiquing a peculiarly American response to representations around AIDS and HIV. I'm referring to attempts, from various quarters, to ensure always positive depictions of the ways the virus has affected the constituency whom Foucault, whether willingly, is often pressed into representing: gay, white, educated, middle-class males.

Although Guillory skillfully teases out some of the scratchier threads in Miller's narrative, it seems he wants to cut the book out of wholly homophobic cloth. Miller insists on his honesty as an outsider. Also, he hardly expects a single reading. In correspondence with me, Miller "hoped that [the book] would be understood . . . as an invitation to think—and to feel—for oneself." Even if, as I wrote originally to him, not everything pleases, *The Passion* remains about as neutral, even affectionate, as possible, while piquing, let's admit, some of the curiosities of us all.

We must be prepared to entertain less than flattering ideas about Foucault, who, as Guillory suggests, doesn't need defending. Nevertheless, Guillory joins others willing to neutralize AIDS and HIV along with those infected, with the final result not of eliminating or managing but of whitewashing. This is far more disturbing than any suspicions Miller might arouse, deliberately or otherwise, because it links a form of political correctness to the moralism of those who have coopted the term for use against us. Might Foucault have behaved in troubling ways? Does not AIDS remind us that death is the passion of sex? And does that thought not add rather than subtract value from Foucault's life? I answer yes, on all counts, in part due to Miller's work.

Yet even before it appeared, the book polarized readers. Judith Butler, for example, commenting in an article found in *The Chronicle of Higher Education* (September 30, 1992), calls Miller's purported link between homosexuality and a death wish "insidious and enraging" (A13). She associates such a link with "the culturally reactionary position of people like Patrick Buchanan." Butler and others, such as David Halperin ("Bringing Out Michel Foucault"), accuse the biography of being strategically unwise. Miller is therefore describing Foucault's behavior in a way that will simply give the forces of reaction more ammunition. In this respect, at least, they seem to be right. Roger Kimball, writing in *The New Criterion*, seizes on Miller's biography as much for what it *doesn't* say as for what it says, just as Butler and Wendy L. Brown in *The Chron'*, and Halperin in *Salmagundi*, attempt to read between Miller's lines, construing the book's ostensibly inherent homophobia.[10]

It's reactionaries like Kimball, however, who to me are far more insidious and enraging than the demure James Miller could ever be. However, Kimball succeeds only in further enraging Foucauldians, whether they care for Miller's book, and giving us back our ammunition twofold. Kimball suggests that academicians like Butler, Brown, and Halperin are "homosexual activists who feel that Mr. Miller was insufficiently reverential" ("The Perversions of M. Foucault" 11). He doesn't name names, which he doesn't hesitate to do for Miller's supporters, like Richard Rorty and Alasdair MacIntyre, two of the contributors to the Foucault/Miller symposium in the Winter 1993 *Salmagundi* who respond favorably to Miller's work.

Kimball's reactionary, ad hominem attack on Foucault via Miller would seem to place itself below comment, if it weren't for the fact that Miller has incited Kimball to a discourse that reveals the empty, insupportable, and impoverished nature of his neoconservatism. Kimball simply tries to discredit Foucault's ideas by indicting him personally, a maneuver Halperin suggests Miller is trying to make with Foucault, without beginning to explore the ways in which those ideas informed Foucault's life. Kimball fears that, since Foucault's behavior was purportedly dangerous, so must be his concepts.

Although the terms of the debate differ, it's reminiscent of the storm of controversy that broke over revelations of Paul de Man's having written Nazi-sympathetic journalism during the war—how the worth of de Man's thinking became submerged in the fallout of political logomachy. Perhaps Kimball has caused some damage to Foucault's reputation and influence. But our having remained silent about his corporeal and philosophical experimentation would not have shielded Foucault or his followers from conservative reaction in any event. It might even have perpetuated an oppressive history of neglect and paranoia. Silence will only be the final death of Foucault, so the more we discuss his life and work—and the problematic Miller has done so honestly and insightfully, in my view—the better armed we anarchists of the body will be.

3) Deleuze and Guattari

Gunshots. Canon fire. Crossed sabers. Charges, feints, retreats. Losses and reinforcements and escapes. The smoke is not clearing. We are still in the midst of battle. We have driven the forces of reaction back to this old field where, we well know, the future shall be decided. Many of us have chosen to side with the French, who once seemed about to take over everywhere, or so the hysterical authoritarians claimed—sometimes to our disadvantage. We may be no longer fond of imperialism, but we raise our cry to charge when it becomes clear that the enemy is worse, has ruled for too long and only wishes to continue doing so. Besides, despite our problems, we bring genuine reform. Setting aside relatively small, though significant, differences, we join a fight that means the survival of our bodies as well as of our ideas. Some say this is to impose yet another form of tyranny. We say their tyranny could never be matched. Here we stand, however, prepared to fight them for what we hope is not the last time. Unless we can undo them utterly!

Could this be what Marshal Ney, arriving too late at Water-loo to make an effective difference strategically, was contem-plating, when he ordered a fateful series of charges on that afternoon in June? The man who had once vowed before Louis XVIII *le [Napoléon] ramener dans une cage de fer,* and who would be executed for the treason of rejoining his former com-mander, now claimed about the attack that *il s'agit du salut de la France* (Logie 30, 127). I cannot imagine this moment in the battle without recalling what is perhaps the most spectacular scene in the most spectacular war movie ever made, Sergei Bondarchuk's *Waterloo* (1971). Nor can I help feeling defeated, myself, by the end of those two suturing hours, much longer in the original cut. But while the charge lasts! At least until the cavalry crosses the plateau and gets repulsed by the calm, organized, and very well prepared squares of allied infantry, in and around which the horsemen must flow, and from which explode the orderly lines of fire cutting them down as they ride.

We view all this through the smoke, from the air, no doubt from the helicopter that, if we think about it, can desublimate this moment with the chopping of its rotors (and which will return in chapter 4). At any rate, it becomes painfully clear that the charge has been a bad miscalculation, exhausting French cavalry and leaving it up to the Old Guard to carry the day. Though stunning and courageous, it fails, helping plunge Europe into one of its most repressive periods, whose effects we are, in a way, still suffering.

As I watch this cavalry running hard against the allies, I construe a becoming-nomad on "a milieu of exteriority, or ex-trinsic relations with nebulas or constellations, according to which it fulfills functions of insertion or situation, such as bordering, encircling, shattering" (Deleuze and Guattari *A Thou-sand Plateaus* 353). "Located between the two heads of the State, between the two articulations . . . pass[ing] from one to the other" (355), the cavalry for those few moments breaks away from the despotic state it is defending, hurling itself at the armies of even more insidiously despotic states, following orders *à regret* (Delort in Logie 127), and riding after a hopeless cause. A part of us wants them to succeed, while another part contemplates the consequences of a victory. So we loop ourselves into this singular event. Maybe we speed back through the scene and play it over and over. Really, its symbolic significance gets nearly too hard to resist, as the charge itself must have been.

It remains consternating to utopians that Deleuze and Guattari's personal military ethics seem so obscure. Expecting from their affirmativeness, plateaus, flows, interconnections, becomings, and other appealing concepts a fundamental warmth and peacefulness, readers are startled to discover them writing so vigorously, and at length, about the war machine ("Treatise on Nomadology," *A Thousand Plateaus* 351–423). That they use a form of warfare as an example of a way of thinking about difference seems troubling enough, but then they clearly privilege a form that exploits continual movement, surprise, treason, pillage, and wastefulness, rather than the orderly, rational, hierarchized systems of most Western military governments, including our own. The latter, by contrast, emphasize such concepts as fairness, ethics, respect for human life, the proper treatment of prisoners, and intervention to ensure justice.

What's more, followers of Deleuze and Guattari use the language of violence in discussing their concepts. Brian Massumi, for example, calls an entire chapter of his *User's Guide to Capitalism and Schizophrenia* "FORCE," dividing it into rounds with pauses like a boxing match. He understands their strategic negotiations between total revolution and expedient accommodation: "Tactical sabotage of the existing order is a necessity of becoming, but for survival's sake it is just as necessary to improve the existing order, to fight for integration into it on its terms" (104). Queer power, for one, must *force* positive change, while taking care not to exhaust itself in hopeless battle after hopeless battle with immovable institutions.

In addition, Massumi locates an aspect of molarity—that organized, transcendent, interior phenomenon D & G contrast with molecularity: paranoia. "If bodies can be duplicitous, passing as one identity while continuing to incarnate another, every body is a potential enemy" (115). For him, the battle cry of this policy is "incorporate or annihilate" (115). That, however, could just as easily be shouted from the horses of the nomads. "[T]he war machine is directed against the State, either against potential States whose formation it wards off in advance, or against actual States whose destruction it purposes" (*A Thousand Plateaus* 359)—only on an anarchic, atheistic, minoritarian scale. The nomad knows when to fight, and when simply to avoid.

But his or her life is perpetual readiness in war-making, even when the band is peaceably spread out across the smooth space s/he has annexed. When it's alerted to move, the band often faces the state's efforts to contain its velocity:

> The State does not appropriate the war machine without giving even it the form of relative movement: this was the case with the model of the *fortress* as a regulator of movement, which was precisely the obstacle the nomads came up against, the stumbling block and parry by which absolute vortical movement was broken. [*A Thousand Plateaus* 386]

Recall again the French cavalry, stymied by the British squares.

Or consider gay people in the U.S. military, willing to serve but only on incompossible terms, already serving but placed under the threat of interrogation from the garrison, already having served but going public with the scandal of their previously silent and imperceptible duty. Deleuze and Guattari obviously remain useful in such cases: they accurately identify the ways in which molar formations like the state attempt to impose their hegemony, while offering rout(e)s between the squares, techniques of resistance that resemble attacking, breaking, and running more than a historically inevitable struggle with an inexorable outcome.

This fresh concept of conflict, of critique, is traceable back to Deleuze's earlier work. Michael Hardt, in *Gilles Deleuze: An Apprenticeship in Philosophy*, is as apt as Massumi to use military terminology, when describing Deleuze's relationships to the philosophers he contested earlier in his career. In the subsection entitled "The Paradox of Enemies" of his chapter about Nietzsche, Hardt attempts to clarify ambiguities surrounding Deleuze's adversaries, some of whom he faces directly (Hegel) and others by means of the figures of his monographs (Christ). Finally, he decides:

> The answer [to the problem of nondialectical negation] will have to be found in Nietzsche's total critique; it must constitute an absolutely destructive negation that spares nothing from its force and recuperates nothing from its enemy; it must be an absolute aggression that offers no pardons, takes no prisoners, pillages no goods; it must mark the death of the enemy, with no resurrection. [28]

This "total critique" becomes even more radically ruining than the daily life of the nomad, locating in Deleuze (at least out of *Nietzsche and Philosophy*) a means of engaging in conflict that is absolute and unmerciful. Later, in a discussion of Deleuze's reading of Spinoza, Hardt extends this critique to the affects produced by interacting bodies, which meet and either find each other "composable" and joyful (unresisting) or incompatible and sad (throwing up resistance that must be bypassed or removed) (94). These are extreme limits of interaction, but in any case "affirmation is intimately tied to antagonism," as Hardt paradoxically has it (115). It is not a happy passivity that would allow for any and all diversities. It is a ruthlessness that dances while it undoes, sings while criticizing, clears an opening for new forces and affects, as Foucault attempted to do with his resistant archaeologies and extreme sexual encounters, and as Lacan adumbrated with the ongoing agonisms of imaginary violence.

Foucault, for example, poses the model of power as a battle against the traditional model involving repression, a hierarchical imposition of authority over a compliant subject. "Power is a war, a war continued by other means," he says (*Power/Knowledge* 90), paraphrasing Karl von Clausewitz, theorist of warfare during the Napoleonic era, who fought at Waterloo after having served as a POW to the French. Power, along with the resistance that is an integral part, operates by means of tactics and strategy (164) that never utterly completes its aim, utterly fails, or disappears (56). It's ongoing and ubiquitous, but that doesn't make it all-powerful. In fact, one of the most important ways that the subject can resist power is to manipulate his or her own body, as I've suggested.

Foucault explored sadism/masochism, toward an ascesis of self-abnegation, compelling however controversial. Lacan suggests a similar pursuit. Speaking about the fundamental alienation of the ego from desire, Lacan refers to "the aggressivity of the slave whose response to the frustration of his labour is a desire for death" ("The Function and Field of Speech and Language in Psychoanalysis" 42). The subject thus engineers this death by ingenious means. He or she may or may not actually die in the process, but establishes death as the linchpin keeping the struggle against authority under motion. Lacan, however, accepts this aggressivity as an inexorable aspect (element, but also image) of the dialectic's entanglements—the death drive—whereas Foucault is more apt either to negate such aggression through personal surrender or to adopt the Nietzschean, masterful tactic of affirmation. The slave remains resentful and hopeless, thereby tragic. The Foucauldian subject, conscious of power's insidious mechanisms, nonetheless offers resistance with the very fact and strength of his own body, its ability to affect and be affected, to submit to forces while creating them.

Deleuze and Guattari also see these forces acting everywhere, maybe even more everywhere than Foucault, since they disperse power more widely and on a more fundamental level metaphysically. Foucault doesn't concern himself as much with philosophical issues of the Deleuzoguattarian variety (for example, the nature of difference in itself), preferring to locate and examine power/resistance in the relations between institutions and subjects. Supplanting the *hierarchy* of power with the *network*, he traces the progress of the paradigm from periods when the disparity between classes was greater (before the turn of the nineteenth century) to periods when the disparity shrank somewhat during the creation of the bourgeois class, with its bureaucracies and fairly local technologies of discipline. But Deleuze and Guattari, especially in *A Thousand Plateaus*, see desire, a concomitant to power, operating even between the "particles" making up both matter and relations, whether social, personal, or ideational. Sometimes these particles clump together to form molar aggregates (such as phalanxes), and sometimes they disperse molecularly (as in wild, hopeless cavalry charges).

The movement back and forth between the molar and the molecular, between reterritorialization and deterritorialization, is what for me characterizes the experience of the body in contact with other bodies, fleshly or textual. The schizo, the particulate, diverse subject, engages in a sort of perpetually losing struggle that, in any case, guarantees that subject a means of escape and renovation. One lives to fight again, despite abandonment, persecution, disease—and even ecstasy.

* * *

Lacan, Foucault, and Deleuze and Guattari, then, provide paradoxical, conflicting, maybe incompatible modes of thought about contestation. Despite their differences, they remain useful by delineating for queer studies a technology of critique that is itself unpardonable and unpardoning. They mold bodies that refuse completion, disobey interdictions, and pursue strife in an effort to create themselves anew.

4

Music into the Body: Philip Glass and Others

Prelude in the Postmodern Mode

One of the most memorable moments during the hearings for the Meese commission on pornography occurred when a member of this venerable, perhaps venal, commission remarked, and I'm paraphrasing: "I may not know what pornography is, but I know it when I see it." Despite the multiplicity of intelligent voices, despite the earnest, and not so earnest, theorizing by critics from any and all disciplines, despite honest efforts to achieve at least what Habermas might call a temporary consensus about just what this latest, latist ism *is*, I think many of us tend still to describe our experience(s) with postmodernism in the phenomenological manner exemplified, perversely, by that commission member.

Whether we handle the smooth, day-glo railings outlining James Stirling's Neue Staatsgalerie in Stuttgart; nostalgize over the deconstructive song-writing of Gang of Four; build narratives to complete, and thereby title, Cindy Sherman's *Untitled Film Stills*; or tease out the meanings, contrary to our better judgment, of Deleuze and Guattari's webs of neologisms and fervent post-'68, antimodernist rhetoric—we say we have encountered, or have been subjected by, *the postmodern*. Of course, this type of reaction is really of little help in identifying, however tentatively, an aesthetics or politics or economy of postmodernism that would allow us to separate personal taste from critical judgment, that would authorize us to shed the brackets and the scare quotes and speak plainly as a porn star about what we see and desire in the postmodern.

Yet, in the Blanchodian sense, as we grasp harder and further for this slippery animal or mechanism we call postmodernism, the harder and further, we find, we must reach and grope even to begin to catch up. An irony results in that as we continue to insist on the provisionality, the tentativeness, the incompletion, the fragmentariness of postmodernism(s) (and I'm thinking here especially of Ihab Hassan and William Spanos), the more imperative it becomes to reify it, especially as certain forms of the movement come under attack from right and left alike. If we don't know what it is that we're defending, it will become indefensible. But if the artifacts of postmodernism we admire are actually resisting our well-intentioned defenses as much as they're resisting accusations of being in themselves either offensive (as the right may have it) or neglectful of lived history (as they left often claims), then a crippling paranoia— a sense of the critic's being a center elsewhere (nowhere important)—is clearly a possible outcome.

Like that member of the Meese commission, we're left with the paradoxical task of *looking* at the very thing we're trying to render invisible, so as to avoid hypostasizing it and letting it circulate insidiously, searching for the outlines of those defining characteristics yet surrendering to the blur of impressions they impart as if the allowance for subjection will in itself convince even the most skeptical of postmodernism's substantiality.

This is why a typography or cartography of postmodernism, which Frederic Jameson, for one, at the end of his influential essay, "Postmodernism and the Cultural Logic of Late Capitalism," suggests as an essential task, seems to me to be a logical way to approach the culture of postmodernism with an aim toward that endlessly deferred definition. However, the "cognitive mapping" to which Jameson refers would appear to resemble the cartography by the Old World of the New World during the golden age of naval exploration, in which the map is more or less drawn *first* and the voyage is made to confirm its assumptions—especially as to where the boundaries lie, beyond which is merely the monstrous. A more useful method of cartography would be to set out on the trip with the *purpose* of sketching a map, which would then be used on the return trips; to draw and redraw the lines every time, not simply to admit to the provisionality of the representation, and *some* sort of map is certainly a provision among many others required. But to apply the most relevant, fair, and, yes, playful critical technique to the postmodern object. (The voyage in question here, for this chapter, might be simply the very act of reading through a list of rather canonical texts on postmodernism—

suggested in the cartography below—in order to start rendering that plan.)

Of course, if we're looking for a *stable* object to locate definitively in our scheme—insofar as it *is* ours—we're not likely to find it. One of the activities that postmodernism has encouraged is proliferation itself, as the many anthologies and anthologylike studies of postmodernism evidence. Stanley Trachtenberg's handbook comes to mind, as does Jameson's own peripatetic survey of postmodernism; plus *Art after Modernism* and its follow-up volumes; *Design after Modernism*; all the collections of critical theory; special issues of scholarly journals, such as *October* and *differences*); the MLA's increasingly eclectic *Profession*; art exhibit catalogs; and so on. (I can't think about what my list includes without thinking about everything it *doesn't* include. The proliferation is immediate and ongoing.) Again, we search among these confusions of discourse for the dominant paradigm, as, for example, Brian McHale tries heroically but not quite completely to do in *Postmodernist Fiction*, only to have the elusiveness of the model irritate and seduce us enough, like a Parthian archer, to lead us more determinedly in pursuit. We may lose the struggle yet discover new ground.

In this context, I think of Oedipa Maas, eccentric character of Thomas Pynchon's novel *The Crying of Lot 49*. I should like to position her as a subject with whom to identify on the postmodern chase. I spoke earlier of the paranoia of the critic. The paranoia in Pynchon's novel involves, among other things, the enumeration of alternatives. It's as if the setting forth of a specific number of explanations will somehow hook Oedipa back into some rational reality. When she finally becomes saturated with images of the Tristero, she, or the narrator, stops to consider what could possibly be going on. She limits herself to, or feels limited by, a "symmetrical four," none of which Oedipa likes. Whatever mystery she has encountered is either dream, hallucination, plot, or fantasy. Why does the narrator call these four "symmetrical"? Because the dream of a potential reality might be only a hallucination; because the plot, as conspiracy *and* structure of events, might be mere fantasy. The two sets of conception or perception, to use Lyotard's terminology, are ranged on either side of her, like thieves, even though the levels of imitation, of impalpability, appear to recede indefinitely.

At any rate, in her utter aloneness, confronting the void, Oedipa wishes she were inebriated, a condition that has haunted her since the very first sentence of the novel: it could desensitize Oedipa to uncertainty. But she begins to feel very real pain, and this is when she gets even more serious about taking control, herself, of the situation—namely, by learning as much as she can about this Lot 49. Since the lot is both an archive of relics *and* an inexorable fate, Oedipa would not necessarily possess it—she'd apparently rather leave that to the collectors, like Cohen. Yet she is confronted with even more either/ors, "waiting for a symmetry of choices to break down," wondering what had happened to diversity. By the end she, and we, can only wait and watch, though by now we feel more of Oedipa's presence as a consciousness with memory, cares, worries, desires, especially in the long paragraphs of internal monolog toward the end, so the suspense becomes even more terrible.

If *Lot 49* is any indication, two realms, to choose only two, seem thus to persist in remaining hopelessly remote from one another, in the postmodern moment. That of the text and that of life. (That of Oedipa and that of the Tristero.) That of abstraction and that of lived experience (Laura E. Donaldson). Of events and facts (Linda Hutcheon). History and historicism (or nostalgia; Frederic Jameson). Pain and language (Elaine Scarry). Text and book (Charles Caramello; or the more obvious choice, text and work [Roland Barthes]). Substance and simulacrum (Jean Baudrillard). Expanded field and rupture (Hal Foster). I and you (Craig Owens). Texts and lumps (Richard Rorty). Slackening and terror (Jean-François Lyotard, who deals in even more binaries, like modern/postmodern, representable/unpresentable, conceived/realized, establishment/avant-garde, Proust/Joyce, Dada/Surrealist, Habermas/Lyotard). Freedom and citadel (O. K. Werckmeister). Realms, locuses, worlds that must be bracketed or enclosed within quotation marks, and almost always in contradistinction to the postmodern, which is allowed to exist without bounds in all its indeterminacy, displacement, plurality—its affects "foreboding, premonition, suspicion, anxiety" and its techniques "fragmentation, excerptation, quotation" (Douglas Crimp "Pictures" 180, 183). (No sarcasm is intended here, but can't be utterly silenced either.) How can these distinctions hold, in a larger world, a rotating, revolving discursive arena so textualized that the consensus seems to need no annotation, at least in academic circles? How can Hassan's famous and often-quoted columns of distinctions between the modern and the postmodern, in *The Dismemberment of Orpheus*, continue to sustain the structure we've erected even for the time being, this columned shanty of po-mo?

Confronted by many of the binarities of postmodernism, readers, writers, critics sometimes appear to feel Oedipa Maas's vertigo and isolation. The question is often asked: Is postmodernism caught in a trap of its own making? See, for example, E. Ann Kaplan's introduction to *Postmodernism and its Discontents*, where she quite rightly fears certain postmodernisms' complicity with mass consumer culture. Postmodernism seems, anyway, to enjoy this odd symbiosis with life, what is nowadays called history, a school subject become a technical term. As Paul Bové remarks, "theorists and critics of the postmodern study and describe the present moment and so enact the present while conceiving it" (3). In the afterword to *The Postmodern Condition*, Lyotard speaks of the contradictory nature of attacks on the avant-garde (73) and also of the proliferation in "rules and categories [which] the [postmodern] work of art itself is looking for" (81) in comparison to the nostalgic, totalizing rationality of reactionary late modernism.

Lyotard's nemesis in this respect, Habermas, distinguishes in "Modernism—An Incomplete Project" between "young conservatives," "old conservatives," which may include many of those Lyotard enumerates, and "neoconservatives," a strange designation for Foucault[1] and Derrida, even stranger for Bataille, who is thus made an embattled writer in these "confrontations," as Habermas calls them (14–15). All of these figures are helping to short-circuit the radical flow of electric enlightenment that modernism, to Habermas, should keep under motion until it has connected everywhere.

Though pigeonholing is hardly definitive, Habermas, along with Jameson and others, does suggest the maneuver that, even at this late date, badly needs to be made: that is, one of typology, or typography, a division of the multiple postmodernisms, a few of them, at least, into categories making the debate—and this is perhaps what the postmodern moment as an ism seems to remain—somewhat clearer, however interrelated those categories are going to have to be even before they're established, and however paranoid the maneuver may seem in the face of the intensifying mystery and trauma that the postmodern world calls reality.

A provisional set of postmodern alternatives might fall not into a symmetrical four but into three ranges of threes, all interconnected. Here is the *deductive* movement:

I. Postmodernism defined
    a. Postmodernism is to be defined.
    b. Postmodernism can be defined.
    c. Postmodernism is not to be defined.

II. Postmodernism characterized
    a. Postmodernism must be obvious.
    b. Postmodernism can be subversive.
    c. Postmodernism is irremediably ironic.

III. Postmodernism used
    a. Postmodernism is applicable to cultural formations following the sixties.
    b. Postmodernism is applicable to any period in Western cultural history.
    c. Postmodernism belongs to those who practice it.

The *inductive* motion would simply move "up," from III to I, from an examination of specific uses narrowing down to general statements. In fact, deduction/induction is yet another postmodern binarity, at least as far as analysis goes—one more opposition to use and abuse, and be disabused of. (These contrary yet complementary movements suggest some kind of circular or spiral diagram—perhaps like those that please structuralists, perhaps better left unconstructed.)

It's apparent that the categories following letters of the alphabet are associative. Thus, a critic who believes that postmodernism is to be defined—that is, it *can* be or *must* be, or both—that is, it is a project to do so—would also be likely to assert that postmodernism is applicable to cultural manifestations of a given era. Therefore it is a *periodic* designation, and it must be obvious in order to be recognized—also, because of inherent properties, because of the *peculiar* self-referentiality of the postmodern moment. Baudrillard and Lyotard, for example, would fall into the "a" category. Jameson, by contrast, would belong to "c," finding it difficult to define postmodernism outside a few—*very* few and curiously re-

stricted—cultural manifestations which are subsumable under the powers of late capitalism.

I wonder: Is it dead, or simply belated, or both, like a zombi
whose Rolex got stolen? To Jameson, and other Marxists like
Terry Eagleton, therefore, postmodernism is a *factional* activity
practiced by those who can understand and manipulate its
ironies. Another Marxist, Dana Polan, echoes this sentiment in
"Postmodernism and Cultural Analysis Today." Hence, it fails
to effect the ground swell of social change seen as necessary to
the Marxist program. Its *ethical conscience* is questionable,
whereas the conscience of the "a" group entails a *consciousness
of consciousness.* The "b" designation, finally, includes writers
like Spanos and even Foucault—those believing postmodernism
can be clearly defined, see it as potentially subversive, since
the *subject* of traditional Western thinking is in crisis, and
therefore, looking back on all or much of history, can apply
postmodern methods, generally archaeological and historical,
to any of its periods; so it's called an *epochal* or *cyclical* point
of view. The motto of this group might be "postmodernism is
where you find it" or "an artifact is postmodern when you know
that it is."

We find ourselves back where we started: at the imaginary
moment of (mis-)recognition in which we're certain that the
image we see is a full and complete representation of the presence we assume always to have been there in the first place.
But it's an enabling illusion as long as it helps undermine
categorical assumptions about postmodernism's supposed affront and assault on the rest of cultural history. Put another
way, postmodernism, whatever else we may say about it, cannot be considered utterly a rupture or utterly privileged if it has
been with human culture all along in some form or other.

Similarly, my typographical categories overlap, and many
theorists and practitioners would have to inhabit more than
one category simultaneously. Certain Marxists, for example,
might agree that postmodernism can be defined (I, b), but dis-
agree whether it can be subversive (II, b) or remains indeterminate (II, c), and wouldn't necessarily apply its thinking to any
and all points in history (III, b). Moreover, it must be remembered that this is a *metacriticism* —it applies more adhesively,
perhaps, to commentators on postmodernism than to its writers, composers, filmmakers, photographers. Of course, on the
other hand, if postmodernism is a glacial change creeping

through culture, it might be possible to interpellate as post-modern any artifact postdating the beginning of that change, according to when it's located.

This outline is a sorting machine, just as potentially unde-pendable and obsolete as any, just as subject to needing an overhaul, and almost immediately, especially in the expansion of its components. It may not make the task of identifying postmodern *works* any easier, but then it seems that postmodern critiques, or critiques of postmodernism, have been generating as fast as their objects. For the moment, it might be wisest to hold as many positions at once as possible, before the domi-nant, if there is one, emerges, if ever, and if even desired.

"With coincidences blossoming these days wherever she looked, she had nothing but a sound, a word, Trystero, to hold them together" (*Lot 49* 109). Oedipa experiences the noncenter, circles of signifiers without a hub, a possibly defunct, possibly fictitious but potentially hegemonic faction without a leader, a triste tryst or sad affair in which nothing of value is fulfilled. The postmodern debate can certainly appear similar, but read-ers are no less drunk or mad than Oedipa in trying to make sense of it while dangers threaten, so long as, clearly, they're being entertained in the meantime.

A Real Reel

Entertainment would seem to have little to do with the pretext of (to) this chapter, an aside, made before the discus-sion proper begins, that would seem to be able to invalidate or at least devaluate the entire project: the story of the assault on, and mutilation of, a young boy in Pierce County, Washing-ton (front-page story by Don Carter in the *Seattle Post-Intelligencer*, February 1, 1990), in which the boy "quietly answered the most intimate questions about a sexual attack" in court. His calm and clear description of the attack, which included strangling, rape, dismemberment—and, astonishingly, survival—is horrific. It's a story in which people are likely to say that language fails beyond simple retelling, in which signifiers for emotional reactions may be as obscene as the crime, and objective description seems enough to evoke the proper response as well as the proper action. A story, in short, that could make a certain sort of postmodern self-obsessive-ness, meaning "almost everything and thus nearly nothing . . . where very little is at stake" (Jencks *What Is Post-Modernism?* 34), an inexpedient waste of time.

The story's levels of discourse, by the time of this writing, are heaped up considerably, from the boy's account of the incident to family and police, to reports to the press, to testimony, to Don Carter's and others' stories, to follow-ups, to commentaries and commentaries on commentaries, and the ensuing, resonant silence. Legislation responding to the story, where the removal of a young boy's penis in the woods would seem to be the one finally unforgivable type of sexual assault (after all, had it been a girl, she wouldn't have lost anything but, perhaps, her virginity; she might still have had an organ with which to enjoy sexual pleasure and, above all, to procreate)—laws made after the fact, when crime, corruption, mistakes are made visible and therefore inescapable from public scrutiny, may be reassuring but are also offensive, especially whenever castration is being considered as punishment for sex offenders. Washington State Governor Booth Gardner's calling the resulting bill a "message to the people of the state of Washington that we are serious about protecting our children and our families from violence and crime" (the *P-I*, front page, March 1, 1990) may thus be noted as one more example of the ineluctably textuality and discursivity of this kind of world, even to nonacademics, even when drastic, irreversible actions are taken *in* it, affecting it in more ways than can be counted. Legislation is a "message"—here addressed to those it protects—that is, those voters whom Gardner "represents" ("we," "our"). It is not addressed to those it admonishes—that is, the criminals, usually, according to recent reports, coming from racial groups whose children and families appear to make little difference, who will swell the prisons as a result of belated and paranoiacal law-making. It is a case of treating the symptom without attending to the cause, without even paying it lip service. And this appears to be as typical of contemporary governments, especially those dominated by conservatives, as it does of certain forms of establishment journalism.

The *P-I* has treated the story with dignity, at any rate. Without being in the slightest way facetious toward this boy, efforts to curb sexual assault, or postmodernism, some readers may find it easy to take the story of the boy's trauma and mutilation as a castration paradigm, loss of the hegemonic center, destruction of the referent, removal of the signified, the phal- excised leaving only the -logocentrism of a disempowered boy and his tale. Yet the boy has lost something that he will never get back. One aspect of his sex life has been taken away. Totally, finally, undoubtedly. While we ken this event (which was real) only through rea(l)ms of texts, which, of course, are also real but maintain a problematic and problematizing relation to their signifieds, these texts *retain* what they assail.[2] If theorists like Hutcheon, then, are to be believed (*Poetics* passim, esp. 144–57), postmodernism can't as often be as radical a force of change as that assailant's knife, no matter how affective, and is not as likely to make its concerns as compelling as those of the boy and everyone who cares about him.

Actually, that kind of catastrophic loss has been dramatized and in front of a mass audience, both in print and on the screen. To take one obvious example, in John Irving's and George Roy Hill's *The World According to Garp*, the biting off of a man's penis in a car during fellatio seems too funny to care much about—whereas the boy's testimony in that Tacoma courtroom causes the direst abjection. Irving's journalistic prose is possibly meant to help authorize his fictional accounts as if they were drawn from real life, a pretense that insults prose and life alike. But mortification sold, and sells, and gives critics jobs.

While the following survey treats in part of senses of loss and recovery, lives and deaths in subjects and the texts they form and that form them, stories like that of the assaulted boy should be running in the background, as if the eyes read one text and the mind thought another, both and neither receiving adequate attention. In which case, for instance, the removal of "Frame-Tale" from John Barth's *Lost in the Funhouse* would signify as little as the potential death of Sheherazade, who not only tells tales to save her life but frames them, too, thereby framing herself. This chapter attempts to show that the lives and deaths, the successes and failures, whether willed or not, of postmodern artifacts can, in themselves, rather than causing a "waning of affect" as Jameson calls it, compel, and compel powerfully. The thing is, not to be afraid, before the exploration has begun.

As the foregoing suggests, postmodernism returns obsessively to the body, and I have chosen just such a compulsion—that in the art, music, and literature movement known loosely as minimalism (and the postminimalism that follows)—to discuss in terms of the affects it produces, and the effects it has, on bodies experiencing it. Minimalism in its earlier, purer forms was perhaps an example of high or decadent modernism (in Jencks's terms), but not a nostalgic return to tonality. At any rate, it was an example of postmodernism's emphasis on the body—its pleasures, pains, subjections, endurances. It *became* a music in and for the body just as surely as serialism, its nemesis in some ways, became a music in and for the mind, explicitly and aggressively. To speak here of a return to tonality in the traditional sense, some kind of neoconservatism, seems irrelevant, since minimalism grew out of musics that were either tonal to begin with (Glass's rejected early work, which nevertheless grew out of a tonal tradition not exactly opposed to serialism, until Glass *made* it so in his new-found language, the one we now associate with his name); or drew upon musics whose idioms bear little relation to traditional Western tonality (Indian, African, Asian).[3] Minimalism cannot, therefore, be said to constitute an astringent, though unruly, modernism, nor some revanchist antimodernism, but in between or at the limits of these forms: a sort of virtual body, instead of either an enclosed system produced out of the mind of mathematics (serialism's hegemony through not only pitch but timbre, rhythm, and the like), or neoromantic auteurism (as in David Del Tredici or John Corigliano).

What might define this virtual body? An entity embodying a cluster of lived experience, offering itself for consumption at the limit between interpretation (the hermetic modernist) and subjectification (the abject hypermodernist), partaking of both but inhabiting neither exclusively. Not quite the projective weapon of the nomad, nor the introceptive tool of the economist (*A Thousand Plateaus* 395). (Post-)Minimalism embodies just such a textual body by enacting certain kinds of subjectifications (intraceptions), while not being so reductive or empty as to discourage reflection ("imaginary passion"; see Rajchman 18). Not quite the mirror held up for our (dis-)identification, but a pane of Glass by which to perceive ourselves, through which to recognize the holder and the context beyond.

Music into the Body: Philip Glass

I begin with a quote—not by Philip Glass, whom I've singled out obsessively to exemplify the pitfalls and potentialities of repetitive music—but by his apparently more purist rival, Steve Reich. Speaking in a text now more than twenty years old about minimalism's enticement to subjection and liberation, he writes:

> Musical processes can give one a direct contact with the impersonal and also a kind of complete control, and one doesn't always think of the impersonal and complete control as going together. By "a kind" of complete control I mean that by running this material through this process I completely control all that results, but also that I accept all that results without changes. [10]

Minimalism appears more or less fully developed early in the postmodern period, in the late sixties, and is often seen (and heard) especially in Europe as just another ism among others. Considered a conceptual period that art passed through on its way to more engaging, personal forms, minimalism defines significant problems around the body as a site of contestation. As Reich suggests, process or minimal or systems music contacts the impersonal as a means toward more direct contact with pleasures of and in the body incited by a return to fundamentals: in Glass's case, to rhythm as basis for—and cause of tension with—melody, consonant harmony, and ritual. The improvisation eschewed by the music (except to allow the performers occasionally to rest) becomes our own response-ability as we wander around, get up to leave, or remain to let the music subject us utterly. As Glass himself suggests, we may even remain to remind the performers of our discomfort, a sort of involved disaffection (see Peter Greenaway's documentary about Glass in his series *Four American Composers*, 1985).

What results can entail new ways of desiring and feeling, as well as the troubling implications of aesthetic and political discipline, as we'll see in the case of Paul Schrader's film *Mishima* and the opera *Akhnaten*, both scored by Glass. Eero Tarasti, in "Le minimalisme du point de vue sémiotique," calls this music *un phénomène très ambigu et paradoxal* (21), a very ambiguous and paradoxical phenomenon. But for Tarasti it's largely a mind thing, a play of signification, whereas for me it's that but also a body thing, playing on the sympathetic rhythms of our biology and therefore both potentially subversive and absolutist.

People seem to respond to this music, and to postmodernism generally, on a visceral level. It's just as likely, then, that some recognize and thereby prefer one sort of postmodernism over another. E. Ann Kaplan, for instance, in her introduction to *Postmodernism and its Discontents*, distinguishes between a revolutionary version and one that's complicit with what Jameson and others call "late capitalism." One theorist will claim that postmodernism can indeed achieve liberation of oppressed human subjects (I think, say, of William Spanos's enthusiasms), while another, such as Dana Polan, maintains that postmodernism is little more than the latest fashion in mass consumer culture to which the administrators of high culture are only condescending, perhaps out of cynical opportunism in the academy. It's difficult if not impossible to take either position exclusively, or to determine whether postmodern artifacts affect only individuals capable of comprehending them or large groups of consumers over which they wash like a tide.

Linda Hutcheon's notion of postmodernism as "complicitous critique" might be useful here as a sort of middle ground and as a corrective to polemical extremes. She holds that, in fact, no postmodern artifact can avoid complicity with the discourse it contests. She holds that the post- is always already engaged in an intimate dialectic with the -modern. This may sound sensible to some, pessimistic to others, but at least it addresses the "suspensive irony," to use Alan Wilde's term, that seems to obtain in postmodernism—certainly in minimalism, with its paradoxes of revolt and complicity.

The case of music makes the task of identifying the oppositional tendencies in postmodernism no easier—music may even complicate matters in that it's often still considered absolute (regardless of whether a piece of music is, in fact, a piece of absolute music), existing in and by and for its own mathematical laws as well as its emotional effects. In other words, paradoxically, it's a personal thing, borne by the impersonal. It would seem that, at least since the Frankfurt School, whose supporters attend to the social text that every score necessarily is, after the irruption and dominance of popular music in our culture, and after the general swing among composers of so-called serious music back toward tonality and accessibility, it would be a simple matter to identify a postmodernism of music.

Indeed, there *was* a modern period in music history, which is considered to be, like the capitalism supporting it, late (see Werckmeister 109ff.). If we, even provisionally, identify the postmodern as socially engaged, intermixed with popular *and* elite forms, and listenable, then we know it when we hear it. But it's not that simple, especially when the music fulfills the

expectations of high culture administered by international capitalism. So there is as much to be disturbed by as happy for,
as Kaplan, Jameson, Hutcheon, and others so strongly imply.

Glass offers just such a contrapuntal case. Both *Mishima*
and *Akhnaten* concern themselves with strong, central, male
(though problematically male) characters who are positioned as
heroes despite who they really were and represented—
authoritarianism, especially. Though neither production was
what anyone would call a huge success, both nevertheless con-
tributed to the repopularization of audience-oriented music and
reaffirmed what had always been true of serious composers—
namely, their ability—even willingness—to simplify their musical vocabularies and cooperate with custodians of culture,
whether high or low. Moreover, Glass *is* usually lumped with
composers thought of as postmodern, at least since he's developed away from his radically minimal (and, I think, more con-
frontational) early phase, of which *Einstein on the Beach* is the
epitome. Admittedly, the score to *Mishima* is quite simply gor-
geous, and potent. *Akhnaten* conforms to the kind of opera that
the established opera-going public demands, with a culture
hero brought down by the bureaucrats. (Is Glass predicting his
own downfall here, hedging his artistic bets against a financially
unstable future?)

Nevertheless, or perhaps indeed, the opera announces
itself as postmodern with its *bricolage* of fragmentary sung
texts (assembled by a multiplicity of scholars, including Glass),
polylingualism, and abrupt telescoping, at the end, into the
twentieth century with a text assembled out of Frommer's
and Fodor's travel guides. Achim Freyer's Stuttgart production of *Akhnaten* as retro German cabaret or expressionist
theater, detailed in the documentary about the opera, *A
Composer's Notes*, would seem only to increase the number
of recognizing responses the opera receives. Meanwhile David
Freeman's more naturalistic Houston production renders
Akhnaten as an *Aida* for the nineteen-eighties and beyond,
but has been less successful.

Glass's music itself bifurcates me. On the one hand, I feel
seduced and swept up in the flow of notes, bouncing my limbs
and swinging my head as much as when I listen to a popular
song. His work, as some like the Belgian minimalist Wim Mertens
(16–17) contend, represents a feminine sexual economy of extended repetition, undulating rhythms of pleasure, and only

gradual but then enormously powerful climaxes—a music that is nonphallic, nonnarrative, and ateleological in the traditional sense, at least in its more rarefied forms. It intercedes in the march of musical progress carried on by the serialists with an affront of simplicity, energy, and startlingly popular appeal due in part to non-Western musical sources, which themselves directly appeal to their audiences. On the other hand, I'm fascinated by the manner in which this very seduction becomes overmastering, suggesting submission to (of course male) figures of dominance, including Glass himself, however much he tries to avoid such authority, and he really does try, in decentered performance practices, an unassuming, almost _dégagé_ personal manner, and a speech pattern that is articulate and swift, much like his music.

Mertens reiterates Marcuse's comment that a breakdown of ego functions, like that caused by repetitive music with its excessive Lyotardian economy of intensive gratifications, becomes but a means for institutionalized power to increase its hegemony (124). Glass's choice of subject matter might raise Marcusean suspicions.

In _Mishima_, for example, scenes from the novelist's life are intercut with dramatizations of scenes from his novels, making it appear that Mishima's life was a sort of narrative he constructed, just like any other. He went by an assumed name. He engaged in theatrical acts of traditional Japanese morality. He had a pretend army of beautiful young men, complete with uniforms and rituals and field trips and codes of honor. The actor who plays Mishima himself also plays a character in one of his novels, and appears in newsreel footage _as_ Mishima _within_ the larger film. The lighting and coloration is bold, tawdry, artificial—as postmodern as can be, to heighten the sense of the film's constructedness, but also to attract and hold the eye's attention—yet another form of command. Might we be led to believe, then, that, since everything within, and, so, without, the film is only a fiction, the facts of Mishima's own politics become unimportant?

Separated from the film, Glass's soundtrack appears to make just such a claim. We can, after all, listen to this music by itself and enjoy it thoroughly, and it's really one of Glass's most effective scores, forgetting, at least during our being sutured in, that it has anything to do with a fascist hero. Now, I wouldn't like to think that Schrader's film and Glass's score are not without their critical edges. At the very least, Mishima comes across as a woefully misguided militarist who seemed never to make it out of adolescence, in the Freudian stereotype of the arrested ego. And certain passages in Glass's soundtrack are frightening or anachronistic or ethnically inaccurate enough—for example, the use of an electric guitar—to make one pause. However, it's finally impossible to dismiss the central figure here as a mere prop or a loon. Had the Japanese accepted Mishima's retrograde plans, the emperor would once again have been at least nominally deified and the society rendered once again feudal and militarized.

Texts like *Mishima* and *Akhnaten* should not be asked to fulfill criteria of political correctness. They leave themselves too widely open to interpretation for such a superficial critique, in any case. We should ask, instead, How well are these highly problematical texts working further to problematize their subjects? To begin to answer, and here I can only begin, I should like to read them somewhat more closely than I have, applying Lyotardian metacriticism—that fluid sort of analysis that seeks in different texts their own epistemological conditions—to *Mishima* and *Akhnaten*. The former, because the subject offers more sheer information to go by, I shall move through with more poetic license, whereas the latter, with its fragmentariness, will be considered more materially, as a commodity with advantages and disadvantages.

Mishima: A Viewer Takes Down Notes

Mishima compelled intersections of life and work. Beauty transmutes to art transmutes to action, the personal becomes the political. Words that change reality in the sense of conscious manipulation of perception exist in a troubled dialectic with the world, which is nonlinguistic, associated with what he called the unconscious mind. The formally perfect artifact, such as Schrader's movie, and the ethically perfect act, which we cannot bring ourselves to imitate, derive from the same authoritarian impulse to be subjected by and to subject, whether the audience or the citizen.

Fear of artifice, the mirror, the mask, of merely looking, merely practicing a martial art, of deceit, similar to the fear of women and the feminine, the undisciplined, of the loss of self—

the emptying out—in sex. Fear of theater as an emptiness, a darkness that surrounds and subtends the action, impels the drastic chance taken under bright light, preferably sunlight, the blood of the Japanese disk, itself representing a violent act of creation. But that action is only the exaggeration of the artifice, the aesthetic spilling into the ethical. The attack and suicide fulfill the spectacular ritual even as they explode it and force ordinary life into an ongoing repressive desublimation of intersubjective violence. "Stage blood is not enough. Poetry [should be] written with a splash of blood." The public rests content with reading it, while the Samurai lusts to draw it forth.

Writing remains insufficient, the feebler half of the tradition requiring the sword to complete it, carry it to its climactic conclusion. Suicide becomes a form of expression, like death and destruction generally. If the American bombers destroy the Temple of the Golden Pavilion, beauty will have been redeemed in its own flames and will have saved the sensitive young misfit from his own desire.

Sex cannot happen; it depends upon initiation rites, speculation, and finally martyrdom, the drive that highlights aesthetic concerns over the body and threatens to allow it to decay merely, through dissipation, the doom of personal beauty's indulging itself—the homosexual's greatest fear. The homosocial bond among the men in the Shield Society thus acts not only to discipline sexual interaction but to ensure death at the moment of greatest beauty, *in* the moment of greatest beauty.

Theater creates beauty but only through fakery, props, mise-en-scène, interchanged roles, stage and pen names, as in the film *Mishima*, outsizing itself such that it foregrounds its own textuality, becoming its own fetish. During the performance of the piece we may look but not touch, allow it to stand (in) for our lack but have to admit its insufficiency as an unnatural article, a gaudy dildo running out of juice. As the music ends abruptly, so do the repetition of this fetish and the hesitation to take our lives into our own hands; as the suturing tears asunder, so do the viscera. But this is finally the act of the solitary, performed when all other avenues of social action have been exhausted.

Citizens must wear identification badges but not so much to separate them as to enforce conformity. If we don't read Japanese, one badge may resemble another, and we notice the same actors playing different roles in different scenes, almost as if they're interchangeable. This is the realm of the imaginary, not the real. Black and white describes Mishima's past life, including passages from his autobiography; color describes the present of the action in 1970; and supersaturated color glows from stagings of scenes from the novels. The real is the naturalistic, the Oedipal the colorless contrasts of old movies, and the imaginary the stylized, hyperchromatic mirror stages of Mishima's fiction.

In the *Kyoko no ie* (*Kyoko's House*) sequence, for example, we see the mommy-daddy-me triangle played out between the mother/prostitute, the absent father (killed in the war?), and the dreamy young son. He seeks the greater masculinity of real action in contrast with the feminine falseness of the stage and its narcissistic idealism, associated with homosexuality. "Stage blood is not enough." The prostitute, as means of masculine sexual expression, holds up a mirror to the man: as a result, he adopts her feminine attributes. His relationship with the older woman, on the other hand, involves violence, blood, and death. The artist (Mishima) thus acts as witness to the real blood of their (double) suicide—like the critic observing culture. The perfection of the smooth skin must be marred by the razor blade. Cuts, bruises, scars all over the young man's body signal the real inscribing itself there, signifying masculinist violence and self-abjection or -subjection, which he performs only in terms of women; with men it involves courtship, honor, love, economic struggle, aesthetics, militarism.

He centers a triangle of women: the mother, the prostitute, and the lover. The mother offers security, a little eroticism; the prostitute, pleasure; and the lover death. It is a cycle of women. Suicide needs an older woman, denies *open* conflict, which he might have with another man. It unites the aesthetic (imaginary) to the ethical (real) in one brilliant act, centering around the fetishes of music, sets, the "silver phallus" of the jet fighter, samurai swords, uniforms, Japanese tradition, the emperor (the "Joker"), the sun-disc, and suicide implements. But suicide also collapses the arena, allowing no more productive conflict.

2. *Akhnaten:* Opera on Film

Akhnaten, renegade from polytheism, tried unlike Mishima to subvert tradition rather than fulfill it. Glass apparently intended to portray the king as a sort of nonconformist reformer, a spiritual leader, the man of religion. Glass wished the libretto to remain fragmentary and incomplete rather than through-composed, rather than fabricating the missing blocks of the narrative, in order to allow the audience a certain freedom of vision. Yet he and his collaborators shape this partial narrative in such a way as to suggest an interpretation favorable to Akhnaten as a tragic hero. In fact, Glass calls the pharaoh's hymn to the sun, in which he identifies with his own image as an abstract signifier of power, "Akhnaten's best moment" (*A Composer's Notes*). He considers his downfall at the hands of the religious establishment as the opera's true tragedy.

Glass admits to Akhnaten's savagery, but underplays it. In *A Composer's Notes*, the documentary of the opera's pre-mieres, his German producers read the pharaoh as a sort of naive totalitarian, surprised by his own power. Glass balks somewhat, yet accedes to Achim Freyer's reading, as well as to Freyer's own authoritarianism, his absolute control over the production as well as the great physical demands he places on the performers, perhaps in keeping with similar demands made by Glass's music.[4] To Freyer's credit, Akhnaten becomes a figure more moved than moving, less an agent of violent change than its symbol, less and less interested in state poli-tics, and more and more sympathetic as lover, father, and rebel. Freyer seems to understand that, in the dispensation previous to Akhnaten's reign, power was dispersed among pantheon and bureaucracy alike, with authority vested in the dynastic name of the father; that, with Akhnaten, power as a cult of personality becomes emptied out and impersonalized under the sign of the sun disk; that Akhnaten's downfall accompanies the restoration of an oligarchy all the more in-sidious for outlasting rebellion and extending everywhere—the dark side of Foucauldian resistance.

It must be remembered, though, that, as pharaoh, Akhnaten remained at least semideified and certainly absolute in his rule, at least nominally. Some historians suspect that it was his mother who actually ruled Egypt—hence the strongly Oedipal pull of the narrative (and *Mishima*'s), from Glass's source in Velikovsky to both Freyer's and Freeman's ménages à trois among Akhnaten, his mother (Queen Tiye), and Nefertiti. His influence was powerful enough to revolutionize religious think-ing and artistic representations—here is where Akhnaten be-comes Glass's hero undoubtedly—as well as to foment fundamental rebellion among those whom he'd displaced—and

here is where the worshipper of the sun-disc becomes inexorably the martyr to the unjust, with their anthropomorphic, bes-
tial deities. The slippage from the Mishima- or Akhnaten-like
protagonist to the hero-composer behind Glass thus becomes
quick. *Akhnaten* the opera itself follows tragic-operatic conventions much more so than its predecessors in the trilogy, with
a conductor (in *A Composer's Notes*, a rather evangelically converted one) and an orchestra performing preludes, arias, a duet,
recitatives, and other set pieces—all within a palatable polytonal
idiom and constrained by Freitag's dramatic pyramid.

Glass has certainly done all he can within late capitalism
to remain the humble pieceworker, ready to fulfill commissions, quickly and often, from rock musicians to opera com-
panies. His performances with the ensemble deemphasize him
as composer; he's just one more player, directing with tosses
of his head, in the old days; now, he barely registers onstage
among his performers. His personal manner conveys a paradoxical sense of detached engagement, or engaging detach-
ment, depending on his interlocutor, I included. Yet, as he
admits, staying home and writing music has provided him
with a living far in excess of the less popular avant-garde's.
For example, the Met paid him $350,000 for *The Voyage*,
putting the lie to Pierre Boulez's claim that you can't live on
repetition forever. Whether Glass's drive to increase harmony
and decrease confrontation is merely practical or grotesquely
cynical remains for the listener to decide, as Glass himself
would no doubt allow.

Many critics on the left, as suspicious of poststructuralism
as of postmodernism (which they see not only as complicit but
coextensive), accuse the present period of being authoritarian
according to the imperatives of late capital and the institutionalized academy. While I don't necessarily agree that forms of
culture other than those discussed above are as insidiously
fascistic, I admit to the possibility that authoritarian (read:
largely patriarchal and white and hetero and bourgeois) elements remain, at least vestigially. Deconstruction, for example,
has encouraged the rise, and demise, of mostly male authority
figures: Bloom, Hillis Miller, Hartman, and, of course, de Man
and *his* own followers, who seem unable to dispel the ghost of
fascism that hovers behind de Man's image. Often, the game of
deconstruction has appeared only as fair and inclusive as that
of New Criticism, with rules, referees, scores, winners and los-

ers—think of the agony in Bloom between potent fathers and their rebellious sons. Moreover, since deconstruction is so heavily invested in that which it engages, it can easily be construed as conservative rather than ruptural: it must in some sense reproduce or recuperate what it seeks to undo, allowing the despised term to continue to circulate. Foucault's emphasis on power, though he claims his emphasis is really on the *subject*, which I think is true, sometimes gets trapped by a similar traduction: that power becomes reified, fetishized, and privileged, even though resistance is part and parcel.[5]

Foucault may or may not be rightly traduced, but others are more open about their tendencies. I think, for instance, of Charles Jencks, the British architect and critic who helped define postmodernism in architecture and painting. In his coffee-table book, *Post-Modernism*, he implies in several places that we can simply elide fascistic elements in postmodern architecture—look at Leon Krier's or Angelo Bofill's massive structures—and celebrate the marvelous symbology of it all, despite the obviously monolithic nature of architectural neo-classicism, resonating as it does with Albert Speer (in Krier's case, there is a direct connection). Humbler, though perhaps no less disturbing, examples exist as well, especially in popular culture. Ramones, with songs like "Blitzkrieg Bop" and the supersensual onslaught of their stage performances; Keith Moon's, the Pistols', and Siouxsie's occasional adoption of Nazi imagery; hard-core skinhead punk; the return to the Ivy League/Wall Street image and ethos among the young during the eighties—all attest to a paradoxical foregrounding and critique of the master/slave dialectic so vigorously rejected by virtually all who identify themselves, or who are identified as, postmodern, whatever their political affiliations.

I would say, then, that where postmodernist music is concerned, the question, again, remains open. Is the individual listener's ecstasy during a performance of *Mishima* or *Akhnaten* enough to begin contesting hegemonic modernist culture? Will it start with the subjection of the body and consciousness, via the thrill of some ludic dominance? It may be that, following Hutcheon, we will achieve liberation *only* through complicity, and therefore Glass and the rest are doing more for us than we can presently realize. As Glass remarks, "I may not know exactly what you're hearing, but I know *how* you're hearing."

Pruit(t) (-)Igoe: Broken Glass, Abandonment, Demolition

Godfrey Reggio's silent film *Koyaanisqatsi*,[6] "without dialogue or narrative structure, produces a unique and intense
look at the superstructure of modern life," as the CD's liner
notes have it.[7] It conveys a feeling of melancholy from the very
opening chords of Glass's music, which Michael Riesman plays
on the organ while the title forms downward from red dashes
drawn across a black background (the organ has traditionally
been an instrument of solemnity and grandeur, in harmony
with the film's awesome panoramas and earnest purposes).
Reiterated descents in the minor on the footpedals, as well as
Albert De Ruiter's otherworldly bass intonation of the film's
title—a Hopi compound whose meaning is not revealed, though
it hardly needs to be, until the end (that is, life out of balance),
crazy life, a life calling for a new manner of living—is quickly
accompanied with a sad, wavering figure in the left hand. A
mournful melody in the treble completes this immediate and
arresting cinematic and musical sense of loss, even before the
movie has begun. Soon Ron Fricke's camera is pulling away
from several Native American figures drawn into a cave wall.
They appear to be human bodies encapsulated or mummified,
dead yet preserved, eternal yet inactive, like that translated
Hopi vision itself, which Reggio and his collaborators exploit.
The cave is located somewhere in the desert southwest where
no human life now moves.

Have the former inhabitants of this *a*human, as well as
inhuman, landscape been driven away? Did they simply move
on? Or did imbalance wipe them out? The suggestion is that
whatever made it possible for humans to live in this place has
been removed. Meanwhile the images of nature left behind
and tracked down by the camera—the broad views of rocks,
crags, mesas, gulches, canyons—remind viewers of the vast-
ness of time and the relative smallness of the person within
this time: life as a universal context for human subjects, no
matter whether they succeed or fail. Those who once lived
here, succeeding, then failing, perhaps, are irrecoverable,
though their descendants live and remember, but—and this is
crucial—so is the relation they used to enjoy with this environment that, presumably, allowed them to consider life in
totality as an equilibrium in the first place. Such, at any rate,
is the vision of Native American life before white imperialism,

with which many people, since a long overdue revisionism as well as the consciousness-raising of Native Americans themselves, have become familiar.

Obviously, though never stated, the film's theme will thus concern human habitations and relationships with surroundings: how people move into spaces, transform them, get transformed by them, and ultimately unmake them, rendering them uninhabitable, though minimally livable, for themselves and their progeny. Reggio dramatizes the violent transition technology forces from the natural world to the human by focusing on destructive, polluting industrial processes: explosive mining operations, smoke- and steam-spewing power plants, massive electrical wires carried by those gigantic anthropomorphic latticework towers that loom over the landscape like the colossuses of modernity. These power lines connect desert to city, whose environment is supposed to remain isolated from the unpleasantness of nature but can't escape the squalor caused by the seizing and diminishment of the land—dangers adumbrated by the Hopi prophesies hymned near the film's conclusion. Even the machinery used in these operations, on a scale seemingly overlarge to be human, looks positively *in*human, beyond the scope and control of mere mortal flesh, which gets dwarfed, for example, by an earth mover as by the wheels of the Juggernaut, and engulfed by the dust it throws up—an image to be reprised in *Powaqqatsi*, but in a postcolonial, Third World context.

In a way typical of the film's technique of simple juxtaposition, echoed by Glass's blocky musical structure, the camera, in another scene, begins closed-up on a mother and child at the beach—two generations, the older asleep and the younger one active. Then gradually the camera moves back to take in more and more of the picture, until it includes the hulking nuclear power plant—one big generator for generations, isotopes for eons, to come—in the background. (*[Einstein] On the Beach* would seem to be the tacit reference here.) The world that these humans have constructed for themselves, then, consists of this tenuous control—harnessing and containment, as if of a savage animal—of natural forces, a delicate balance in itself, for the purposes of comfort and convenience, perhaps even survival, because people have become almost completely dependent on electricity since its introduction as a widely available utility, requiring the speedy depletion of resources, at the turn of the century, side by side with express desires for leisure and rest from the labor that makes this kind of life possible.

By the time Reggio moves decisively into the city, its attenuated or accelerated paces are frightening, amusing, mesmerizing. It seems that human life has developed so far away from any respectful and sensible relation with the surrounding world that there is little hope for socioeconomically sound reconnections beyond high-tech exploitation. Although the movie and its music appear to locate in nature itself a certain sense of melancholy, at least near the beginning and end, this is only because they have to serve in part as a monument to loss—loss of the balance implied by the Hopi word lending itself to this vision. As an instance of technological production, *Koyaanisqatsi*, first in a series of films moving from alienation back (or ahead) to some type of recuperated relation with life (the second is *Powaqqatsi*, more of a travelog through various human societies and the ways in which they succeed or fail to form social and natural wholes during imperialism), is therefore an electrical and electronic lament from the machine itself, a thousand points of light on a screen that cannot but deny facile attempts by privileged politicians and their reckless constituents to ignore or trivialize that wreck of a life that progress has produced and reproduced.

Koyaanisqatsi is thus an immanent critique, rather than a postutopian lament. This is not to claim that some perfect relation even once existed, even apart from white Western perceptions of Native American life—apart from readings of its texts, which exist in a state that might be called fragmentary by Eurocentric standards—or that, were this relation actually recoverable, it would even be desirable in a contemporary, diversified, automated context: only that a more perfect union with the natural world could be made as possible as seemingly impossible by the highly developed technologies to which the so-called First World has been accustomed, and by which the more as well as the less developed worlds have been made subject.

One of the most thrilling, and chilling, dramatizations of this kind of subjection in *Koyaanisqatsi* comes during the "Pruit Igoe"[8] sequence. As Glass's abruptly loud, intense "broken"[9] music plays, the camera, riding in the aircraft that the music is, in a sense, meant to drown out, soars over this ill-fated workers housing project: an eerie counterpoint between the zealousness of the shouted "Ba!" syllables in the Glass and the utter inertness and desolation—the silence, of the apartments in the project, all of whose windows have been broken and left swung out—results, creating a tension like the one that must have preceded the blowing up of three central blocks in 1972. Flying overhead gives us a certain mastery, but also positions us as impotent gods, able only to witness, perhaps to celebrate, destruction. Pruitt-Igoe was designed in the high-modernist International Style by Minoru Yamasaki, who designed the World Trade Center. Tom Wolfe calls Pruitt-Igoe "classically Corbu" (81), in other words, à la Corbusier's Unité d'Habitation (1947–52), a concrete "social condenser" as Kenneth Frampton says (227).

The complex opened in St. Louis in 1955. Pruitt-Igoe expressed typically shortsighted and idealistic notions of the architecturally modern. These might best be summarized by the godfather of modernism in building, Walter Gropius (the "Silver Prince," to the mordant Wolfe), who sought salvation through architectual "honesty," in his _New Architecture and the Bauhaus_:

> The most admired cities of the past are conclusive proof that the reiteration of 'typical' (_i.e._ typified) buildings notably enhances civic dignity and coherence. As a maturer and more final model than any of the individual prototypes merged in it, an accepted standard is always a formal common denominator of a whole period. The unification of architectural components would have the salutary effect of imparting that homogeneous character to our towns which is the distinguishing mark of a superior urban culture. A prudent limitation of variety to a few standard types of buildings increases their quality and decreases their cost; thereby raising the social level of the population as a whole. Proper respect for tradition will find a truer echo in these than in the miscellaneous solutions of an often arbitrary and aloof individualism because the greater communal utility of the former embodies a deeper architectural significance. The concentration of essential qualities in standard types presupposes methods of unprecedented industrial potentiality, which entail capital outlay on a scale that only be justified by mass-production. [37–38]

Ominous notes are struck here, especially the homogenizing, the deadening, power of standardization effected by the cooperation of big ideas with big money. At any rate, as Wolfe delights in pointing out, Pruitt-Igoe did nothing if not _diminish_ the "social level of the population as a whole." The workers who were supposed to occupy these buildings had already moved out to the suburbs, making room for "recent immigrants from the rural South" (Wolfe 81; his dapper urban conservatism is clearly in recoil from the soil). Nevertheless, the concentrated uninhabitability of this prophetically disunified habitation could hardly be considered generally appealing, least of all to critics like Jane Jacobs, who, soon after Pruitt-Igoe's inception, must have it in mind when she writes of "the city's [St. Louis's] largest project, fifty-seven acres of mostly grass, dotted with playgrounds and devoid of city streets, a prime breeding ground of delinquency in that city" (100).[10]

Wolfe delights also in the collective response of Pruitt-Igoe's last remaining inhabitants when asked by a project task force what to do with their home: "Blow it . . . *up!* Blow it . . . *up!* Blow it . . . *up!* Blow it . . . *up!* Blow it . . . *up!* Blow it . . . *up!*" (82). If the reiterated, percussive "Ba!" of the Western Wind Vocal Ensemble singers echoes the shout for destruction (it's as if the Glassian syllable is a massed Scroogian rejection of good intentions loud and stiff enough to raze the project), viewer tension gets finally released: Pruitt-Igoe crumbles dramatically, along with other architectural failures, in a heap of dust on the screen, descending along with Glass's broken scales.

Gropius, whose own public housing proposals—such as the Project for a Group of Ten-Storey Blocks of Dwellings (Gropius 93), virtually indistinguishable, "standardized" as he euphemistically calls rational monotony, from Corbusier's chic Unités—had already anticipated *Koyaanisqatsi*'s flyby, though not its depressing discoveries:

> With the development of air transport the architect will have to pay as much attention to the bird's-eye perspective of his houses as to their elevations. The utilization of flat roofs as 'grounds' offers us a means of re-acclimatizing nature amidst the stony deserts of our great towns; for the plots from which she has been evicted to make room for buildings can be given back to her up aloft. Seen from the skies, the leafy house-tops of the cities of the future will look like endless chains of hanging gardens. But the primary advantage of the flat roof is that it renders possible a much freer kind of interior planning. [30]

Those "leafy house-tops," those "endless chains of hanging gardens," returned like a potlatch exchange to a female-

gendered[11] nature on flat (and, what should be much to
Gropius's consternation, rotting) roofs, therefore, don't come off
simply as memories of a glorious past age: it is clear that they
never existed except in the doctrinaire imaginations of International Style theorists and builders. Granted, much of their work
is beautiful, especially the individual houses, especially the
ones they designed for themselves to live in, and their techniques could not be wholly rejected without a nostalgic and ill-
advised return to less advanced technology that would not
answer public housing concerns, though it might be right for
separate dwellings—true as well for the technological advances
of modern music.

However, and this is where the minimalism[12] of Glass is
hardly complicit with the repetitive modernism (or late modernism) of constructions like Pruitt-Igoe, *Koyaanisqatsi* serves as
a decisive indictment of that avant-garde proposing to redeem
society with a utopian culture of art from which it has become,
curiously enough, alienated. Art, as human production, certainly can participate in the alienating processes and procedures of socioeconomic relations. This is what postmodern
productions like *Koyaanisqatsi* are at pains to suggest. The
"unity which is life itself" (Gropius 24) remains a myth, like the
"unité" of Corbusier, like the reality of realism against which
certain forms of modernism reacted, that therefore can never
be recaptured, even as it is reproduced, in cultural artifacts.

The last inhabitants of Pruitt-Igoe responded to the project
by trashing it and finally calling for its removal, willing the loss
of their own domicile because it had never satisfied practical,
or even impractical, expectations. It was indeed an object to be
destroyed, despite, implicitly, its cool rejection of another avant-
garde's (for instance, Dada's or surrealism's) playfulness, engagement, demythologizing, resistance. And Glass's music only
increases enjoyment in the drama of Pruitt-Igoe's undoing, while
actually helping intensify panic over the death(s) of the city.

Schaefer calls *Koyaanisqatsi* (the soundtrack) "[one of
[Glass's] best scores" (85), and it is. The additional music for
the film, by music director Michael Hoenig, although more or
less in a minimalist idiom, is left out of the soundtrack album,
making the latter in its own right a tightly constructed, rounded,
satisfying experience, like *Glassworks, The Photographer,
Mishima, Songs from Liquid Days, Dancepieces, Powaqqatsi, 1000
Airplanes on the Roof*, and the trilogy operas, which either edit

out some of the live material or were studio albums to begin with. One reason for the success of these works, in spite of the inchoate or, often sudden, beginnings and abrupt endings, concluding only by the force of concluding themselves, that can dismay listeners of the more conservative classical music programs, aside from the challenging though popular, nonatonal musical idiom, is the way in which they marry the, say, Freitagian, masculine sexual curve of most Western classical music since the development of sonata form with the reputedly more feminine, open-ended forms of Eastern musics (Rockwell 112).[13]

The *Koyaanisqatsi* soundtrack overall has a rising and falling action, returning in the postcoital "Prophecies" to the music of its beginning, the title track (very much as Foucault does in *L'ordre du discours*), so that the mind hears the second track, "Vessels," once again. The music keeps looping around and around like those tracks of the (post-)modern world whose irreal dramatization in the film puts the pixellated (and pixilated) simulations of video games, included in the film, to shame; cycles of connection, disconnection, and reconnnection are played out in the music (see Berg 136).

The track following "Pruit Igoe" is called "The Grid." It is perhaps the most famous event in the movie. As the film, and the soundtrack, gain speed, hurling people, vehicles, clouds, through the city, the music builds up a potent motoric, sexual rhythm, which, when precipitously halted, shatters the alpha state that the film is supposed to induce in the viewer—utter subjection, suturing, jarred into a kind of postcoital abjection only too aware of its alienation from what it views. (The Brechtian technique answers Glass's interest in the progressive—to use Glass's term—existential and absurdist theater of modernism [*Music by Philip Glass* 4].) And what it now views, in fact, is the same New York City, from directly above, but slowly, quietly. Thus a "close match between film and music" (203), due in part to Reggio and Glass's interdependent composing, is made.[14]

Of course, the alpha state, the mesmerization, can be broken in other, less intentional and less spectacular ways. *Koyaanisqatsi* is circulated as a cult film, a midnight movie, an art-house film, often around college campuses (and now as an opportunity for the ensemble to tour again). But is this the target market, is the film reaching those people who scurry through it, can it catch up with them? Or does it address only a "concerned minority," as

Jencks calls it (*What is Post-modernism?* 14)? And then there is the question of reproducing the film itself, diminishing its auratic sound. Prints can be scratchy and faded, ruining the detail; the stunning stereo production, squeezed through tinny PA systems, can come out mushy and insipid. Even in the home, the music can pop and rumble (on LP), drop out (on cassette), or skip (on CD) and perform its own "phase-shifting pulse-gate" experiment more in the manner of early Steve Reich (Schaefer 78).

The *Koyaanisqatsi* CD, while beautifully packaged, is homogenized by the bar code on the back and by typographical errors not the least of which is the misspelling of Pruitt-Igoe and of Glass's publishing company. The reiteration of "Original Music Composed by Philip Glass" throughout the packaging may be Glassian, but poses more questions than it answers. Finally, the very attraction of Glass's music, once repeated a few times, is at issue: his peculiar type of repetition—though not without precedent, as has been frequently pointed out—within movements, within works, and across numerous works (Glass's prodigiousness astounds but also unsettles [Schaefer 80-81]) may not only be an acquired taste but one to be indulged infrequently; otherwise, saturation (instead of suturation)—and disaffection, like the kind often shown to Glass now that he's become so popular—can occur.

But the fact that Glass's music tends to polarize listeners, to absorb them or push them away, suggests its ultimately compelling nature and that of minimalism in general. Minimalism is, paradoxically for its name, thick, absolute, monumental, often simply in its time scale: for instance, Glass's *Music in Twelve Parts*, Laurie Anderson's *United States*, Warhol's *Empire*, and for that matter Barth's "Frame-Tale" and Goldstein's *The Jump*, discussed below. Also in painting and sculpture, such as Donald Judd's vast, untitled concrete constructions, the monumentality of "gestures that are repeated with little or no difference, or slightly more extended actions that appear to exhaust themselves" (Crimp "Pictures" 179; a sound, if partial, working definition of minimalism)—also here a species of subjection occurs in which the self applies itself, as it were, to the work, or the work substitutes itself for that human self. Seduction in reverse is definitely possible: "the subject acts insofar as he is acted. *There are no subjects except by and for their subjection* ("On Ideology" 244 and 249 [Althusser's italics]). Barthes would suggest that the act of listening, like that of reading, wouldn't necessarily mean *captivation*; one would have to listen away from the music occasionally, as one looks up from the book, occasionally—like that listener alienated by sputtering machines or headache—otherwise one might remain unaware of the enjoyment (24). Music, like reading, or looking, *comes* to an *end*. But Althusser's subject, freed from that self-consciousness in order utterly to be subjected, sounds more like the listener a listener of Glass (or any great music) becomes, one who first establishes the terms of subjection (like Althusser's first definition, an author of actions ["On Ideology" 248], a kind of sadist)—for instance, by going to a concert—but then gets subjected beyond all the fantasies of masochism: an experience of death that either eliminates or convinces as only such an experience can, by enacting an undoing that the subject cannot but be conscious of, and *merely* conscious of.

This undoing, after it is done, certainly has changed people, but usually hasn't disabled or killed them; *Koyaanisqatsi*, while it subjects viewers and listeners utterly, must also leave them with a message that only their conscious minds can apprehend and thus make a basis for change outside the self. Glass's music may often sound as if it will never end, but once it does, it just as often makes the ensuing silence, or applause, an utterly dissatisfying substitute, determining the subject by emptying it out, hollowing itself into the listener in order to create a lack, which it would then fill with itself, so that, upon ceasing, the music leaves a *dreadful* lack utterly unlike that left by the satisfactions of narrative music. Responsibilities return. But then they do, and must.

In the meantime, however, thought might cease. Certainly the demands placed on the body for performers and listeners alike can preclude reflection and impose a kind of absolute music involving precision (just getting the notes right, as Dora Ohrenstein emphasizes in Greenaway's film, and counting the proper number) and endurance (the repetition of physical movement that grows more and more challenging). Circular breathing, for example, necessitates a surrender to one's instrument. So while serial (academic or uptown) music insists on the authority of the intellect, minimalism insists on the body, enacting a ritual of concrete subservience upon the players, who nevertheless are allowed to rest—if not upon the listeners, whom Glass allows to wander or depart. Performing this music, though, at least the earlier pieces, means to deemphasize the centrality of the composer. Glass, for instance, retains the name, but retires as much as possible from the cults of personality forming around him. (He doesn't hesitate, though, to defend his copyright, as in the case of Jim McBride's *Breathless* remake, rearranging music from *Glassworks*. And contrary to Boulez, he has indeed lived quite well on repetition, if not forever.)

Musical minimalism thus compels us to reexamine our corporeal relationship to the appreciation and consumption of music, just as visual minimalism often places the body in a sculptural space it's unaccustomed to (for example, Richard Serra, whom Glass once worked with and defended in the notorious case of *Tilted Arc*). Its repetitiousness not only seems to echo that of daily life, which includes listening to music to pass the time, but refers to the consumption of the media it's recorded on, encouraging the machinic processes of selection, shuffling, repeat play—and repeated purchasing (Attali 87ff.). Is minimalism then, a cyborg music? Does it interface the body with the machine, or with machinic action? After all, it has largely depended on electronics and amplification—as well as reiterated movements in the appendages. Music, musician, machine, and music appreciator thus form a peculiar oneness comparable only to that found in popular forms. Minimalism shares more with rock 'n' roll than it does with Rachmaninov, a composer Glass likes, to our surprise. Maybe the current swing in alternative popular music toward ecstasies of repetition (techno) will help block the backlash against minimalism.

Testimony from Glass, and many others, couldn't prevent the removal, and thus the destruction, of Serra's *Tilted Arc* by office workers. To them the modern and the postmodern are indistinguishable if not unimportant, and need be rejected in favor of a humanism already crushed by their bureaucratic working environment and all too painfully disanaesthetized by Serra's *Arc*. The postmodern is more than some reactionary puritanism, though some of its forms would install a new order and encourage compliance with existing institutions. Glass wins commissions but shuns the academy, and his voice is disincluded from MIT's publication of the testimonies around Serra. Glass has paid rock back for its allegiances, in the "Low" and "Heroes" Symphonies, populist works if ever he wrote them. The uptown won't acknowledge him, while downtown sometimes becomes sarcastic (for instance, King Missile's "Glass" positioning the minimalist composer at the piano as a kind of demented lounge act). Time for nonserious music to do more than pay tribute—Colourbox's "Philip Glass," The President's "Philip," Prince's synthesizer pastiche on *Lovesexy*, even fellow Juilliard student P. D. Q. Bach's "Prelude to *Einstein on the Fritz*" and Thomas Wilbrandt's "The Minimal Event"—and insist on the residence of music in the flesh, where it lives most fully.

Glass's works are therefore helpful test cases in any investigation into the successes and failures of postmodern artifacts to delight and instruct, to convey senses of loss and recuperation without moralizing or utter banality. In short, to entertain subjects while interpellating them and calling upon them to interpellate themselves, to formulate and enact their own resistances, in and through the body, to the works of capitalism and culture.

Poststructuralism and Postmodernism

As I mentioned, there's a largely phenomenological manner in which the popular—and, sometimes, not so popular—imagination apprehends the very postmodernism that engages us so intensely and which we struggle to define, or struggle *against* defining. As with the Meese commission on pornography, "We may not know what *it* is, but we *know* it when we see it!" Similarly, I believe, we may tend to slip easily from the postmodern to the poststructural and back again, with only the post- to hang on to as we slide from what seems like an aesthetic realm of discourse (the former) to a philosophical one (the latter).

Some critics maintain these discourses to be discrete, not only because of discontinuities between them but because of a tradition—dating back at least to the taxonomical division of the discourses in the eighteenth century—that insists upon keeping them separate. Andreas Huyssen, for example, reads poststructuralism as a theory of modernism only tangentially related to postmodernism, which he prefers to see as a breakdown in the divisions between high and low, elite and popular, right and left, and so on. In fact, Huyssen speaks of "a kind of dubbing where the poststructuralist language is not in sync with the lips and movements of the postmodern body."

I shall return later on to dance with the body of a recognizably postmodern text. Suffice it to say that we're both inside and outside our own time, at the same time, and this is both impossible and absolutely necessary. The archive may reveal to us that which has made certain of our discourses coextensive. As Foucault says:

> This *a priori* is what, in a given period, delimits in the totality of experience a field of knowledge, defines the mode of being of the objects that appear in that field, provides man's everyday perception with theoretical powers, and defines the conditions in which he can sustain a discourse about things that is recognized to be true. [*The Order of Things* 158]

But the archive also forces us to realize how far out of that archive we need to climb just in order to see how deeply embedded we are within it.

The twisting and turning and backtracking and supplemental maneuvers I've just made in these last couple of paragraphs are meant as a demonstration, albeit a crude one, of my contention that, given the inexorable fact of our being poststructuralists in a postmodern age, and vice versa, the two realms of discourse are just as inexorably intricated. We may hope, with Foucault, to be inside and outside at the same time; we end up *there* already and hoping again to be *here*. I think there's been a crossing of influence, an interpenetration of the two discourses, in which one has responded to the other's manifestations with deepenings and extendings of substance, sophistication, and power. To speak of them separately, even (or especially) in comparison, is already to ravel and unravel their particolored threads with the posts of our textual weaving.

But let's for the moment return to these embattled posts, for clarification. Generally poststructuralism is construed as a continuation and critique, mostly French (Derrida, Lacan, Foucault), of structuralism: a critique of the sign, as it may be gnomically put. A critique of the givenness of structure, of the assumed naturalness of expression, of the self-presence of the enunciating subject, of the unassailability of truth, of the privileging of speech, of the fullness of desire, of the absolute power of repression; also, of other, mostly French, writers

(Saussure, Lévi-Strauss, Barthes). Postmodernism (not only French) denotes, on the other hand, some kind of contested legacy of modernism. A critical response to certain modernist assumptions: the autonomy and inviolability of the text, its ability to subsume ambiguities under an organic wholeness, its submission to the tradition, its emphasis on formal concerns over social and historical and economic ones. The postmodern contest would not be possible without modernism's example—on the level of form (structure rendered visible) as well as content (alterations in the sexual climate, for instance).

Thus, both discourses carry on particular traditions within their own realms ("tradition rightly understood," as the very modern Schoenberg and Gropius defended their own seemingly iconoclastic forms of composition). These discourses are not intended to break absolutely with their objects of critique. Deconstruction, as an example of poststructuralism, perhaps the most strenuous example, must recuperate that which it undoes; it must be closely engaged with its object in order to do so. Hence certain of its critics have called it a new orthodoxy of close reading, even though it is not at all meant as a *closed* reading, not as a method at all, even though it closes with that which it reads. Deconstruction depends absolutely on a rigorous, some might say peculiarly French, rationalism, even as it overstrikes Descartes. For a similar example of postmodernism, we may take a book of criticism like William Spanos's *Repetitions*, a text that is quite obviously an absorption and dissemination of poststructuralist theory, notably Foucault's, though Spanos's playful, convoluted, intricate style may recall Derrida himself or Lacan rather than Foucault's *raréfaction*. Spanos wishes for a criticism of opposition to dominant culture, a Foucauldian countermemory able to exhume and restore marginalized discourses, which can then be used for a "positive disassembling, not a nihilistic annulment" of aesthetic modernism. Spanos actually critiques deconstruction for becoming easily formulaic, institutionalized, and academicist—not "worldly" as Spanos, echoing Said (by means of Foucault), would prefer.

Yet what is one to make of Spanos's "[h]ermeneutic . . . (destruction)" outside the institution? How can a criticism so heavily invested in obscure texts engage interestedly (à la Heidegger) with the "world"? Whose interest is being served?

Hardly the preterite with which Spanos sympathizes. The point here is not that Spanos's proposals are without their own kind of energy, excitement, playfulness, slippages, indiscretions, ambiguities, suspensions, deferrals (as in Derrida, whom he repudiates), but that Spanos cannot even begin to put his proposals into practice without accepting the terms and conditions that poststructuralism has helped to establish. His postmodernism of "being there" therefore becomes a poststructuralism of always being elsewhere. Spanos's text is indeed perhaps more of an example of postmodernism, as I've abused him, than a setter of poststructural example.

We can see from these writers that poststructuralism and postmodernism share intentions along with methods, as revealed even by their signifiers. The game of naming our period and its practices continues, for example, with Derrida's *Carte postale*, in which the message is assumed to be what it represents and to arrive at its destination, but only reveals its fictitiousness and either never arrives or arrives only in a mangled, almost illegible, form. Thus to post the message as its originator is always already to be behind it, to postdate it. The similarity of being belated tells us something not only about the investments by these discourses in what preceded them, but about the very episteme that links them together and renders them compatible in the same period and under similar conditions.

In his own post-Kantian way, to broach yet another belatedness, Jean-François Lyotard, in *The Postmodern Condition*, asserts that texts *determine* the conditions and criteria under which they are to be read. They define limits that restrain utterly nonsensical, abyssal plays of signification, a danger that poststructuralism avoids with extreme and, perhaps, ironic vigor, and, more importantly, define limits that enable these texts to be read *at all*. It remains unseemly to bring assumptions to certain texts to which those assumptions are irrelevant or unuseful. I would like to offer my own example of a critique that plays (with) a text that is in itself playful and meant to be played, to demonstrate the intrication of the posts at hand—exemplification, rather than exposition, being my preference for addressing the question of poststructuralism's and postmodernism's similarities.

Two Versions of the Fictionally Minimal: Barth and Bernhard

1. *Framing Posts, Re/fusing Barth's "Frame-"*

As an early artifact of postmodernist fiction, John Barth's *Lost in the Funhouse* gets problematic even before it is read. The pronoun should be in quotation marks. It might be asserted that the real text of any text is not really locatable, hence an ideal but not prior text must be projected, however provisionally, in order for different people to talk about the same one and for some of these people to forward authoritative readings. Barth problematizes textuality by foregrounding issues involving the physical act of reading, of handling a text, and therefore the corporeality of language (at least of language play), its formation in and through subjects. In this way, the text is *felt* before it is read (or red, as the case may be), *apprehended* before comprehended (if ever).

For instance, what is the reader expected to do with "Frame-Tale," whose title is one-fifth as large as the entire—well, what should it be called, what genre does it fit, what genres does it invade and burst asunder? If the piece were actually cut from the book and fashioned into the Möbius band[15] that Barth would like to see as the book's guiding metaphor, a number of difficulties would arise. For one thing, Barth's tale without a tail would no longer be attached to the larger text: it would be removed from the series which (paradoxically) it initiates, of which it proposes to serve as the frame (which is literally impossible), becoming itself a witty remark in the quodlibet that it forms with Derrida's infamous dictum *Il n'y a pas de hors-texte* ("there is no outside-the-text").

"Frame-Tale" would no longer be one tale in a collection, but two texts, at least: the title, instructions, and "(*continued*)" signs left behind in the bound *Funhouse*, and the strip of paper that has been cut from the book and fastened end to end, twistedlike, or left flat, discarded or recycled (my edition as a whole seems to be printed on dingy recycled paper—environmentally sound, perhaps, but often difficult to read). Second, the strip, once excised, would adapt a life of its own, if retained, as a conversation piece, initiating and attracting commentaries involving its own self apart from the text of which it is yet, in a sense, a part, while the book is left incomplete but also visibly consumed beyond normal wear and tear, looking, in a way, for its lost element, or, as Jameson might have it, its lost referent (Baudrillard might lament that it isn't even looking). Most readers, it could be said, are loath to bring the shears to these unnumbered pages one and two of Barth's work, if only because they would rather keep track of one Funhouse instead of two, would rather be free of the burden of ignoring or accounting for the separate piece and apologizing for its cut origin. Wouldn't anybody? Readers hardly hesitate, though, to write their names and marginalia in books, to blacken the edges of the pages with grime from thumbs, to dog-ear the corners, especially if the books are paperbacks, because, after all, doesn't this (ab)use make them appear more to be parts of life as it is lived entirely?

The strip, of course, is not symmetrical, although its ten words are divided equally between its two (flat) sides. Typographical constraints may be determining this distribution. It helps that the text is printed in all capitals, and in a large point size, making it more readable but also stretching the words to the length of the page: a minimal text maximized, "the shortest short story in the English language" on a large scale ("it's endless" according to Barth). As Douglas Crimp says of Jack Goldstein's minimalist film _The Jump_, "Time is extremely compressed . . . and yet extremely distended." In "Frame-Tale" the first word of the second phrase ends the first phrase; so the strip is continuous not only across the seam but within the text in total. Barth's book (or perhaps it should be called this Barth book, meaning this reproduced text in particular and not any particular copy),[16] in _The Chicago Manual_ sense of the word _book_, everything between and including the covers, operates with just this kind of disorienting Funhouse ambiguity, starting on the outside, which is not the beginning, as is quickly detected, and moving through the initial, traditionally unpaginated pages. The name John Barth appears always above the title, even on the spine, as if the latter were a dependent adjective clause to the former: "This is John Barth, lost in the funhouse" the book appears to announce, but which John Barth? And what is a John Barth?

On the back of the half-title page, a list of Barth's books, _not including_ the present one, appears, and they're not even called books or works, but consist only of titles in small capitals under the words "_by John Barth_" (one of these not/works, _LETTERS_, does in fact have a title in all capitals, but this is

apparent only from outside the *Funhouse*). And as if the subtitle, "Fiction for print, tape, live voice" isn't presumptuous and
somewhat pretentious enough—despite Barth's disclaimer in
the first of the appended "seven additional author's notes (1969),"
most people will never experience these fictions as intended—
there comes the daunting copyrights page, where it is virtually
impossible to locate either the book's origin or the edition's
publication date. The pieces aren't arranged in the order of
original printing. Some were obviously written when it became
apparent to Barth that a work of short fictions was called for.
Barth's multiple, interconnected forwards and author's notes,
themselves looping without end around and around this very
water-obsessed author's anchorless "Doubleday Anchor Edition," are of little help. He says, "The reader may skip all these
frames and go directly to the first story . . . called Frame-Tale"
(the reader is not yet inside the book proper, or so it would
seem). This is a frame that, as has perhaps been exhaustingly
demonstrated, provides a defective thread for guiding the lost
out from the author's nest of angles. Readers are indeed framed
by this tale, fooled into ceaseless implication with a narrative
physically of their own making.

The extent to which Barth can be said to be carefully plan-
ning this deception, however, problematizes the problematics of
the *Funhouse*'s frame with/out a work. Certainly, this is all in
fun. But whether Barth is his narrator or not, whether or not
readers in fact cut "Frame-Tale" from his book and perform a
Möbius strip-tease, are finally immaterial relative to Barth's
reinscription of a long masculinist tradition of stunning literary
performance. One patriarchal critic, plus followers, have made
it the basis of an entire theory of creative development. Those
in the canon supposedly subsumable under this theory include, most prominently, Joyce, Wilde, Byron, Sterne,
Shakespeare, Chaucer, the authors of the Arabian Nights,
medieval cycles of romances, and the Greek myths—plus many
others whose tragicomic work plays openly with language as
language as performance as its own plenitude, a raison d'être
without which there would be no reason for being, without
which many academics would have no reason for writing. Here,
Charles Caramello's book on books as books and texts, *Silverless
Mirrors*, becomes unavoidable: "For Barth as a writer writing in
the intertext, originality (the need to seminate rather than to be
disseminated) remains pressing" (115). Barth had, in "The Literature of Exhaustion" (*Atlantic*, 1967), expressed anxiety over

just such putatively debilitating detumescence in literature generally, then answered himself with "The Literature of Replenishment" in the same magazine thirteen years later. The terms of this refilling are troublesome, though, not least because of the monotonously male gender possessed by the waterbearer:

> My ideal postmodernist author neither merely repudiates nor merely imitates either his twentieth-century modernist parents or his nineteenth-century premodernist grandparents. He has the first half of our century under his belt, but not on his back. Without lapsing into moral or artistic simplism, shoddy craftsmanship, Madison Avenue venality, or either false or real naiveté, he nevertheless aspires to a fiction more democratic in its appeal than such late-modernist marvels (by my definition and in my judgement) as Beckett's *Stories and Texts for Nothing* or Nabokov's *Pale Fire*. He may not hope to reach and move the devotees of James Michener and Irving Wallace—not to mention the lobotomized mass-media illiterates. But he *should* hope to reach and delight, at least part of the time, beyond the circle of what Mann used to call the Early Christians: professional devotees of high art. [quoted in Jencks *What is Post-modernism?* 7]

At last, the Barth of "*About the Author*," final (?) page of the Doubleday Anchor edition of *Lost in the Funhouse*, emerges from his office at Johns Hopkins and into the dim hallway lighting—smily and engaging enough, but unconvincing as a guilty academic whose generational schemas for literary inheritance, and haughtiness, belie his democratic sentiments. Humbly he would have a certain public embrace him, taking care not to crush the modernism under his belt, as he reaches for the sophisticated, the meticulous, the incorruptible, the knowing—those who still have all their brains and can read literature. But this includes nearly everybody. Caramello, in fact, doesn't go so far as to indict Barth for this doublespeak, remaining himself caught up in merely formal poststructuralist concerns:

> To the extent that *Funhouse* oscillates between print and live voice, with tape mediating—to the extent that it strives to "have it both ways" formally—it strives to have it both ways philosophically: to have a decentered writing as a continuation *and* a negation of centered speech. [118]

Barth hardly interrogates this endless doubling-back, as Caramello claims: he puts it into print, puts his name on it, puts it before the reader, who must stand gazing at its lures, in line behind the person on the cover of the paperback, and hopes that person is "invigorated" (in the "Foreword," a forewarning in its own right) by this meretricious construction, which could just as well be avoided as a hall of mirrors where the only images, come to find out, are those of the builder gazing across at one another.

This *Funhouse*, meant to decenter and multiply readers, then, ends up marginalizing them, alienating them, sending them back out into themselves, as the man with the funny smile urges them in. They're present for *his* pleasure, apparently, decidedly, to be trapped forever in his everframing antiframes.

2. *Bernhard's* Nephew: *The Body of Consciousness*

Barth's "Frame-Tale," superlatively short, nevertheless provides an opportunity to descant at length, maybe to infinity. Thomas Bernhard has also composed short pieces, though none so reductively minimal (or so grandly total) as Barth's "Tale." Bernhard's smaller books, which he often wrote simultaneously and with great prodigiousness, offer similar opportunities, however—ones that engage the body more directly and forcefully, more concretely, than Barth's rather abstract "Frame" or even Bernhard's own miniature narratives.

Bernhard's libidinal economy of prose, identified, correctly, by Stephen Dowden as minimalist and relying on spoken Austrian German and musical repetition (4, 1),[17] involves a "horizontal"[18] reading experience not unlike that of listening to Glass, scanning Deleuze and Guattari's plateaus, or of imagining the end(s) of the Möbius band. In fact, his prose becomes the ne plus ultra of the fiction of the body, obsessing over illness, consumption, impotence, and death; driving this obsessiveness to the limits of personal affect and physical endurance.

Bernhard became legendary for his vituperative persona, in Dowden's words "a grand master of contempt and malediction" (2). His narrators like to make pronouncements that are certain to polarize readers. You surrender or you retreat; Bernhard won't allow any conditions. In *Wittgenstein's Nephew*, the sarcasm sharpens its edge when Bernhard's narrator leaves behind the histrionic prop of the persona and directly attacks existing individuals, institutions, publications—whatever deserves Thomas's wrath. Bernhard himself steps into the audience of his drama—in this case *The Hunting Party*—becomes irate at the production, and leaves before the curtain, refusing to believe his friends claiming success. *Ich hatte naturgemäß ein Ganz anderes Stück geschrieben, als das, welches diese niedertächtigen Schauspieler und also Verräter ihrer Kunst, bei dieser Uraufführrung gespielt haben* (157–58) ("Naturally the play I had written was quite different from the one that was actually performed by these unspeakably perfidious thespians" [96]). He agrees with Paul Wittgenstein's assessment of the production as a flop because Paul is to be respected for telling the truth, even if he seems already dead, the prose modulating, as it does, from one sequence or key to another without transition, reminiscently of minimalist music. And it is just as ambiguously totalizing.[19]

We might think we're hearing a strong, central authorial and authoritarian voice in Bernhard. Through sheer force and outrageousness, however, this voice paradoxically gets multiplied and dispersed into narrative affects whose theatricality bases subjectivity—or creates one—on or through performance, repetition, obsessiveness, rather than stable verities supposedly traceable back to Bernhard himself. The truth-effects of the actor—Bernhard's own arrogant stunts (for example, his refusal to accept the Grillparzer Prize), his rather staged mode of absolute critique (sitting among the audience while the literary officials on the dais hunt around maniacally for their awardee)—instead of the expression of truths we either succeed or fail to understand, even appreciate: these are what we experience.

Bernhard achieves his effects with narrative structures of return, compulsive repetitiousness, suspension, and aggregation, much like Glass's, establishing planes of intensities, which not only make reading Bernhard an act of compulsion itself but oppose, explosively, traditional ideals of centrality (of voice), development (of character), resolution (of conflict), fame (Bernhard's, which he often refused), and perhaps even pleasure, as typically construed in, say, realist, linearly narrated fiction.

Often Bernhard's reiterative, antinarrative structures, helping concretize the writing itself, draw upon the litany, with its repetitions of syntactical constructions and trancelike effects:

> *Wie der Paul, hatte ich, wie ich sagen muß, meine Existenz wieder einmal übertrieben und also überschätzt und also über*

*das Äußerste hinaus ausgenützt gehabt. Wie der Paul, hatte ich
selbst mich wieder einmal über alle meine Möglichkeiten hinaus
ausgenützt gehabt, alles über alle Möglichkeiten hinaus
ausgenützt gehabt mit der krankhaften Rücksichtslosigkeit gegen
mich und gegen alles, die den Paul eines Tages zerstört hat und
die mich genauso wie den Paul eines Tages zerstören wird,
denn wie der Paul an seiner krankhaften Selbst- und
Weltüberschätzung zugrunde gegangen ist, werde auch ich über
kurz oder lang an meiner eigenen krankhaften Selbst- und Weltüberschätzung zugrunde gehen. Wie der Paul war auch ich damals
auf dem Wilhelminenberg in einem Krankenbett aufgewacht als
ein fast völlig zerstörtes Produkt dieser Selbst- und Weltüberschätzung, und vollkommen logisch der Paul in der
Irrenanstalt und ich in der Lungenanstalt, also der Paul auf
dem Pavillion Ludwig und ich auf dem Pavillion Hermann. Wie
der Paul sich jahrelang mehr oder weniger fast zu Tode gerannt
hat in seiner Verrücktheit, so hatte ich mich mehr oder weniger
jahrelang zu Tode gerannt in meiner. Wie der Weg des Paul
immer wieder in einer Irrenanstalt hatte enden müssen,
abgebrochen hatte werden müssen, so hat mein Weg immer
wieder in einer Lungenanstalt enden, abgebrochen werden
müssen. Wie der Paul immer wieder ein Höchstmaß an
Aufsässigkeit gegen sich und gegen seine Umwelt erreicht hat
und in die Irrenanstalt eingeliefert werden mußte, habe ich selbst
immer wieder ein Höchstmaß an Aufsässigkeit gegen mich und
gegen meine Umwelt erreicht und bin in eine Lungenanstalt
eingeliefert worden.* [*Wittgensteins Neffe* 32–33]

(I am bound to say that, like Paul, I had once more overstated
and overrated my existence, that I had exploited it to excess.
Like Paul, I had once more made demands on myself in excess
of my resources. I had made demands on everything in excess
of all resources. I had behaved toward myself and everything
else with the same unnatural ruthlessness that one day destroyed Paul and will one day destroy me. For just as Paul
came to grief through his unhealthy overestimation of himself
and the world, I too shall sooner or later come to grief through
my own unhealthy overestimation of myself and the world. Like
Paul, I woke up in a hospital bed on the Wilhelminenberg,
almost totally destroyed through overrating myself and the world.
Paul, quite logically, woke up in the mental clinic, and I woke
up in the chest clinic—he in the Ludwig Pavillion, I in the
Hermann Pavillion. Just as Paul had more or less raced himself
almost to death in his madness, I too had more or less raced
myself to death in mine. Just as Paul's career had repeatedly
been brought to a halt and been cut off in a mental clinic, so

mine had repeatedly come to a halt and been cut off in a lung clinic. Just as Paul had again and again worked himself up to an extreme pitch of rebellion against himself and the world around him and had to be taken to a mental clinic, so I had again and again worked myself up to an extreme pitch of rebellion against myself and the world around me and had to be taken to a lung clinic.) [*Wittgenstein's Nephew* 19–20]

This particular passage goes on a bit longer. Even as an excerpt from a single sequence in a little book, it exemplifies Bernhard's peculiar narrative strategies, and summarizes the concerns of the text as a whole.

First, the passage calls into question the authority of the speaker, who is negotiating points of view between the truthful (autobiographical) and the false (fictional), doubling the book's genre along with himself. But, as usual, Bernhard isn't content to allow the voice a mere doubling. Other forms—the allusion (to Diderot), the eulogy, the broadside, the medical report, the confession, along with the litany—with the varying sorts of subjectivities they construct, combine here.

Bernhard, the narrator, in *Wittgenstein's Nephew* avoids positioning himself as the kind of authority he vilifies in the figure of the physician. Although comically content to play the role *des Unscheinbaren, Rücksichtsvollen, Unauffälligen"* (26) ("of the considerate, unobtrusive, self-effacing patient" [15]), only because to do otherwise than play the docile body would be to weaken oneself physically, he repeatedly indicts the doctors, nurses, and attendants. As in his other books, this criticism seems to encompass the whole of Western medicine and the purportedly enlightened science it represents. Despite his admiration, even love for, Paul Wittgenstein, the speaker resists applying humanistic notions either to Paul's condition or his own, preferring to involve Paul in an agony of (dis-)identification requiring repetition-compulsion, abdication of mastery, and the symptomatology of paranoia—all unrepentantly (he refers to Ludwig Wittgenstein as "a shameless philosopher," to Paul at one point as "a shameless madman" [62–63]—rebels against their family's authority). He will be the patient who describes for an other, not the doctor who prescribes and proscribes *as* the other. He wishes Paul well, yet can or will do little to correct what he sees as the sheer fact of madness, and ultimately abandons him, rather shamelessly. Unlike Freud, whose ghost haunts these clinics, or, say, in our own day Oliver Sacks, who remains the still, sane center of a Frankensteinian world of neurological cases offered for our sympathizing consumption, Bernhard implicates himself as always already ill, no better or worse than Paul, who mirrors Thomas at almost every moment, whether in or out of the hospitals.

Though Bernhard is the motivated writer—perhaps helplessly so—Wittgenstein is the larger mental talent. Though Bernhard is level-headed enough to construct the narrative Paul can't, Paul furnishes its exemplary subject and retains the greater reputation. Though Thomas's finances are stable enough to keep him alive and perpetuate his career, Paul has the more to expend, enabling himself to entertain friends, usually themselves members of the aristocracy, and distribute wealth in amounts irrational to his conservative family.

Sehr oft habe ich gedacht, er *ist der Philosoph, nicht ich,* er *ist der Mathematiker, nicht ich,* er *ist der Kenner, nicht ich* (94) ("Very often I would think: *He's* the philosopher, not me, *he's* the mathematician, not me, *he's* the expert, not me" [57]). Bernhard must, in a way, hold himself apart from Wittgenstein in order to maintain his mental health but also to preserve an autonomy, itself at least partially defined by Bernhard's competition—understated but implicit throughout, possibly even motivating the narrative, informing each one of its mad sentences.

He must, though, *find* Paul first, who lies abed in an adjoining ward. A corridor links the two friends, establishing a sort of Möbius band where ontology, the dominant paradigm of modernism, in McHale's terms, and epistemology, the paradigm of postmodernism, have been inscribed on either side. Now, the two concerns—for being and for knowledge—have been twisted back on one another: a single continuous surface appearing as two. Bernhard attempts to move along this corridor, from one clinic to the other, to *be* in a place where he knows his friend will *be* and will *recognize* him:

> *Ich war damals absolut zu weit gegangen, der Pavillion Ernst war ja schon zu weit gewesen. Ich hätte schon vor dem Pavillion Franz umkehren sollen. Aber ich wollte ja unbedingt meinen Freund sehen. Erschöpft, vollkommen außer atem, saß ich auf der Bank vor dem Pavillion Ernst und blickte durch die Baumstämme auf den Pavillion Ludwig.* [17]

> (On this occasion I had gone much too far: even the Ernst Pavillion was too far—I should have turned back when I got to the Franz Pavillion. But I was determined to see my friend.

I sat on the seat outside the Ernst Pavillion, exhausted and completely out of breath, and gazed through the trees toward the Ludwig Pavillion.) [9–10]

In spite of prohibitions against wandering, in spite of (decrepit) physical obstacles, both within and without, in spite of trepidation against visiting a friend who will show him an excess of affection—and in spite of the digressions these hindrances cause—Bernhard, and the narrative, persevere. Or rather, Paul does, since he's the one to reach the other side first, in spite of greater restraints. Setting himself in motion, the narrator finds instead that it is the friend who arrives while he sleeps, just as I choose *Wittgenstein's Nephew* to read only to find myself seized by the gripping tale.

Paul laughs about the coincidence of finding Thomas there, and the two promise to exchange visits halfway between the wards, but succeed only once in doing so, when Paul can scarcely do anything but weep and shake, while Thomas barely survives his thoracic tumor to return home and lose track of his friend. The twist, crossing itself, where the two men's being-as-ill passes their (renewed) knowledge of one another, becomes that bench in between the two clinics: site of abjection and only slightly effective rebellion against medical discipline.

It is in such an imaginary, and, of course, real, space when epistemology and ontology combine, when knowledge of oneself as a separate subject grounds one's sense of being in the world. The rivalry resulting from this (dis-)identification is what perpetuates the momentum of narrative and evades the absoluteness of symbolic orders:

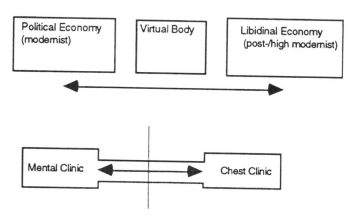

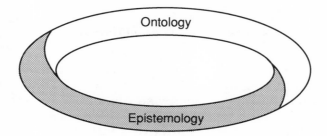

Paul seems the one who can't escape from the loop. He resides in the *Ludwig* Pavillion, always being reminded of his (in-)famous uncle. Sometimes he convalesces in another hospital named after another relative. He can't help making a spectacle of himself and incurs the eternal resentment of the Wittgensteins, who refuse to intervene. Illness and alcoholism drain his finances and wreck his personal life, returning him to the care of physicians who can't properly diagnose or treat him. Finally, it seems, Paul is incapable of simply dying, and appears frequently as a sort of overdressed corpse. Eventually Paul resides directly above, instead of across from, his friend, who has decided to avoid him. Having arranged themselves into a dissonant chord, the two must part company and the narration must stop. Bernhard, at the very end, admits never to have visited Paul's grave, but his text, its long unbroken rectangle[20] laid out from Thomas's awakening out of anaesthesia to the end of their *Friendship*, substitutes for the interment while keeping Paul's memory alive.

Indeed, Bernhard's narrativity fulfills an aesthetic that Poe, fellow son of Baltimore to Glass (who has often set his work to music) famously set forth nearly a hundred and fifty years ago:

> If any literary work is too long to be read at one sitting, we must be content to dispense with the immensely important effect derivable from unity of impression—for, if two sittings be required, the affairs of the world interfere, and every thing like totality is at once destroyed. ["The Philosophy of Composition" 15]

At the beginning of that same article, Poe refers to Godwin's compositional procedure with *Caleb Williams*, which, Poe insists, involved "working backwards" before writing forwards—so that a seemingly coherent effect and inexorable plot result actually from a nonlinear process of shaping and reshaping.

(Similarly, you may listen to the twelve parts of Glass's *Music in 12 Parts*, which moves gradually back from harmonic stasis toward modulation, in any combination or order.) Despite all the interference from the world, Bernhard realized with Poe the significance of the body-as-reader itself, in the act of reading, and composed texts for its pleasure, pain, and perseverance.

I hope by these examples to have shown the potentialities and limitations not just of a certain kind of poststructuralist manner of reading, but of attempts to lash these two posts into a fascicle with which to symbolize a new order of things in contemporary culture. I assume that my own performativity, my exultation and overinvestment in "Frame-Tale" have become apparent enough to help undermine the very project of fastening poststructuralism and postmodernism together inextricably, yet also to demonstrate my joy in tying the threads. As for *Wittgenstein's Nephew*, it should stand as an eminently postmodern counterexample to Barth's high-modern avant-gardism, and help restore the compellingness of the flesh itself to writing's frame.

Postlude: Death of the Text

I read in Althusser an implicit idea: subjects can hail themselves. Subjection does not always have to occur from outside, much as outside objects become necessary, and are often uninvited. If the postmodern self is indeed schizophrenic as claimed, resistance of this kind must be possible. But it might be disunified postmodern artifacts that teach that multiple self how to muster oppositional agencies even against those forms of power and knowledge that authorize artifaction from the start.

Paul A. Smith's critique of Althusser's figure of the "'individual subject' [as] no more than the bearer or support of ideological practices that are inscribed upon it" (17; Althusser therefore lacks a theory of agency) is well taken. Smith says, "there seems to be no reason to suppose that there exists a unifiable subjectivity" (18). This he sees as the result of Althusserian interpellation. He suggests possibilities of resistance that lie beyond even the unavailable real of Lacan; that is, beyond the strange dialectic of self-consciousness and overdetermination inherent in the latter's thinking ("The unconscious is neither primordial nor instinctual; what it knows about the elementary is no more than the elements of the signifier" [*Écrits* 170]) but already present in Althusser ("History 'asserts itself' through the multiform world of the superstructures, from local tradition to international circumstance" [*For Marx* 112]). Maybe even beyond that failure "to produce a 'subject'" that Smith correctly identifies as often occurring (37; partial failures may, actually, be more interesting, and more usual).

Smith establishes his own binary opposition, diverse forces and positions/consumption/Lacan vs. unified force and unified position/production/Althusser, whose tension is delicately balanced at best. He could be accused of eliding ideologies and ideology, of privileging literary texts as interpellators (there are equally if not more compelling ones, indeed) just as Jameson privileges assembly lines as real work; or Bové, despite himself, privileges the "literary critic." (Again, his quotation marks are intended to question the identity of his particular profession, and not that of the category itself.) And Smith's resistance comes fairly close to sounding like nostalgia for the last instance or residue—even if not humanistic, it seems to base itself in a need to intervene, just as postmodern critiques of humanism have to base themselves on a traditional paradigm. Smith thereby betrays a certain fear of the text oddly analogous to Barthes' "pleasure": "a cinematic or literary text is never addressed at a reader it knows and thus can never articulate itself with its reader in a predictable fashion" (34). Aside from being rife with questions it cannot answer, this would argue for near-complete despair in the production of certain of these texts, despite the personification, the personality, it lends them.

It might be possible that, because of his apparent fear, Smith misunderstands the usurping force of subjection in the consumption of these texts—how people get overtaken by them, how personal subjectivities can be replaced with the texts', however temporarily, and that this event in itself can be subversive and liberating, as well as motivating to act. Besides, what's the essential difference between being overdetermined by diverse forces operating inside and outside subjects, and by ideology, finally, when both might entail an endless search and rescue of those forces for the purposes of analysis, whether Marxist or Freudian?

For Hutcheon, who has come to believe that "the post-modernism of the 1970s and 1980s offers little cause for either despair or celebration" (*Politics* 10), the present moment has no more power than that of "complicitous critique" (2) and "cul-tural 'de-doxification'" (7). She wonders, with Bové, if post-modern theory isn't "entangled in its own de-doxifying logic" (14) and asserts that it's finally an indeterminate debate. Postmodernism argues that the way out is the way through; yet it may be that when theory, and the self that might apprehend it, silences, and is filled with unknown otherness growing out of difference without opposition, the grounds for a new politics are laid. Barthes, Foucault, Reggio, Glass all enact this estab-lishment of contingent foundations. As one of the narrators of Kathy Acker's *Don Quixote* says, "The self must be more com-plicated than life and death, more complicated than duality" (190). And more complicated than the obscenity or pornogra-phy that Acker's work has undoubtedly been considered. It is more likely the "poverty, alienation, fear, inability to act on desire, inability to feel" (190) of evil enchantment in a postmodern world. It is the enchantment that must have confronted the boy in those Washington woods, before something was taken from him that could not just be put back.

One last word, one that involves a medium not discussed here: photography. What Lyotard calls "pornography," a reuse of the rules of visual representation for the gratification of mass expectations, is perhaps what Abigail Solomon-Godeau would place in the category of postmodern photography (75–85; though, obviously, pornography has art photography pretensions). Here, too, however, occurs a resubsuming of the popular avant-garde into a type of hermeticism, despite postmodern photography's moves toward "pointedly critical ends" (82). Solomon-Godeau quotes from Barthes's "Death of the Author," which sounds hopelessly circular by now: "The book itself is only a tissue of signs, an imitation that is lost, infinitely deferred" (81). She recognizes correctly the revolutionary potential in this position, and sees clearly that it might not always be taken advantage of, but doesn't critique the disjunction between Barthes's re-writing of New Criticism (via structuralism) and a postmodern photography that is so far from being closed that it actually dramatizes its relationships with outside forces.

The real that photographers once thought they were simply framing within the picture, which, curiously, was supposed to

achieve the "autonomy, self-referentiality, and transcendence of
the work of art" (85) apart from that reality, is itself getting
called into question—though not denied. In fact, it's just another take because, by Solomon-Godeau's lights, the postmodern
photograph is engineering its own recuperation:

> As an indexical as well as an iconic image, the photograph
> draws the (represented) world into the field of the art work—
> thereby undermining its claims to a separate sphere of exist-
> ence and an intrinsic aesthetic yield. [77]

Does this not have ominous overtones? If the modernist art
object recoiled from the world's attempts to absorb it, the
postmodern object, to Solomon-Godeau, makes an attack its
best defense, but possibly to swell and encompass all reality,
all knowledge, like a cancer, insidiously, until it has become its
own self-enclosed cosmos. Think of Bové when he says, "Theoretically and ideologically, [scientific criticism] will show to all
those counterhegemonic groups that no alternative hegemony
is consistent with human aspirations for liberation and equal-
ity" (20). It is easy to read in this remark the often exclusionary
politics of the defensive intellectual who claims to have found
the hegemonic critique of reality and who is reluctant or incapable of admitting any other, a problematic idea alone requiring
another whole critique.

So when the text, *as* text, becomes everything, it becomes,
in Jencks's terms, nothing—dies just as painfully as the author
or the subject. And when the text has thus been exploded, the
shards reassemble into a wholly new kind of aesthetic object,
as the subject struggles to remake itself in terms of being and
knowledge forever changed.

5

Skeletons in the Closet:
Paradox, Resistance, and the Undead Body of the PWA

Preface

In January 1989 several physicians, working in a number of different Northwestern medical institutions, made an alarming discovery. My partner, Charles, had a brain tumor the size of an orange in his head. During consultation two days before surgery, some of these physicians speculated about the nature of the tumor: Was it cancer, or merely an abscess? Without a biopsy, no one could tell. But the assumption was that since Charles was gay and had a growth in his head, it must have been the overripe fruit of the tainted male seed. AIDS. Or, to be more accurate medically, toxoplasmosis, an opportunistic infection often found in persons with AIDS.

A doctor asked Charles's permission to test his blood for proteins reactive to HIV (I wondered if they'd already given him this so-called AIDS test). Charles consented skeptically, knowing, to put it in his own words, that he did not have AIDS. Nevertheless, Charles and I waited impatiently for the results of the test to come back, as people often wait for any definite diagnosis, however bad, so they can move on to the next step in the course of an illness and its treatment. And when later one of the doctors languidly informed us that he was negative, we were relieved, even though we knew that the physicians all along had been reading AIDS into Charles and identifying his unnamed brain tumor as an undeniable symptom.

Doing so was actually nothing new. In Charles's case, particularly, a GP had assured him that his headaches resulted, perhaps, from the stress caused by being in a homosexual relationship; Charles was thus misdiagnosed, nearly too late. Such a reading of the body has, of course, a peculiar history.

Doctors in the nineteenth century often believed that a lesion on the brain caused degeneracy, which was passed down through successive generations by means of sperm (see Drinka 49–50). Charles's physicians simply applied this theory deductively, narrowing their search from a general set of (visible) symptoms to a specific (invisible) source, from the pathological identity to the pathology. It's called *presumptive diagnosis*.

After yet another tense wait—for Charles to emerge from his operation, from the anaesthesia mimicking death, the zombification of Western medicine, and into intensive care— the surgeon sat down across from me in the waiting room, backward in a chair, and worried over his previous (provisional) diagnosis: How could it *not* have been AIDS? He had been so certain. It was as if he were disappointed. I was just glad Charles was alive, since he was given a fifty-fifty chance of surviving the operation itself. (The surgeon's concern about his reputation eased my fears. I figured Charles must have been OK if the greatest brain surgeon in the United States of America was no longer so worried, apparently, about the *body* of the person with whom he had, for the past seven hours, been more intimate, in a sense, than I had.) But the whole event had been a lesson in the power of the gaze, medical or otherwise, to construct a peculiar subject on the basis of self-identity, to mark the body with a script whose authors would prefer not to revise.

My subject is this body, glanced by language. It refers to the past, like a living artifact; and points forward into the future, like a prophecy unaware of the full power of its desire. It's Foucault when, referring to a previous paradigm shift, he seems eerily to predict "a new experience of disease ... coming into being which will make possible a historical and critical understanding of the old experience" (*The Birth of the Clinic* xv). That understanding begins with a strangely familiar question.

Introduction

Roughly fifteen years after AIDS has emerged in bodies and in discourses alike, how should we theorize the political unconscious of the syndrome, an unconscious that subsists, for example, between the gay male body and the socius that would disown it? It's a question that refuses to die. Not because no one has found the correct answer, but because formulating the question, repeatedly and in various contexts, has become an act of resistance in itself.

For hermeneutic purposes, I use the term political unconscious in the Jamesonian sense: "interpretation in terms of the collective or associative" rather than of "individualistic categories" (*The Political Unconscious* 68). When I speak of the gay male body, it isn't as an entity in isolation, but one that is always already caught in the network of interpersonal relations that Marxism *and* psychoanalysis assume. I don't, then, share Jameson's bold claim for Marxism as being the "only . . . philosophically coherent and ideologically compelling resolution to the problem of historicism" (19), any more than I share Tim Dean's claim for psychoanalysis as "the *only* contemporary theory equipped with a rigorous concept of extra-discursivity" ("The Psychoanalysis of AIDS" 92). Jameson's notion of an immanent social field, determining in a certain sense the ways textual bodies come to be formed, remains helpful in any discussion of AIDS writing, whether on the page or the flesh; while Dean's insistence on the operations of the *objet petit a*—the lure of desire along the insignification of language—begins the indispensable work of properly signifying AIDS on a grand theoretical plain.

However, I don't follow Jameson or Dean into quite the same defiles of the signifier, though their ideas point in positive directions. For example, I broaden the Marxist/psychoanalytical term to include the suggestion of unconsciousness: a condition brought on among public officials when confronted by a health emergency involving despised minorities, who somehow are disincluded from the socius, or virtual social body, which those officials are elected or chosen to represent. Also, the term *unconsciousness,* for my uses, becomes a *positively* threatening condition, because it foretells, like a nightmare, the awakening of the mind and body from a death too quickly foretold and too comfortably trusted.

To address the question I originally asked—how to theorize this particular political unconscious—we might review hegemonic and counterhegemonic AIDS commentaries, the first of which typically represent the gay male body as other, slipping into feminine, black, poor, immoral, and conspicuously promiscuous; and the second of which represent it as self—that is, unproblematically male, white, salaried, upright, and ostensibly restrained. Yet this work has been done and continues to be done by archaeologists and genealogists more diligent than I, some of whom appear below. Whatever we say in this regard only supplements their efforts, regardless of our theoretical framework.

Another approach might be to offer the definitive reading of these differing types of representations, once and for all, possibly by means of psychoanalysis, of homosexuals, AIDS, and homosexuals with AIDS. We'd employ the mode of the deplorer, the mode of negation, as well we should—as well we have, since, almost immediately, persons with AIDS began to be deployed by neoconservatives, among others, as objects of disavowal of everything and everyone evading tidy, disciplinary categories. However, establishing such a reading can mean establishing a criterion of discursive correctness that is anything but unconscious and nothing if not, like fundamentalism, simplistic and hypocritical. I've heard of people walking out of director Gregg Araki's movie, *The Living End* (discussed below), because the PWAs in the film weren't accepting their seropositivity with quiet dignity and grace, and because the film refused until the last frame to resolve its darkly comic ironies. But such expectations are precisely what condemn us all to a fate worse than death: a living hell of moralism.

My approach, then, will be quite different: to read the scripts of this very real trauma—as well as the imaginary spectacle that AIDS has in large part become—as another round in the ongoing debate between representations of deviant sexuality, a conflict that is as old as Oedipal myth and as new as the latest media panic. This approach in itself might also sound like nothing new, fraught as it is with the psychodynamic concepts which theorists have employed so effectively against certain AIDS representations. But I'm less concerned with duplicating such work (e.g., Dean) than with proposing a scandalous and, I hope, fortifying point of view based on some of the vexed rhetorical questions pursued by the discipline: What cost to real desire does analysis exact, though it help us survive? Does our struggle within the chain of signification (the symbolic order) enmesh or unbutton us? Do we reenter the labyrinth of the imaginary to face this time an even greater rival?

I propose that AIDS, itself a paradox that crosses a number of hotly contested dimensions, has mobilized paradoxes which, paradoxically, rewrite a familiar yet unforeseen political unconscious. This, rather than simply maintaining the present dispensation, offers vital possibilities for resistance to the syndrome as well as to often intransigent institutions, themselves offering little more effective resistance than that of crass disavowal, of murmuring no to concern as well as to a cure. The person with AIDS remains a scandal, even after several years of attempted sanitizing and normalization of his or her image for the so-called general public or for academicians. That image, a sort of skeleton constantly emerging from the closet of discretion, is a complex one. Its very complexity—intricating health and sickness, joy and sorrow, life and death—resists closed categories and facile truths. When we struggle ceaselessly to make sense of AIDS and the suffering it causes, we should resolve to *manage* its paradoxes, dramatized by the undead in body and spirit, rather than try to resolve them for (our own) good. When we decide to negotiate these at times abstruse complications, we actually take matters of flesh and blood into our own hands.

Almost at once, unlike our government, intellectuals began this task of crisis management. I'd like to discuss the AIDS paradox in terms of theoretical writing around representations—work by Douglas Crimp, Paula Treichler, Donna Haraway, Leo Bersani, Susan Sontag, Simon Watney—and later to focus on a couple of American films, *Longtime Companion* and *Parting Glances* (with a nod to *The Living End*). I find in these theorists attempts at coming to terms with images of the body and sex during AIDS as productive of life as well as death. In the films, we encounter these very images as characters, who possess varying degrees of vitality—either existing in a sexual wasteland until the end of AIDS, or living with AIDS until death and beyond.

Aids in Theory

Many have claimed repeatedly, and within a variety of disciplines, that AIDS does not exist apart from its representations. For example, Douglas Crimp makes a point of the constructedness of AIDS at the start of his introduction to *AIDS: Cultural Analysis, Cultural Activism,* by now a canonical text in the literature of AIDS resistance. Not wanting to deny the brutal realities of AIDS for the many persons it affects,

Crimp asserts that only by recognizing and deconstructing the often pernicious ways in which AIDS gets represented can we begin to determine our own destinies in and through those representations (3). Crimp does not argue the enlightenment faith, shared in part by such figures as Foucault, that once a problem has been rendered visible, it has been rendered less powerful to do harm. Crimp argues instead, actually *with* Foucault, that making everyone *see* what has been repressed opens up both persistent paradoxes and possibilities for change. In another text Crimp calls for both mourning *and* militancy as necessary responses to AIDS; the former becomes fuel for the latter. Militancy, our acting as agents of history, doesn't simply negate or make null the ubiquitous structures of mourning ("Mourning and Militancy" 18). We not only live but keep ourselves alive through paradox.

Paula Treichler takes a similarly complex approach. In "AIDS, Gender, and Biomedical Discourse: Current Contests for Meaning," she acknowledges that ". . . AIDS is real, and utterly indifferent to what we say about it" (195). At the same time, she asserts that "'AIDS' does not merely label an illness caused by a virus. In part, the name *constructs* the illness and helps us make sense of it" (195). It's paradoxical to think of AIDS as both indifferent and an effect of *différance*, but the paradox itself frames most discussions of AIDS and serves as a sort of dialectic useful in overcoming it—not in transcending it, but in managing it back into practical absence. As Treichler says, "Our names and representations can nevertheless influence our cultural relationship to the disease and, indeed, its present and future course" (195).

Writing out of a tradition different from Crimp's but similar to Treichler's, Donna Haraway, in her article entitled "The Biopolitics of Postmodern Bodies: Determinations of Self in Immune System Discourse," remarks, "Bodies ... are not born; they are made" (10). Denying that scientific bodies are given, she says, "bodies as objects of knowledge are material-semiotic generative nodes" (12). Haraway suggests at least a couple of provocative extrapolations. One is that *AIDS was not born; it was made.* The other is that the body as a "material-semiotic generative node" may seem as far from the stressed and convulsed body of the person with AIDS as possible. Imagine yourself at your lover's hospital-bedside. Your lover is about to die; your lover has chosen to forego anaesthesia, and writhes in agony because Kaposi's Sarcoma has covered the linings of his lungs with lesions. You wish to provide support in his final moments; you yourself are convulsed, but by the enforced intimacy of primal separation from the dying.[1] You whisper into his ear: "Take heart. After all, your body is no more than a material-semiotic generative node." But since pain has, in Elaine Scarry's sense, effectively muted your lover, he's unable to lift himself from the mattress and reply, "This isn't the time for coyote cyborg rhetoric."

The paradoxes of intellectualizing during a health emergency remain. They may seem at times distasteful, yet in the absence of a strong, effective response from the government and its agencies, theory—as well as the activism it can inspire—numbers among the few weapons left us in the fight against AIDS. Theory is not just a guilty pleasure or luxury. (At least it's cheaper to obtain, and more effective, than AZT.) Treichler points out this uneasy doubling of philosophizing and crisis-response in her text (196). Leo Bersani, also, in "Is the Rectum a Grave?," expresses a peculiar guilt over intellectualizing in the midst of such a health crisis, or "war zone," as Treichler terms it: "The only *necessary* response to all of this is rage" (201). But AIDS offers Bersani one more opportunity out of a history of opportunities, derived from culture as well as personal experience, to reveal the virtues of self-humiliation through sexual drama pressed to the extreme. In Bersani's words:

> AIDS has literalized [the potential for death] as the certainty of biological death, and has therefore reinforced the heterosexual association of anal sex with a self-annihilation originally and primarily identified with the fantasmatic mystery of an insatiable, unstoppable female sexuality. It may, finally, be in the gay man's rectum that he demolishes his own perhaps otherwise uncontrollable identification with a murderous judgment against him. [222]

Bersani's language causes a scandal in a number of senses: the certainty of death from AIDS, which is not a certainty that anyone can count on, fortunately; the recirculation of some relatively stable signifier of female sexuality, however provisionally and critically; the metaphorization of the (almost exclusively) gay male rectum and the occlusion of the body of the PWA, even after Bersani's repeated emphasis on fleshliness; and, finally, toward the end of his article, the romance of sacrifice in the figure of the gay male, which echoes Simon Watney's valorization of martyrdom at the end of his book, *Policing Desire* (148), as well as Susan Sontag's interpretation of becoming infected with HIV as a kind of unknowing act of suicide, in *AIDS and Its Metaphors* (26).[2]

All these critics mobilize paradoxes useful in discussing the body of the PWA. Haraway says that bodies in general "can be reasonably thought of in terms of disassembly and reassembly" (15). In practice, however, these procedures can occur only within the laboratories of multinational capitalism, sustained cynically by humanistic self-interest. That is, insofar as the types of biomedical research Haraway describes get perceived as profitable, their benefits eventually reach my body after the new paradigm has been converted into capital for institutions, and not before. Treichler, speaking on behalf of our bodies, still firmly under medical scrutiny, claims that we should continue vigilantly to read into linguistic structures that are never completely within our control (192).

In psychoanalytical terms, we insist that no one speak for *us* by discovering the *failure* of signification. Bersani, focusing on the anus as a hot site, is able not simply to resolve but to subvert a Freudian master-servant dialectic by means of a masochism primary to all sexuality. Homosexual experience can thus offer that mysterious general population of heterosexuals a *jouissance* always already present within their sexually ambiguous selves. Watney wants bodies to increase in value after they perish, not so much as saints' relics but as martyrs entire, of the kind who inspire the living. Finally, Sontag implies that one can act as the agency of one's own undoing while remaining unaware of doing so. Her begging the question—assuming suicide, the result, to be the cause of the cause, HIV infection—sounds like an example of pernicious homophobia. But it seems as unconscious as her self-contradiction: when doctors construe her having cancer as itself pathological, they act insensitively; when Sontag construes infection as suicidal, she demonstrates compassion.

Whether she knows it, Sontag's logic, like that of the others I've mentioned, operates supplementarily. The metaphors of AIDS supplement AIDS itself. That is what she suggests by her very use of the conjunction *and* in her book's title. It's as if the metaphors can be simply be excised, to reveal AIDS in all its anatomical horror, or at least in its plain reality. Of course, as

the logic of the supplement continues operating, the supplementing element threatens to *supplant* that which it was merely
intended to substitute for or append (Derrida *Of Grammatology*
144-45). Metaphor is all we're left with. AIDS does not exist
until metaphor fleshes it out, proliferating the paradoxes.

With Haraway, the monstrous postmodern body, made
permeable and flexible by infection with HIV, becomes the *agent
provocateur* in debates over traditional notions of hygiene. With
Treichler, the alien other, like the unconscious, comes stalking
back to implicate even those who have analyzed it to death. For
Watney, the dead body of the PWA rises up and returns to
exhort survivors, overwhelming us with its absolute claims to
authority. And for Bersani, the annihilated ego begins to murmur again, to haunt the body of the gay man through which
it had been silenced and removed, making it possible for the
critic to speak about that very experience. As for Sontag, how
can we avoid replying at this point to her call for an end to
metaphor-making except to reclaim the (paradoxical) power of
metaphor (*sinthome*) itself? "Giving up on harmony, on the
ideal [of symmetrical relations, between gendered subjects or
signifiers/signifieds], opens us up, paradoxically, to greater free-
doms" (Ragland-Sullivan 68).

Now, paradox is not proprietary to the intelligentsia. Take
for example the Conservative Family Campaign in Britain,[3] or
Proposition 64 in California, each of which has proposed the
quarantine of persons with HIV infection and AIDS. The inherent contradiction of these and similar efforts is that only *some*
are at risk at the same time that *all* are at risk. In other words,
only some people are considered to be risking their lives, but
all people are risking their lives in allowing the risky few their
basic human rights, claimed only by those with the privilege of
dispensing them. Conservatives have liked accusing gay men of
deliberately spreading disease among us, meaning those who
consider themselves not only unaffected but honored to be so.
Gaetan Dugas—otherwise known as Patient Zero, the reputed
progenitor of AIDS in North America—becomes the prototypical
villain, fucking with murderous abandon.[4] Other villains, or
vectors as they're sometimes termed, include prostitutes, who
are also called reservoirs of disease even though they have
more experience than many in preventing its spread. Along
with villains we have also had victims, and the victimhood and
innocence of different people with AIDS has by now been well

deconstructed,[5] even though these insidious concepts seem to be outlasting all attempts at emptying their oppressive signifiers.

As all these kinds of paradoxes proliferate, resistance, paradoxically, becomes increasingly possible and even, to use Bersani's stressed word, *necessary*. But, to touch again, briefly, on the ubiquitous notion *that AIDS does not exist apart from its representations* or, as I extrapolated from Haraway, *AIDS was not born; it was made*. Packed into the logic of this assertion lies its opposite—namely, that AIDS actually *does* exist apart from its representations. In other words, to say that AIDS does not exist, holding in abeyance, for the moment, the inexorable contingencies of representation within language, equals asserting that it does exist but that we cannot locate it, the acronym as purportedly stable signifier cannot body it forth even as it convulses the body with terror and pity—as well as compassion and rage. Maybe, then, it's no contradiction to posit the existence of AIDS as a kind of absence over which the veils of representation are cast in order for its existence to be revealed or, more fundamentally, called forth. And this is hardly different from asserting that the queer body must itself be clothed before it can socialize, must get inscribed with various, often conflicting and contradictory discourses before it can get re(a)d as an object of identification or disavowal. In fact, if the body did not exist in the ways we've liked to think, neither would AIDS, which opens that body to the possibility of infection without itself infecting it. Rather, the body hosts, transmits, and expresses *HIV infection,* as we stress each time AIDS gets mistakenly described as an STD. But the body performs these operations in a seemingly infinite number of ways, medically, socially, and linguistically.

In short, AIDS does exist apart from its representations. But only an accumulation, an overaccumulation, of representations will make AIDS, and the bodies of persons with AIDS, radically *visible* and therefore *viable*: granted life, authorized to be written and read, allowed to mingle, or condemned to wither away, or condemned *for* withering away. However, perhaps AIDS will remain only ever *virtual*. Once we remove the veils, we can no longer find AIDS or the body it inscribed, as, ironically, the AIDS-phobic often hope, even though we're sure it is there, like a dead person living in the mind, like the deceased who doesn't know that I dream him alive, like a corpse brought back from the dead but under his own control, like an outcast zombi in revolt against a fate worse than death: the capital punishment of identity's and agency's elimination.[6]

I don't mean to drive my argument so far as to suggest that AIDS is nothing *but* metaphor, which a casual glance at the ways in which the dominant media have generally represented the syndrome may lead one to believe. I simply want to emphasize two conceits: that it is vital for us to read metaphor vigorously and to write metaphor aggressively, never allowing others to monopolize it. Also, to remember with Derrida that metaphors, and the concepts they supposedly dis-/close, are closed with each other in an unending dialectic without sublation ("White Mythology" 268). Or, as Derrida more directly puts it elsewhere, "I don't believe that the opposition between concept and metaphor can ever be erased. I have never suggested that all concepts were simply metaphors, or that we couldn't make use of that distinction" ("Jacques Derrida In Discussion with Christopher Norris" 72–73). A limit-point of linguistic functioning must be maintained, even in the presence of the direst physical distress.

Which puts me in mind of Foucault's apparent stoicism toward his own infection. In the Foucauldian sense, we render the intangible tangible in order to reveal its emptiness, its ability to be transformed easily and continually, to be filled with whatever significance we choose. As Foucault remarks, "We must make the intelligible appear against a background of emptiness, and deny its necessity" ("Friendship as a Way of Life" 209). The most perverse, delightful, and hopeful irony is that even after the queer subject, the queer body, has been killed as a result of AIDS plus inadequate, sometimes hostile, methods of combating the syndrome—even after death, that supposedly emptied locus of discourses returns, fully inscribed, to haunt the resistant as well as the indifferent, the negative as well as the positive (in a number of senses), helping to continue proliferating promiscuously the discourses that surround and shape the bodies of those with and without AIDS. Even after finding a cure for the body, medicine won't cure AIDS; even after providing life-saving education, activism won't stop the spread. AIDS has become a structure like the Sedgwickian closet, or even more so, like socialization in general: not given but imposed, not desired but inescapable, not to be cozied up to but disciplined. It reshapes the flesh from which it hangs.

Lacan has famously remarked: "For the symptom *is* a metaphor whether one likes it or not, as desire *is* a metonymy, however funny people may find the idea" ("The Agency of the Letter" 175). AIDS is—to employ the stressed Lacanian copula—an anatomy of the unconscious of contemporary sexual politics.[7]

The Skeleton in the Closet

Hence the first word in my title, skeletons, which has carried with it a polyvalence at least since romanticism that is applicable to the aesthetics of our own time. What I mean to evoke is the varied meanings of the term *anatomy*, whose etymology denotes cutting up. History has added flesh and blood to, and subtracted them from, this abstraction: the study of animal or plant structure, the structure itself, dissection, the body dissected, skeleton, the human body, and any minute examination of a particular object. In spite of Haraway's dismissal of "internal harmonic principles" as agents of biological growth (10), the romantic trope of the anatomical or inorganically whole body persists, and in multiple ways, during postmodernism, perhaps especially because of AIDS.

I think Haraway has the subtractive model in mind: pare the dross of discourse down, like Pygmalion, and the essence, the life, the germ as it were, will manifest itself. This is the model she rejects, and rightly. But an additive and therefore beautifully corrupt romantic model, the segmented Frankensteinian or Promethean body, an assemblage of disparate parts, is obviously crucial, not only to the romanticism she repudiates but to our own postmodernism, repeating as it does the satisfying yet inadequate fantasmatic imaginary of primary identification in Lacan, an image that haunts this discussion of the relationship between hegemonic and counterhegemonic AIDS discourses ("Aggressivity in Psychoanalysis" 21). Such a model is useful in theorizing the gay man's body as it gets intersected by these discourses, since, to make a long, anguished story short, most of the dominant discourses would rather flay the queer body of the significations it chooses for itself and overwrite it with their own than dare recognize themselves in those supposedly merely artificial, constructed images called queer.

As dis(as)sembler, I want, therefore, to add yet other veils to this already multivalent skeleton. The hidden secret, the scandal bound and gagged and stuffed away. The wasted body of the person with AIDS hosting the tiny cryptosporidium and unable to sustain it*self.* The undead, the personality embalmed in the texts of the Quilt, autobiographies, encomiums, photographs, testimonies, articles, memories, songs, symphonies, musicals, plays, invectives, living bodies, conference papers, journal articles, anthologies, dissertation chapters. It is this persistent, insistent subject that I find myself most concerned with, because s/he denies that emptying out, marking for death, and discarding of the queer body that hegemonic discourses—heterosexist or otherwise, originating wherever—have typically attempted to enact. In the realm of film, as I'll soon show, *Longtime Companion* provides an example of dominant reinscription. *Parting Glances* provides perhaps the best counterexample, even after many years when so much has changed AIDS and AIDS has changed so much.

However, back momentarily into my title's closet. As Crimp, drawing on the work of Eve Sedgwick, suggests in a lecture originally delivered in the spring of 1991 at the University of Washington, entitled "Right On, Girlfriend!," the closet is a social structure we carry with us everywhere, whether we're out and about or into our personal spaces (6). It serves as a mask for the masquerade of appearing straight, or at least not declaring our queerness, itself a paradox, as well as a prison for our desires. In a sense, like cyborgs requiring recharging, we depart from the closet and perform the tasks of living only to return and plug ourselves back in, and shut down—a cyclical, rhythmical movement of repression and liberation and repression. We're living queers and skeletons in our closets, too: outing ourselves continually and creating a scandal by refusing to die away, drawing power from our resistance to the closet's strictures, like vampires, the undead, seeking blood and the darkness (at least, with David Wojnarowicz in *Close to the Knives*, in the unsafe yet prophylactic abandon of the imagination, if not with material bodies).[8] Among those terrorized by ambiguity, it has become even more scandalous to capture this representation than to give it more attention by deploring it. I embrace that scandal as I embrace the scarred body of my lover.

Beyond the familiar colon in my paper's title, lie the paradoxes of AIDS, some of which I shall now help proliferate, hoping to anatomize unitary and thus ironically *partial* views of the queer body with AIDS no matter whence they come. The PWA is, of course, my subject here. The extent to which the person with AIDS and the queer subject coextend needs to be theorized, and this chapter can only begin to do this. But what does it mean to be overinscribed, to engage paradox? I mean simply the overdetermination of any body by discourses whether self- or other-generated; I mean the ways in which the body becomes re(a)d with the incisive styluses of language. An agony of resistance designates what I take to be the combative nature of intersubjectivity—in other words, a contest between subjects whose originary identifications serve to initiate lifelong rivalries with images both pleasing and threatening.

And to continue my rather promiscuous playing on words, I would call our crisis the AIDS emergency, had I more room for the title. I want not only to place its drastic nature in the proper perspective, which our political representation in general refuses to do, but to remind us that the crisis is, unfortunately, only just emerging, coming out of an immersion in the bodies of millions. The worst, along with the best, is yet to come.

The Paradoxes of AIDS

AIDS has mobilized individuals and coalitions not just to combat the syndrome but also the opportunistic infections of homophobia, sexism, racism, ageism that traverse our bodies and the body politic. AIDS has hailed the immune system, bestowing upon it the status of a subject, one that recognizes, remembers, and responds. AIDS has mobilized paradoxes down to the smallest level, too. HIV itself is the hugest paradox, despite the fact that it can be seen only with an electron microscope, Haraway's eye of science. HIV can lead to the death of organisms millions of times its size. It is both alive and dead, a limit point of biological functioning. It is both pure information—rewriting the DNA of its host cell backward as a kind of hegemonic agent, like a cyborg—and a counterspy who forms a fifth column among the body's defense forces. HIV has become the double agent of AIDS, yet some, like Peter Duesberg, consider it harmless per se (42–44 and passim). Others suggest it's incapable of acting alone. Researchers such as those at the National Academy of Sciences hold this view (Nichols 97).

Positivity to HIV infection results from detection of protein antibodies to the virus, now often bestowed with the pleonasm of "HIV virus" along with the pernicious metonym of "AIDS virus." In other words, part of one's corporeal identity comes to be defined by the presence of antibodies which, like signifiers, imply the absence of the objects—in this case "the virus" rendered back to a singular concept—that they signify.

Being positive can mean initiation into medical protocols based on an inability to locate positively the source of the condition, whereas being negative entails *not* manifesting antibodies—a double negative, one that should logically resolve into a positivity. But it only means that one is probably not positive, a designation to which we queers, like the German filmmaker Rosa von Praunheim, have happily begun to add our own valences.

If some gay men, in the spirit of such defiance, feel that injunctions to practice safe(r) sex express but the newest technology of discipline over their sexual behavior—bending them to a regression to pre-Stonewall secrecy and self-denial[9]—they should consider that the scale of sexual safety has itself been contorted, so that the usual progression of attributives twists back under the low technology of safety. Safe is safer than safer, which is riskier than no (abstinence). In other words, the hierarchy of safe > safer > safest is replaced with 1) safest (no) > 2) safe > 3) safer.

1) The absence or avoidance of sex represents the safest possible behavior. 2) Sex present and accounted for but without the exchange of our precious bodily fluids becomes the absolute limit of safety. Expenditure, a common representation of queer sex that doesn't produce anything, nevertheless allows for the exchange of *some* value for another, such as time for danger, making *all* sex only comparatively safe. 3) Sex with expulsion of fluids halted by protective barriers, thus interfering with the exchange of other values, like safety, represents responsible simulation of previously nonlethal exchanges.

Delany would seem to think that what's worse than these injunctions against risks—their disciplinary content—are the very subjects of the enunciations: his constituency among gay people, already disciplined by having become such subjects, their bodies snatched by an invasive morality that would maintain absolute discretion between corpuses, whether material or discursive. Thus, safe-sex educators become resident aliens. We've seen them before, but they're behaving differently now, in public and in private. And what they enjoin often seems neither concrete nor familiar, satisfying itself with vague directions—for example, "Always use a condom," without specifying how, where, or when, and rather paranoid warnings—"always use a condom for oral sex," despite the street talk naming sucking as safe— but not always properly intervening. (One of my favorite dreams is to travel back to the late seventies in a time machine and begin exhorting people, gay men in particular, about the dangers of a new virus. But then I awake to the realization that I'd probably suffer the same fate as Cassandra.)

The new discourse of safety subtends the grammar of description. Similarly, it extends the risk implicit in sex into the realm of real danger, posing the potential foreclosure of (sexual) life against risks once understood as not only desirable but quite often necessary. When the Commendatore in *Parting Glances* returns as a ghost, he still plays the role of the reprobate son, rather than the avenging patriarch, and makes only banal and incomplete remarks. Nick, in response, bolts from the confines of his tiny apartment and heads for a party, probably in order to get laid.

It isn't just that language can't be clear enough. It's that words remain inadequate to paradoxes they help form, and, above all, fail to resolve the paradoxes of my body's behavior. AIDS has scandalized our culture in part because it graphically demonstrated that failure, revealing bodies with glorious histories of deviance. Such bodies appear to us on the screens of our collective fantasy as well as in the flesh. In the cinema and on television, there have been waves of interest in AIDS and persons with AIDS. Productions have varied widely in approach, quality, and budget, where more money does not equal a smarter film. As with the exponential increase in AIDS discourses, selecting our focus becomes harder year by year.

To be fair to all three films I'll discuss, I should emphasize that each represents a different generation of people with AIDS and occupies a distinct genre. *Longtime Companion* seems to speak to and about the first and second generations of PWAs— the first ones to be identified as having a particular disease syndrome and to deal with the initial waves of infection and

death (early-to-mid-eighties). It is a solidly Hollywood friendship flick, in the manner of *The Big Chill* and *Diner*; it's aimed
at an audience slightly older than I.

Parting *Glances*, on the other hand, is definitely about my
generation, those who began to experience directly the effects
of AIDS somewhat later (mid-to-late eighties) and who found
ways to live longer as well as to represent themselves and
others as more than (at times) comically resistant to syndrome
and representation alike. The film remains a part of the domestic black comedy and party movie genres, like *Who's Afraid of
Virginia Woolf?* and *The Boys in the Band*, which also more or
less adhere to the three classical unities—time, place, and
action—and end with cathartic revelations.

Finally, *The Living End* speaks for a decidedly younger crowd,
the perhaps fourth generation of people with AIDS and their
friends and families, whose anger, dark humor, and fatalism
both offer new promise for resistance and challenge the values
of safe(r) sex. As many have observed, Araki draws on the genre
of the rebellious road film—from *Easy Rider* to *Thelma and
Louise*—pushing his characters into a suburban wilderness to
pursue flight lines of ecstasy and terror. These generations and
genres maintain discrete distances from each other as much as
they overlap. So, to counterpoint the three films to one another
is, in a sense, unfortunately to forget their very different purposes and audiences.

Hollywood Characters

I'd now like to take two examples from these popular films
as contrasts in resistance to erasure. Both *Longtime Companion*
(director Norman René 1990) and *Parting Glances* (director Bill
Sherwood 1986) depict the return of the dead from AIDS, but
in significantly different ways. *Longtime Companion*, in reenact-
ing the typically empty Hollywood gesture of cathartic pathos at
its conclusion, reinscribes hegemonic discourses that would
seek to void, forget, and trash the PWA. By contrast, *Parting
Glances*, in allowing its gay male PWA to refuse roles assigned
him by the oppressive narrative of transgression, punishment,
and repentance, desublimates such *Don Giovanni*like moments
of terror and pity through a bathetic reaffirmation of living, and
thus opens wider possibilities for resistance.

The action in these two films returns continually to the beach, which becomes the scene of the hedonistic, carnivalesque lifestyle once led by persons who are now dead or scared away, or at least overcautious, who have forsworn their former or potential promiscuity. "The season's over" as one character in *Parting Glances* remarks, with hardly suppressed bile. In *Longtime Companion*, characters often assume and therefore disavow promiscuity as a cause of AIDS in others, right up to the very end. The character who once acted in a soap opera called *Other People* announces at an AIDS benefit: "I used to be one of those 'Other People'."

Early in *Longtime Companion*, panning across a Fire Island beach party in 1981, the camera moves quickly from tables crowded with empty beer bottles, to people dancing on the sand, to gay men cruising each other on the deck. By the end of the film (late summer 1989), that same beach has been emptied of everyone except for three survivors, a gay male couple and their woman companion, musing on tomorrow's obituaries and the possibility of the epidemic's end, as daylight fails and the season winds down. After the main character, Willy, stresses his desire to "be there" when the syndrome is "cured," all the dead from AIDS who had once frequented the beach come running back down the boardwalk, and a sunlit reunion of old friends ensues. The group seems to include more diversity of gender and ethnic background than the film previously includes—one thinks also of the gender and ethnic tokenism of the party scene in *Parting Glances*, which is as well primarily a movie about gay white middle-class men, a depiction that perhaps helped reinforce the construction of AIDS as a disease belonging in particular to this group. Then, suddenly, the undead from AIDS disappear, and Willy reiterates his desire to "be there." The three people, which it seems must include a woman to stabilize somehow the disruptions possible from an already stable gay male couple in a Hollywood film, depart the beach and leave it utterly empty, as the lyrics of the accompanying song inquire, "Do you remember when the world was just like a carnival . . . ?"

Longtime Companion thus leaves us with the impression that longtime companionship, not returning to but turning one's back to the beach, in some way protects people from the ravages of promiscuity and its attendant lack of commitment; we never see actual sex, safer, safe, or otherwise, in the film. Lisa,

Willy and Alan's friend, triangulates their relationship to suggest, I think, a possible heterosexual model for commitment—is this the family romance fictionalized?—which Willy and Alan are assumed to emulate. *They* survive, and remain privileged to continue enjoying, however minimally, the beach, which is now curiously empty of the living.

In *Parting Glances*, to the contrary, the single character with AIDS not only *returns as a person living with the syndrome* to the beach where he had once played pranks, where he proposes striking out on a new adventure overseas, but refuses to "Repent!" as his friend—in the guise of the Commendatore from *Don Giovanni*—bathetically demands. The dream-work that armors Nick's dead friend Greg, as the reprobate Don's patriarch, as knight of the living dead PWA, implodes bathetically when the Commendatore lifts his visor and puffs on a cigarette, remarking on the tedium of heaven and the importance of staying alive *for that reason*. Greg derides Nick for Michael's "turning [him] into an opera queen," an immanent critique, in a way, of Nick's enforced identification with Giovanni. Any suggestions about the ravages of "trashing it up," as Robert, the Ken doll character, calls it, are silenced, as Greg vanishes with an aposiopetic form of advice conveyed from Nick's dead mother: "'If you go an a trip, make sure to take—'."

When Nick first spots the knight blocking his hallway like bad period decor come to life, he blinks, dons his leather, and leaves to attend the going-away party for Robert that he was previously avoiding. Many of the characters, Robert particularly, have been making excuses for not keeping in touch with Nick, and Nick himself kisses, touches, and hugs people to reaffirm his aliveness and interrogate the denials of those who assume themselves either to be at risk from the slightest touch or to be unimplicated by AIDS at all. Now that the knight has conversed and vanished, Nick sets out for the private beach where he will play a cruel prank on Michael, leading him to believe he's going to commit suicide but actually testing Michael for his loyalty and sense of mischief. Michael more than passes the test, and the two of them leave the beach empty, but as living, unruly, and unrepentant queers turning their backs on despair. Here, at the end, the beach is only the beginning.

Such an empty locale provides the backdrop for the finale of another film about PWAs, *The Living End*, "An Irresponsible Movie by Gregg Araki" (1992). Araki's subtitle cues us to his intentions: not to make a film that would appeal to Hollywood, members of the Bush administration, who were still in office when the film was released and are interpellated as "fuckheads" after the end credits, or critics concerned with crudely positive representations of persons with AIDS. However, Araki does appear to hail viewers who share his anger, frustration, rebelliousness, and sense of black humor. All these are affects of the drifter, Luke, one of the two main characters with HIV, who often makes a speech about his "missionary" position in society while lying atop his lover Jon, the other main character.

Luke's mission, in fact, is to have none that's socially responsible. Being positive authorizes him to reject conventional notions about work, family, money, sex, property—everything subverted by him and Jon while on the lam. "You really wanna go back to your 'I'm HIV-positive and everything's normal' hunky-dory life?" he asks Jon, while refusing, himself, ever to go back. Luke, rather, pushes, in the literal as well as figurative sense, endlessly forward—in a death drive—away from every kind of propriety and toward the ultimately vital end of *jouissance*: murder-suicide during orgasmic anal sex with Jon.

This act fails only because Luke's pistol has run out of bullets. He's been a killer throughout the film: a beautiful man, who evades the funny, cock-baiting dykes; blows away gay-bashers; offs a cop; proposes to inject George Bush with his blood at gunpoint, and offers Jon a "killer" anatomy lesson in men, bisecting Jon's torso with his finger, as might an autopsist.

Luke and Jon's beach, wherever it might be, "Wyoming, Siberia, Pluto?," is the site of their pact's nonfulfillment, and it frames the film by repeating the wasteland seen at the beginning, where Luke sprays graffiti and twirls to lob the empty can at the dead city of Los Angeles in the distance. The beach is an antiplace that's everyplace, a flat, minimal, yet universal stage for Luke and Jon's dire drama of eros and thanatos. The silver crucifix dangling from his neck, Luke places the barrel of the pistol in his mouth, as if to fellate it, while forcing the bound Jon's cock up his ass. After Luke fails to shoot, Jon at first frees himself, strikes Luke, and walks out of the frame, only to return and embrace his lover. The camera pulls far back to reveal their utter aloneness in the void.

The dialectical symbolism couldn't be more telling: the romance of life, in the person of Luke, who rewrites murderously homophobic graffiti wherever he finds it, with death, or

Jon, who venerates the suicide, Ian Curtis, of Joy Division. The affirmation of gay love, which comes to represent *all* gay love, there on the edge of the earth, utterly apart from the heterosexual social systems that support it. Luke seems rootless, while Jon leaves his friend Darcy, home alone with her unfaithful boyfriend Peter. The double meaning of fucked as penetrated as well as killed. Being on the beach as both absolutely empty— the depopulated land—and full of possibility: the live ocean; the sound of the surf continues through the closing credits.

Even seemingly defeated and abandoned, Luke and Jon remain stoical and validated in their arrogant love. Speculating whether he and Jon met in a previous life, Luke remarks, "Death is a lot like coming." They've come to die, but survived. Folding back the imperative on Jon's bumper sticker, Choose Death, the two of them have elected to become agents of their own mortality.

Parting Glances and *The Living End* thus continue to affirm the possibility of depicting the body with AIDS as vital, complex, hard to discipline, and productive. In *Parting Glances*, Nick gets angry at his lawyer for assuming he won't be alive for Nick's upcoming tour, and stars in an MTV video where he sings, troping over Frank Zappa and the Mothers of Invention, "We're only in it for the drugs." Above all, these films depict bodies that need not rewrite oppressive scripts reiterating denials of sexuality, representing traditional domestic arrangements, or rehearsing narratives of reprobation and repentance. *Longtime Companion* speaks, on the contrary, for those who view the body of the PWA as irremediably other and remote, regardless of the sexualities they declare.[10]

In a telling moment, Willy and Alan are lying together in bed. Alan asks, "What do you think happens when we die?" To which Willy replies, "We get to have sex again . . . I hope." I would like to think that Willy means the dead body is still somehow cathected and promiscuous, even as I know that what he suggests is the living body's refusal to allow itself these pleasures.

Parting Glances and *The Living End* therefore remain two of the few widely distributed films that reject this doom: the death of the body or the refusal to accept difference. Unfortunately, despite such repentant attempts as *Philadelphia*, it seems it will be a while before Hollywood learns to (de-)part with the glance.

Addendum

When I was finally allowed into the intensive care unit, I saw that the physicians had cyberneticized Charles. He lay immobile in the bed, with connections running from every part of his body to monitoring devices nearby. His head was bandaged like a mummy's. He complained especially about the catheter. He was glad to be awake, and wanted me to touch him, which I refused to do because of the risk of infection. He was angry. I guess that risk would actually have been pretty small, but at the time, Charles appeared so vulnerable that affection seemed like a form of danger. Affection, infection: distantly related words reunited in the popular mind.

Charles chided me, and I regret that I didn't dare touch him when I should have. And I recalled that we hadn't played safe when we first fell in love, willing to forget what we couldn't forget any longer.

Epilogue

The Virtual Body of Aesthetics

Toward the end of chapter 4, I disussed the death of the text. If the author, or subject, as traditionally understood, has died, or at least lies on his or her deathbed, we must reconsider the status as well of the text that embodies its maker(s). By now, we have rejected the hermetically sealed organism of romanticism and modernism; also, the structurally impeccable tissue of signs of one kind of postmodernism, the organism's mechanical simulation. Since the body has rewritten itself, it has reformed the text it uses to record experiences at the limits of the tissues *in* the flesh.

Deleuze, writing about the baroque, reverses the chronology: "If the status of the object is profoundly changed, so also is that of the subject" (*The Fold* 19). "We move from inflection or from variable curvature to vectors of curvature that go in the direction of concavity." Movement toward the limit of subject-ification falls back on (*se rabat sur*) the virtual body of the postmodern entity.

Deleuze implies a neobaroque in contrast with the supposed neoclassicism of high postmodernism. Two paintings, their subject painting itself, will provide examples. The first is Max Ernst's *Surrealism and Painting* (1942). A huge, double-

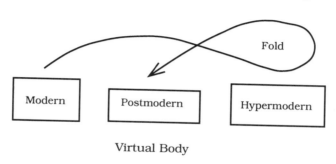

Virtual Body

headed, emulike figure reaches a brush to a canvas, which contains outlines of natural forms, like leaves, overlaid with intersecting curves. At the same time, the figure nurtures what appears to be offspring resting atop a box of household tools, themselves outlined as if by spray. While the beast paints, it seems to be renewing itself, such that the offspring are difficult to separate from the larger body. The painting in the painting, foreshortened by the right-hand edge, doesn't represent anything so much as complement the live, curvilinear forms of the beast, constructing an artifact inside an artifact. The "Painting" occupies the same space as the "Surrealism." Gone is the recognizably human author, but so is the stable, personal artwork. In their places, a new kind of creator as yet not fully formed, and an incomplete, overinscribed aesthetic object, stand. Ernst refers, therefore, to an unexplored and challenging future.

The second example, Carlo Maria Mariani's *The Hand Submits to the Intellect* (1983), turns back to an irretrievable past, in horror of anarchy. The more or less square canvas depicts two virtually identical figures, both of ambiguous gender in classical style: one seated on a marble sphere, the other on a cube. Drapery covers the genitals, folding around legs and shoulders. Each figure paints the other, the left-hand figure, the more masculine, aiming the brush at the heart of the right-hand figure, the more feminine, who daubs the head of the companion. The bodies attract sexually but only as classical statuary, and neoclassical advertising, like Calvin Klein's, do, in an icy eroticism that sublimates lust into an aesthetic appreciation of the body become commodity.

Mariani's painting thus exemplifies, even epitomizes, a species of postmodernism that appropriates an earlier style, itself impersonal, in a gesture of impersonality—a high-modernist criterion. It pushes this gesture to its limit, or rather encloses it in a cramped, symmetrical space it can't escape from. *The Hand Submits* resembles a triumph of drafting, yet, despite their efforts, that triumph doesn't belong to the figures, as the "Painting" does to Ernst's beast. We see through the painting, as it were, to Mariani himself, attempting to recapture the author by means of the formally perfect artifact. We recognize postmodernism as a period, instead of a possibility. We apprehend the body as cold, white, generic, and discrete. I prefer the multiform, almost nonchalantly creative body of

Ernst's surreal chimera: negligent of the human, in control of its productivity, pointing toward possibilities lying ahead for the body and the text alike.

Wordsworth attempted to foreclose the body, meanwhile preserving the fleshly text purportedly defeating it. The speaker of "Nutting," raising and lowering his crook, draws sine waves of sexual violence in the air.

Godwin and the Shelleys parceled, reassembled, and electrified the body, diseasing the organism of its own most oppressive period. Frankenstein and his creature, and Falkland and Caleb Williams, crossing and recrossing each other's paths, chase each other into an indefinite future.

Glass and others have pushed the body's envelope of endurance and ecstasy, seducing it with feminine wiles of the disciplinarian. As the arpeggios rise and fall, the plateaus of *jouissance* intersect and draw us ever upward.

And AIDS has produced for the body a new unconscious that has paradoxically helped it awake to startling potentialities. Experience takes us down to the realm of the dead, returning us to the living utterly altered.

In every case, the text has captured, stored, and perpetuated the body's attempts to re-create itself, registering the dangers it has braved, protecting its memory, and proliferating its effects on the experiments it undergoes. Our bodies become permeable and unruly, while the texts they encounter record changes wrought by the survival of limits. Just as the body doesn't simply submit to outside forces but actually regulates and resists them, the work of art doesn't so much imitate nature as create virtual bodies both determined by and determining (un)natural power. Every body takes the greatest risks. This book, I hope, has testified to that unsettling reality.

Notes

Chapter 1

1. "Nutting" first appeared in this edition positioned between the conversation poem called "The Fountain" and the Lucy poem beginning "Three years she grew." They form a trio of poems that dramatize various kinds of rising (life) and falling (death) action. Wordsworth ultimately collected "Nutting," according to his final arrangement of the oeuvre, as one of the poems of the imagination. The version I here discuss can be found in William Wordsworth *Poetical Works* 147. Henceforth I will cite line numbers of poems from this collection parenthetically in the text.

2. Crawford opposes the sororal to fraternal modes, which are at any rate not negligible. In fact, at least one other narrative with which "Nutting" resonates is the story of Cain and Abel. Wayne Koestenbaum mentions Cain several times, even according him the honor of being "[i]n Harold Bloom's terms . . . history's first strong poet" (10). The theme preoccupied the romantics. Wordsworth and Coleridge were to collaborate on "The Wanderings of Cain," but could not finish the poem. Koestenbaum accurately associates the story with the poets' own fraternal rivalry. Byron developed the Cainite myth into a closet drama. Because it is a primal act of transgression in Western culture, Cain's crime becomes for Wordsworth and others a paradigm for the individual imagination's violence against a world not wholly of its own creation; a certain sacrificial economy among men (recall the Christ/Abel of Coleridge's poem, which he could not, or would not, finish in time for the second edition of *Lyrical Ballads*), an exchange involving the penetrative-receptive action of anality; defamiliarization (Cain, like Wordsworth's heroes, must become a fugitive, disrupting and then fleeing from the familial order); as well as the act of violence implicit in the reader's search for delight and instruction, or meaning, in the text.

3. At least one precedent exists for a male bower in English poetry, one with which Wordsworth and Coleridge might indeed have been familiar: Richard Barnfield's notorious *The Affectionate Shepheard*

Sicke for Love, whose male speaker beckons Ganymede toward "my pleasant Bower Fild full of Grapes, of Mulberries, and Cherries" (quoted in Bruce R. Smith 100). Coleridge, for his part, knew "Nutting," since Dorothy Wordsworth included a draft of the poem with a letter to Coleridge late in 1798, along with early versions of the skating and boat-stealing episodes from what came to be called *The Prelude*. See Reed 259, 331, quoting Dorothy, who describes "Nutting" as "the conclusion of a poem of which the beginning is not written." It is difficult if not impossible to avoid thinking of the poem, then, as an *end in itself*. Wordsworth described it as "intended as part of a poem on my own life, but struck out as not being wanted there"—an intriguing note that almost seems to confer the power of desire upon that life-poem. "*The Prelude*" itself had rejected the disturbances of "Nutting" (Gill's edition of Wordsworth 694 n. 153).

4. Virtually every book-length study of the poem, dating from before the sixties to the present, includes some take or other on "Nutting." This might not strike us as unusual for literary criticism, especially of Wordsworth, except when we survey the diverse ways that "Nutting" positions critics hermeneutically—how, as Foucault might say, the poem incites critical discourse. To read "Nutting" is thus inevitably to navigate a wilderness of commentary, as much as to construe the poem's tropes. At first, critics approach the poem gingerly—as if obeying its ultimate imperatives—and discuss it only in terms of Wordsworth's struggle with his relationship to nature, based on his own gloss (he associates the poem with recollections of nutting expeditions in the vale of Esthwaite; see Michael Mason's edition of *Lyrical Ballads* 377). When critics begin to talk about the poem's sexual implications, they emphasize rapine, but consider the state of the speaker over the bower's, almost to excuse the boy's act as auto-erotic. Hence, David Ferry attributes "practiced libertinism" to this sexual prodigy (24). And David Perkins remarks that "the child has ravaged the hazel bower, but to call it a 'ravishment' expresses mainly the weightiness of the child's feeling, his thrilled fascination and sense of guilt" (185). Perkins suggests, as well, an autoerotic response in the reader. Bloom claims that Wordsworth "transcends the directly sexual element" by displacing it onto the maiden, implying that the poem is a sort of preparation for actual sex (*The Visionary Company* 30–31). Arac, for his part, boldly confronts the issue of self-abuse: "by the turn to female sexualization composing the scene, the poem displaced youthful autoerotic fantasies, the symbolic masturbation Freud recognized in what Americans would call 'jerking off' branches" (45). He quickly shifts his discussion, however, to the castration of the phallic mother. Earlier, Arac notes the critical attention the poem has received as a result of its sexual content, "still acknowledged, though with some embarrassment" (44)—an affect of masturbation, not of rape. Michael G. Cooke, in *Acts of Inclusion*, remains one of the few critics

finally to touch on, however carefully, what he calls the "sub-her-maphroditic" posture of the bower (141).

5. Throughout, my discussion is indebted to Owens's theoriza-tion, which, although it draws on Coleridge, is not concerned with the aesthetics of romanticism. My own essay is an allegory of reading in itself, written by a postmodernist; so it cannot help, in allegor-ical fashion, but to read romanticism through the palimpsest of postmodernism.

6. See Luce Irigaray, "Commodities Among Themselves," *This Sex Which is Not One* 193.

7. See Pipkin's "Wordsworth's 'Nutting' and Rites of Initiation" for a discussion of the trope of leavetaking.

8. Bataille's position is perhaps no less heterosexist than Wordsworth's, Coleridge's, or even Koestenbaum's, despite his posing the crucial question, "Must homoeroticism justify itself by mustering analogies to childbirth and reproduction" (25)? Yet Bataille is probably the most radical in locating sexuality generally in a ground where growth and perpetuation maintain no more and no less a trajectory toward some telos than nonreproductive sex (see especially "The Solar Anus"). The "hetero" in the "heterogeneous" Bataille valorizes must remain a cause for some wonder, however.

9. Magnuson emphasizes rightly that "Nutting" is also contem-porary with the Lucy poems, the Matthew poems, and some of the early material for *The Prelude*, such as the skating and boat-stealing episodes, in which the speakers experience guilt and sorrow out of (sometimes quite deliberate) alienation. We might well speculate that, since Coleridge privileges the organic symbol over the mechanical al-legory (in the de Manian sense), he derided "Nutting" and encouraged Wordsworth to shun(t) it from what we now know as *The Prelude*, into which it couldn't properly be synthesized. Was this, then, Coleridge's own act of (self-)preservation—that is, did he denigrate the allegory precisely because it all to fully embodied (translucently, again in de Manian terms) Wordsworth's poetic triumph?

10. Her own experiences are deemphasized almost to the point of denial. Similarly, in "She Dwelt Among the Untrodden Ways," the "difference" that Lucy makes to the speaker is not just that the poem would not *be* without the occasion of her death, but that this female subject must remain "unknown" to all but the speaker, who shares as little as possible with readers. Wordsworth's typically isolated images—here, the violet and the star—disembody Lucy while keeping her sin-gular and unattainable, apart from sublunary life. In "Three Years She Grew," nature presumes to absorb Lucy, perhaps generously, for its own child, the *différance* between them constituting nature's forms and Lucy's existence alike. But the speaker's melancholy tone in the

last lines—"The memory of what has been, And never more will be," the familiar Wordsworthian complaint—reveals the guilt of his identification with that nature which has foreshortened Lucy's life by overenergizing her, giving her the impossible duty of becoming nature's perfect mirror, itself an already outmoded doubling of poetry's image in the prose prefaces. Finally, in "A Slumber Did My Spirit Steal," Lucy has passed decisively into the natural world, into its deep immortality, its permanence, turning with its diurnal and seasonal rounds, in order to assuage the speaker. This may seem like "abundant recompense" ("Tintern Abbey," l. 88), the favor Lucy pays the speaker back; but it remains to be asked whether the cost to Lucy has been too great, especially since the speaker considers only the cost to himself.

11. I should note that, while Shaviro does not elaborate on the nonhegemonic/homoerotic conjunction specifically, he nowhere associates Bataille with such poets as Wordsworth. He prefers Emily Dickinson and Wallace Stevens. Shaviro mentions Bataille's heterosexism and "virility" (*Passion and Excess* 37, 96), but doesn't investigate them to the point of revising Bataille's economy of desire from "nonhegemonic" to counterhegemonic, which I feel it must remain so long as 1) Bataille's economy banks on basically heterosexual investments, and 2) it gets used as an *alternative* to a sexual hegemony that it may contest but cannot supplant. We gay critics—including Bruce Boone, to whom Shaviro refers—might well learn from Bataille, perhaps disturbed at the thought, however, that once again we shall be forced to take with shame our own (queer) opinion from another (straight man), as I (and Shaviro) do by referencing Emerson, and as I do by plundering Shaviro (see his "Masculinity, Spectacle, and the Body of *Querelle*," where, upon viewing Faßbinder's film, he admits "it would be futile for me to try to write about it without registering the force of [its] seduction" [159]—exactly how I feel towards "Nutting," but from a reversed subject position). "Nutting," in any case, may be homoerotic, but is hardly nonhegemonic, as should by now be all too clear.

12. William Wordsworth, *The Prelude: 1799, 1805, 1850* 7, n. 7. The frequency with which Wordsworth uses "hung" might be overlooked if he had not devoted so much space to a discussion of forms of the verb "to hang" in the preface to *Poems* (1815). Interestingly, Wordsworth uses the description "milk-white" at least one more time, in reference to the ill-fated pair of swans in "Home at Grasmere" (l. 323), which Modiano recognizes in MS D as a pair of males. One of them, representing Coleridge, must be sacrificed so that Wordsworth can choose the more proper domestic companion—Dorothy (Modiano "Blood Sacrifice, Gift Economy and the Edenic World: Wordsworth's 'Home at Grasmere'" [forthcoming in *Studies in Romanticism*]).

13. Crawford's insightful reading also assumes the bower to be female, or at least feminized.

14. This bit of folk wisdom has formed an exchange, to choose one instance, in *Waiting for Godot*:

ESTRAGON: What about hanging ourselves?

VLADIMIR: Hmm. It'd give us an erection.

ESTRAGON: (*highly excited*). An erection!

VLADIMIR: With all that follows. Where it falls mandrakes grow. That's why they shriek when you pull them up. Did you know that?

ESTRAGON: Let's hang ourselves immediately! (12)

Beckett recognizes with Wordsworth the potential destruction caused by a form of sexuality that is estranged; out of bounds; associated with crime, punishment, and death, and shared among males.

15. The most brazen example is, without doubt, "There is an Eminence," third of poems on the naming of places. "This Peak" [l. 5], "this lonely Summit" [l. 17], retains the poet's "Name" as if to keep it apart from the woman whom the speaker loves—an embarrassing inscription, so to speak, of the narcissistic stereotype of homosexuality: "double talk," indeed.

16. "Either we flee the event in terror; or else we are lulled with assurances that it is something to which we are already 'appropriated,' that is already our own" (Shaviro *Passion and Excess* 33).

17. As de Man remarks, "allegory exists entirely within an ideal time that is never here and now but always a past or an endless future" (220). De Man's deconstructive (indeterminate) language itself embodies allegory's ironies.

18. Speaking of landscape with a male appearance, Koestenbaum identifies such in at least two other texts: Lang and Haggard's *The World's Desire*, where some rocks are covered with brush like a man's hairy limbs; and Browning's allegory, "'Childe Roland to the Dark Tower Came,'" where cockle, spurge, thistle, bents, dock—just to name a few phallic plants—populate the desolate scene (158). In "Nutting" the speaker feels confident enough "to smile / at thorns, and brakes, and brambles" (ll. 12–13).

19. See the Gill edition of Wordsworth 694 n. 153.

20. As well as a reminder of our own postsexological biases, in which we strive, often against our better judgments, to sexualize as well as to anthropomorphize plants and animals.

21. Arac terms this highly charged anticipation a mere pause in the action (41).

22. As Jean H. Hagstrum points out, "In the alternative version of *Nutting*, the poet addresses his sister as Lucy . . ." (98).

23. See also Hartman 73.

24. Arac identifies them as ode, epic, and tragedy (39), but I think the complex might be denser still, in effect to overload the structure so that it collapses inward. "Nutting" thus remains a sort of romantic ruin, which Owens associates with allegory as formally synthetic (206). The poem has a picturesque quality Wordsworth—unlike Coleridge—would have utterly rejected (see Modiano *Coleridge and the Concept of Nature* 9) had he not been so scrupulous to collect as much verse as possible for his oeuvre—itself a lengthy supplement to the grand philosophical poem never completed. Instead, "Nutting" occurs in the *Works* as a fragment among fragments: not a discard but a record of its own discarding.

25. "It should be remembered that allegories are frequently exhortative, addressed to the reader in an attempt to manipulate him [*sic*] or to modify his behavior" (Owens 225).

26. I wonder whether Coleridge's response to Otway was conditioned by Otway's personal reputation, such that Coleridge's using this minor poet's "Lutes, laurels [or "lobsters" in the 1817 edition], seas of milk and ships of amber" as an example of the concatenating fancy, rather than the organic imagination, looks like the sublimation of a common complaint against sodomites: that their affections are artificial and their loves unproductive (chapter 4 of *Biographia Literaria*). Indeed, in chapter 14 of the *Biographia*, where Coleridge discusses the cogenesis of *Lyrical Ballads*, he glancingly refers to the "disgust and aversion" accompanying the reading of homoerotic poetry (172). This homophobic shibboleth was common in the poets' day—even the otherwise liberal Percy Shelley repeated it—particularly as a result of their increasing social, philosophical, and moral conservatism (Crompton 284), itself resulting, partially, from disaffection toward the French Revolution. Crompton provides a detailed and admittedly sober account of the regency period's spectacular punishment of sodomites. Their gibbeting cannot but recall Wordsworth's first example of a spot of time in the 1805 *Prelude*: the emptied site of a hanging (ll. 278–301.) The cruel spectacle of this punishment might be all the more reason for Wordsworth to sublimate his feelings toward his rival through an eventually marginalized poem, which thus becomes a sort of trace of the unspeakable. But how, though by talent, might Coleridge have incited such a discourse? Although his was still the Age of Sensibility, when members of the same sex were likely to express mutual affection openly (Holmes

99n.), it was also one of sexual differentiation when male sexuality, as such, separated from the female qualitatively, became rationalized (invisibilized), such that same-sex attraction was just as openly disciplined because it threatened to collapse the distances of the homosocial power hierarchy (Laqueur 196–97). Holmes, despite clearing Coleridge of suspicions, discusses his subject quite suggestively, especially in terms of his submissiveness to authority (101–2, 285), his acquisitiveness in intellectual property (193, 232), his initial avoidance of parenthood (223)—characteristics arrayed around the symbol of Coleridge's habitually agape mouth, an erotogenic zone of internalization (130, 219). Hazlitt was one of the first to notice: "His mouth was gross, voluptuous, open, eloquent" (46–47). Contemporary portraitists drew and painted him this way—without exception in Holmes's illustrations. Coleridge's volubility, what Deleuze and Guattari might call a deterritorialization of the mouth's incorporation function, constitutes an expulsiveness of improvised discourse supplementing the elaborately composed but rarely completed plans of the notebooks. What Coleridge cannot create, to become a legendary poet, he assimilates and disgorges, to become a legendary talker. In reading Judith Butler's _Gender Trouble_, I note that Nicolas Abraham and Maria Torok identify the empty mouth, "which becomes the condition of speech and signification," as the literalized site of mourning over loss (68)—in Coleridge's case, that of his poetic potency?

27. It is almost as if Wlecke anticipates Scarry's argument when he terms the Coleridgean sublime a sort of "sacred horror" in which individual autonomy, and thus the very sense of self, gets rendered null (see Wlecke 73–94).

28. See Paul Smith _Discerning the Subject_ 37.

29. Ivor Winters defines "the fallacy of imitative form" as follows: "the procedure by which the poet surrenders the form of his statement to the formlessness of his subject-matter" (54). On the contrary, "Nutting" plans and executes its seduction with the care of a Richardsonian landowner.

30. Deleuze and Guattari _Anti-Oedipus_ 171.

Chapter 2

1. William Godwin, _Caleb Williams_ 341.

2. Mary Shelley, _Frankenstein_ 229.

3. "Talk about beauty and the beast—she's both," as Inspector Briant cornily remarks about this replicant murderer turned nightclub entertainer. Zhora, like all replicants, inherits the curse of the

cybernetic human laid down by the likes of Victor Frankenstein: her already fugitive life must be destroyed in order to protect real humanity.

4. See, for instance, Maurice Hindle's introduction to the Penguin edition of *Frankenstein* (7).

5. I might go as far as to claim that Mary's aesthetic reiterates an Aristotelian distinction between the efficient cause of the male and the material cause of the female. The former, the active principle, provides the soul for the latter, the passive, corpselike body (see Laqueur 28–30). Mary maintains such an aesthetic as an ideal away from which her creative striving tends to fall. Percy, for his part, seems content simply to embellish Mary's text, in a manner suggesting effeminacy and homosociality, as well as mere assemblage rather than perfect mimesis (see Vickers 36–37, quoted in London 260). London claims that the Frankensteinian "body renders visible the culture's sexual codes and mechanisms of identification, mechanisms that would seem to provide little space for women" (263). However, I argue that, in fact, Mary was attempting, by the very act of *Frankenstein*'s creation, to open that space. Whether this act "can do [little] more than demonstrate masculine preeminence" (London 264) is an issue lying beyond the scope of this chapter, though I would hope Mary was more able than London says.

6. The suggestion of haruspication, though beyond the scene of this inquiry, would be worth investigating. The novel's frequent appeal to augury, omens, fate, foreshadowing, fear, premonitions, is ironic in the light of Caleb's foreknowledge. He knows the entire story already, before he sets pen to paper, though he is obviously obliged to stage the drama of narrative anticipation. But perhaps the real drama of discovery lies in Godwin's writing, in which Caleb is a self-being constituted as pages accumulate on Godwin's desk at the same time as Godwin himself is (re)constituting his own fictional presence, both as narrator and published author.

7. "It was merely a day perished from the calendar" (*Caleb Williams* 338), he says, with a heavy irony he can hardly avoid conveying. Life becomes important only insofar as it is labored, filled with text.

8. See Jean Baudrillard *Simulations* 98. Mary will do much the same in *Frankenstein*.

9. Quoted in Small 49–49.

10. Nitchie goes as far as to remark, "In spite of . . . tributes to her 'masculine understanding,' Mary had no illusions on the matter herself" (22).

11. Mary Shelley *The Last Man* 1.

12. Laborde 9: *L'abondance, la diversité, la richesse du génie de madame de Genlis ne méritent-elles pas autre chose que le profond oubli dans lequel son oeuvre a sombré?* ("Do not the abundance, the diversity, the richness of Madame de Genlis's genius merit something other than the profound oblivion into which her work has sunk?"). Translations of all passages in French are my own.

13. Percy Shelley *Shelley's Poetry and Prose* 174.

14. Caleb himself becomes a text, *The Wonderful and Surprising History of Caleb Williams* (*Caleb Williams* 301; introduced earlier at 268).

15. It seems a horror to Frankenstein that his creature is a segmented composite, like a bug. References to chimeras, mythical assemblages, abound in the text, also.

16. Compare Terry Eagleton's discussion of Saussure: "The signifier does not yield up a signified directly, as a mirror yields up an image . . ." (*Literary Theory* 127). Though Eagleton is writing backward to Saussure (early structuralism), he does not in the meantime write through the nonstructuralist Blanchot, and consigns him to an endnote (221). By contrast, in *Of Grammatology*, Derrida refers to a "dangerous promiscuity and a nefarious complicity between the reflection and the reflected which lets itself be seduced narcissistically" (36).

17. The shudder before orgasm—sometimes surrender in refusal, sometimes a matter of technique—becomes both orgasm's prolepsis and its completion.

18. Grimes is also Sadean: "He regarded both injury and advantage merely as they related to the gratifications of appetite; and considered it an essential in true wisdom to treat with insult the effeminacy of those who suffer themselves to be tormented with ideal misfortunes" (*Caleb Williams* 58).

19. In fact, suggestions of Falkland's transformations are made sooner, in the narrative of his rivalry with Malvesi in Rome (volume 1, chapter 2): one of many instances in the novel when characters undo each other with overpowering eloquence, one that often renders others silent.

20. Variations on the word *penetrate* occur at least eleven times.

21. A comprehensive reading list would have to include at least twenty-five authors.

22. Quoted in Nichie 49.

23. Falkland, on the other hand, is caught up in the logic of jealousy, which occurs when one cannot love what the lover loves, when one is somehow barred from possessing what s/he possesses—such that, if one could seize it, one could no longer be jealous, but also no longer loved. Falkland attracts Caleb toward him, thus, precisely by attempting to deprive him of his liberty, which he must nevertheless continually guarantee him.

Chapter 3

1. See James Miller 350.

2. I originally entitled this book *Beyond Recognition*, to play on the double meaning of a step past Lacan and of destruction to the point of nonidentifiability. In 1992, however, four editors conspired to publish a selection of Craig Owens's work and called it *Beyond Recognition*. Though we'll never know who happened on the title first, I accede to their priority, especially because of Owens, who has influenced my own work.

3. One of the components of the queer gaze is assumed to be the *furtive*: it attempts to look, perhaps even engaging attention, duplicating itself—possibly even possessing, in some sense, the object of its operation. Yet, at the same time, it is thought to be concealing that very operation in a furtiveness disguising a sexual interest. "I'm looking but I'm trying not to let you know I'm looking, because that would be to expose my intentions, my interest, whereas I'm supposed to be looking disinterestedly or at least without certain forms of interest, such as sexual." The returned look often functions, not as acknowledgment of interest, but as pretense to discovery and therefore as threat of exposure: it marks the object as nonidentity, as object out of reach, a sort of seduction where mere acknowledgment, but not engagement, is acceptable, followed by abandonment, which is a privilege typically granted the heterosexual male, who positions himself as the one who chooses the desired object, not as the one who is himself chosen as an object of desire, always feminine. The queer male gets feminized in such a play of gazes, looking as might a straight female who hopes to attract by her attentiveness, suffering in abjection, in deprivation, in lack of the proprietary male principle. Often, also, when the straight male receives the queer gaze, he deflects its attention away toward a proper object, like a passing female, no matter how unappealing otherwise, the idea being both to break any possible identification between subject and object, and to redirect the look toward an object deemed the correct commodity for males in general, the female. It becomes a kind of discipline not unlike that perpetrated by various media dominated by

straight males. Here, the operations of the queer gaze, if visible at all, are dramatized as incorrect, wrong, unnatural, perverse, laughable, pathetic, infantile, stunted—even potentially dangerous, in terms of AIDS, where cruising marks the beginning of a slippery path toward promiscuity, infection, disease, and death. The subsequent emphasis in popular culture on look but don't touch—for example, Calvin Klein's icily discrete human statues—has seemed to bear this out. Even if one makes oneself an object to be desired, one carefully regulates the subjects of that desire, such that some are encouraged while others are discouraged. "I'm seducing you for myself, not for you," to paraphrase Carmen. This, aside from functioning to maintain sexual arousal while keeping fulfillment a distant possibility, provides an alibi for moralizing in terms of personal danger: one should not be demonstrating certain forms of desire because they carry with them the potential for self-destruction and the spread of infection. Thus, the desire is itself diseased—it's just that AIDS has been the ultimate confirmation of its pathology. Sex aversion takes perverse forms, allowing itself the luxury of reverting to normative heterosexuality, actually described that way, to its own detriment, as a supposed refuge from the dangers of abnormal desires. A crisis occurs when the straight male object, under menace of attention from the queer male gaze, perceives that his return look can no longer work to expose what it fears, what it hopes is hidden and will remain so, but that, in fact, the desire motivating the gaze openly and unabashedly continues to cathect with its object, and joyfully. The result is frequently a heightened paranoid response generalizing to all queers, which attempts to reestablish the authority undermined by queer interest in a bad object-choice. Open discussion of this danger also works to recruit support for normativity and to confirm the lack of similar threats posed by peers. The concerted return look of the homosocial but homophobic tribe tries to outnumber and overpower the gaze of the openly desiring queer subject. The public space becomes off-limits to the play of the eyes that implies too much damage. The play is allowed only in private, in the dark, unless between proper subjects kept apart from the potentially infectious improper ones—I think of the U.S. military's fears about queer recruits somehow infecting straight men and women with their desire, even though it's assumed to be naturally repulsive. There's a time and place for every lust. When it reveals itself in the wrong ones, it breaches social norms and dashes expectations based on safety and reassurance. From a homophobic point of view, then, queer desire is undifferentiated and not discriminating: the same pathological condition existing everywhere, which cathects with each object it encounters, however attractive. The homophobe must believe that this is so in order to figure the queer as unitary and comprehensible, such that s/he is less easily contended with.

4. There are two titles and two texts, in English, involved here. The original French title is *L'ordre du discours*, the English translation of which, by Rupert Swyer, called "The Discourse on Language," is reproduced in its entirety in *The Archaeology of Knowledge and The Discourse on Language* (215–37) and in a truncated version in *Critical Theory Since 1965* (148–62). (More will be said about the differences.) Page numbers of citations from Foucault's text, given parenthetically in this introduction, will refer to both editions, respectively.

5. Said says that the "constituted subject [is] fixed indecisively in the eternal, ongoing rush of discourse" (287) and "discourse does violence to nature" (289). Foucault himself, in another text, says, "We must make allowance for the complex and unstable process whereby discourse can be both an instrument and an effect of power, but also a hindrance, a stumbling-block, a point of resistance and a starting point for an opposing strategy. Discourse transmits and produces power; it reinforces it, but also undermines and exposes it, renders it fragile and makes it possible to thwart it. In like manner, silence and secrecy are a shelter for power, anchoring its prohibitions; but they also loosen its holds and provide for relatively obscure areas of toler-ance" (*The History of Sexuality* vol. 1, 101).

6. Yet the voices have replaced white space with ink, helping the speech along; and, by the time they begin, have already implicated the speaker in *some* discourse, however limited by the terms of the dialogue.

7. Whose meanings proliferate and scatter immediately upon the effort to read the word.

8. I would revise the prefixes of these attributives to non, since sex isn't necessarily *against* (anti) that which it doesn't fundamentally support.

9. Neil Bartlett says, "Repetition is the basic formal principle of our desire. We repeat sex, we repeatedly compare bodies (whether we touch them or not). We look like repetitions of the same form. We shape our romances (brief or long) by talking of One who will end the sequence of Numbers. We go *regularly* to places of entertainment. Our music is repetitious. It is the apotheosis of repetition" (252n). Deleuze and Guattari, for their part, see in courtly love the possibility to avoid "a law of lack or an ideal of transcendence" in favor of "singularities that can no longer be said to be personal, and intensities that can no longer be said to be extensive" (*A Thousand Plateaus* 156). In other words, they posit a kind of love in which Foucault's experimentation ceases to be quaint or old-fashioned and appears, on the contrary, as quite metaphysically as well as physically potent. "The slightest ca-ress," they say, "may be as strong as an orgasm."

10. Halperin doesn't want to silence Miller, but admits that he "might wish to intervene, to the extent that [he] can, in the process by which that 'truth' [about Foucault's personal life] is produced and distributed as well as in the institutional practices through which it is made to signify" (76). In other words, Halperin is as willing to seek an invidious truth in Miller's book as Miller supposedly was in terms of Foucault's books. Functionally, then, how do Halperin's and Kimball's approaches differ? Miller has provided his own answer in the title of his response to Halperin: "Policing Discourse."

Chapter 4

1. Perhaps Habermas has in mind Foucault's troubling defense of the nouveaux philosophes, especially of the repentant Maoist, André Glucksmann (see James Miller 295ff.).

2. This section is entitled "The Problem of Reference." It should be noted that here Hutcheon offers her own typology: five different kinds of referentialities.

3. Glass claims that the "Low" Symphony in part picks up where his preminimalist tonal music—a "conservative mode"—left off back in the sixties (Stearns 10). Here, perhaps, he breaks decisively with the earlier aesthetic, and admits that a useful personal idiom, arpeggiated repetition, has been pressed into the service of late capitalism: of opera commissions, special events, collaborations, executive production of record labels—the machinery of labor and notoriety, no less effective, even if somewhat less _affective_, for all that. At any rate, it could be argued that minimalism remains basically tonal because it accepts the tempered scale; it must, in fact, do so, in order to accommodate the fingers in what began as a largely keyboard- and woodwind-oriented music. Glass himself insisted on the tonal nature of this music partially in response to the "heavy European didacticism" (_Music by Philip Glass_ 13) of serialism, partially to continue a tradition alternative to Schoenberg's rightly understood tradition of the avant-garde, partially from exposure to the music of Ravi Shankar and other non-Western musicians.

4. These demands have by now become legendary, but it's worth noting that when I read this part of the chapter during a conference at the University of Oregon, a musician approached me afterward and remarked how difficult it was to perform minimalism because of all the counting involved, an effort foregrounded by the chanting of numbers and solfège syllables in _Einstein on the Beach_, contemporaneous with the counting out ("One two three four . . .") before punk songs.

5. Is it Foucault who fetishizes power, or his critics in interrogating him? See Butler *Gender Trouble* 124 for a quite strategic defense against such an interrogation, contra Monique Wittig.

6. In his listing for the soundtrack, John Schaefer calls this "an otherwise silent film" (85), which it is not: background noise of the outside world—wind, shoes, traffic—is audible, though faint.

7. For that matter, the film isn't "non-narrative" as Glass terms his own music (Rockwell 113): its narrative simply isn't narrated, though it certainly has a rising and falling action like the prophetic penultimate image in the film—a rocket exploding in midair, after lifting off at the very start, one of its boosters tumbling slowly back to earth.

8. This is how the soundtrack album misspells the name of the housing development.

9. That is, music written for diverse instruments, but the term could just as well apply to the compelling suddenness and syncopation in the score.

10. And Hutcheon remarks, "it must have been tacitly assumed that the intellectually underdeveloped should allow the architects to arrange their lives for them" (*Poetics* 27), then refers to Pruitt-Igoe.

11. This is, in fact, a case of willfully mistranslating the German pronoun, just as Gropius calls the architect he.

12. Hal Foster argues that minimalism "might in fact [be] the scene of a shift in sensibility, the very *brisure* of (post)modernism ("Re: Post" 193). Glass's own movement out of modern American symphonism through protracted harmonic extensions to a more varied, populist tonality workable for opera parallels general movements toward postmodern rewritings of classical forms in various mediums and genres. See Griffiths 297. Indeed, resisting it for years, Glass has finally accepted the descriptive term *minimal*, at least as it applies to his earlier work (liner notes to *Music in Twelve Parts*). Is he excusing that style to those familiar only with his later work, from which he wants clearly to distinguish it?

13. Brian Massumi, drawing on Gregory Bateson, quoted by Deleuze and Guattari, provides a fitting description: "a plateau is reached when circumstances combine to bring an activity to a pitch of intensity that is not automatically dissipated in a climax" ("Translator's Foreword" to *A Thousand Plateaus* xiv). Bateson had discovered in Balinese culture, where the gamelan orchestra is apparently played mostly by men, whose youthful erections had been laughingly teased by mothers to approach but not achieve orgasm, a "libidinal economy quite different from the West's orgasmic orientation" (xiv). Perhaps this economy accounts for Glass's use of women's voices in

such works as *Music in Twelve Parts* (Joan LaBarbara, Dora Ohrenstein) and *Dance Nos. 1–5* (Iris Hiskey, Dora Ohrenstein), where the (supposedly) more consistently intense sexual economy of the female can please like a protracted orgasm. Desirable would be a model of libidinal economy independent of culturally confined, and often prescriptive, interpretations of female sexuality. One possibility might be to use the *male* voice as Glass has used the female. Todd Levin, on Glass's Point Music label, has done just that, in such highly libidinally vocal pieces as "Anthem" and "Prayer."

14. The sequence called "The Grid" has also become perhaps the most influential in an influential film. Aside from Ron Fricke's travelogs called *Chronos* and *Baraka*, and aside from Pearl Jam's "Alive" video sampling of *Koyaanisqatsi*'s crashing silver waves, and aside from a promo for Bill Moyers's *Healing and the Mind* that uses Glass's music for "Clouds," a number of visual texts have reiterated Reggio's "Grid": most notably and lavishly, the video for "Television, the Drug of the Nation," by The Disposable Heroes of Hyphoprisy; the grids and motoric racing of the Disney film *Tron*; the brief wordless film retrospective *Pieces of Silver*; a MasterCard television ad, shown on MTV in 1993, encouraging people to use their cards in the supermarket; a 1993 television ad for Oatmeal Crisp with Raisins (New York City scenes); a television ad for the 24-Hour Wake Service (1-900-976-WAKE) that makes even the home seem like a hotel room; a 1993 Seattle television ad for *Almost Live vs. The Workplace* (people scurrying about Grand Central Station, presumably commuting); and a 1993 KIRO Newsradio (Seattle) television ad suggesting we listen while we drive. A television ad for Incognito perfume (Cover Girl) uses the beginning of *The Photographer* as a background to heterosexual beach scenes. Interestingly, "The Grid" itself recalls William Friedkin's *French Connection* (1971; cinematography by Owen Roizman), particularly during the famous car-chase scene; as well as René Char's *Entr'Acte*, where Satie's repetitive music punctuates accelerated scenes of urban life. The movement becomes delirious, involving the viewer—and listener, if live music accompanies the film—in a sort of minimalist absolutism, suture or tearing away, that Char probably intended either to enlist the like-minded or offend the bourgeoisie. In the imaginary, the fetish stands in for the lack (*béance*) threatening close identification; but it can also signal that very breach. In minimalism, the mind serves as a conduit to the body, which determines not only how the work is performed but how it's consumed, according to how successfully the fetish closes the opening. Just as often as minimalism attempts to suture, however, it attempts to tear the wound apart again. A piece might begin *in medias res* and end abruptly, at the moment of greatest ecstasy. The music might become syncopated, even modulate unexpectedly, or become suddenly louder. For example, toward the end of Graham Fitkin's "Loud," the syncopated patterns

shift among the six players, who are already dispersing authority with their gender parity and lack of center, such that the music prevents a rise toward peroration. Fitkin, obsessively concerned with structure as such, the very antithesis of the improviser, achieves this effect only through careful calculation, *composing* in order to discompose: the minimalist aesthetic summarized. The final movement of Steve Reich's *Four Sections* performs a similar feat, in obstinately refusing to modulate into a symphonic apotheosis despite the opportunity provided by the ultimate union of the orchestra's four sections: the tease beckoning toward more intensity not relief, even after ending. We're used to hearing finales as resolutions of earlier conflicts, but only because musicology has taught us to apply the extramusical to the absolute, to write a descriptive program or exploit a literary one, rather than emphasize musical strategy in itself, which the more public musical forms (e.g., opera or symphony) use quite unashamedly to fulfill or flout social expectations. Along comes minimalism, flattening the narrative, extending the flow, and then cutting it short, not only to evince a new economy but to foreground music's inherent paradox: it remains indeterminate, but maintains distinct use-values within and without the self eclipsing all other mediums.

15. Brian McHale prefers the fuller, more satisfying image of the klein bottle for postmodernism, in which the literature of replenishment, as Barth calls it, would therefore serve a tonic that postmodernism could not contain. The foregoing discussion of Barth might support McHale's contention that postmodernism is a paradigm shift from the epistemological to the ontological (in other words, "What do I do with this bottle [or {tale}]? Set it on the coffee table?"—a dubious, and easily trivialized, contention, for sure). The following discussion should argue with Linda Hutcheon that, on the contrary, in postmodernism as perhaps never before, "any meaning that exists is of our own creation" (*A Poetics of Postmodernism* 43).

16. And not the typescript Barth sent to his publisher or the incomplete book being an assemblage of previously published material that had to be augmented by additional work, as yet unwritten, to form a collection, which the book is *and* isn't or any ideas Barth may have had for any such bound volume of interrelated shorter pieces.

17. Dowden also refers to Bernhard's "difficulty" as "modernist," although it seems more *postmodernist* in the sense I've been describing in this chapter. Bernhard's texts are far from the hermetic, fragmentary, mind-oriented artifacts of high modernism, or at least the high-modernist stereotype. Phillip Lopate, in his "On Not Reading Thomas Bernhard," also mistakenly calls Bernhard a modernist ("avant-garde"), though he associates him with Glass, Robert Wilson, and Burroughs—rather snidely (77).

18. I'm thinking of Jane Gallop's notion of the feminine sexual economy, often applied to minimalism, as metonymic—contrary to the vertical or upright, erect, paradigmatic, harmonic, metaphorical movement of the masculine economy—and therefore horizontal: syntagmatic, diachronic, melodic, slippery (*Reading Lacan* 114ff.). Gallop appropriates this lacking feminine movement to counter the privileging of the plenitudinous masculine one, making what is latent quite visible and open, like the minimal P.J. Harvey's "Sheela-na-gig" forever holding apart her labia in an act of defiant lasciviousness. Minimalism scandalizes because it usurps the (typically male) fetish—the riff—radically simplifies it, and multiplies it to lengthy ecstasy, democratizing the phallus, thereby robbing it of uniqueness and self-satisfaction. Rather than developing material to resolve some conflict, minimalism extends it to explode that very dialectic. It flattens affect (à la Jameson) by oversimplifying and insisting upon each constituent element of the music as the hook. Glass, in Greenaway's documentary, has listeners asking, "Where's the hook?" It establishes a feminine trajectory toward fulfillment. To use Gallop's terms, it makes that which is patent come out and surrender the obviousness of its autonomy. (But see Eric Tamm's book on Brian Eno, which describes a certain type of minimalist aesthetic as vertical, emphasizing the timbral effects of harmonic coloration, as well as Craig Owens's essay on *Einstein on the Beach*, linking Glass and Wilson's procedures to the vertical, poetic movement of metaphor in modern linguistics [10].) It has been men, almost exclusively, who have been credited with this accomplishment. Is the appropriation of the feminine any more appealing to women than, say, the appropriation of queer sexualities by straights for *their* own purposes? Does minimalism fascinate itself with female sexuality as a way of reasserting a masculine form of authority, a performing and listening discipline? Do we become disciples to these (mostly male) figures? Female minimalism has tended to emphasize the virtuosic, orgasmic voice (Meredith Monk, Dora Ohrenstein, Joan LaBarbara, Laurie Anderson, Anna Homler). Male minimalism has tended to emphasize instruments, especially those manipulated by the fingers: keyboards, certain winds and strings; or, in the case of rock 'n' roll minimalism, the guitar—Helmet, with its shorn, sinewy, rarefied, jagged, cut metal—or to exploit that (usually female) voice. The hook remains a fetish insofar as without it the piece would represent a lack all the more despicable for not being absolutely an absence. Minimalism foregrounds this possibility. Glass's song "Changing Opinion" ("Refrigerator Song"), for example, dramatizes the search for the artificial hums filling the void of the night, as when one wakes, hears the fridge cycle off, and realizes that the hum has been there all along. Repetition of the sound fills us in a similar way. The response: irritation and flight; or suturing. That is, the repetition either pushes you away because it is indeed foregrounding the fetishistic nature of the music, and therefore *all*

music, in such a way as to diminish its value by multiplying it without conventional variation. One thinks of Lacan's veiled phallus, operating only when hidden. Or, the repetition invests one in its economy by insisting on the fetish as the last instance before a hateful silence—musical absence, lasting four minutes and thirty-three seconds or longer—holding "one thing after another" (Judd), the making of a noise and then moving on (Feldman), "what you see is what you see" (Stella)—against nothingness. What results is a hypostasized fetish that no one can own, which thus anyone can claim as *his or her* own: anyone could repeat it or bend his or her own hook. Hence the multiplication of (post) minimalists themselves, in an age Jacques Attali has termed one of composing: "the right to make noise, in other words, to create one's own code and work, without advertising its goal in advance . . . that is, the right to compose one's life" (132). The ultimate musical fetish, the single note, has often been called meaningless outside some clearly defined harmonic system. However, the single note exists apart from 1) silence, from which it is absolutely different; and 3) any other note or chord, to which it belongs. As 2), the single note exists between silence and music, a sort of difference in itself as a singularity—alone but not negatively unique, but not common, as in Deleuze. In addition, the single note, or chord, held for a long duration, sets up its own libidinal economy making it meaningful, as in La Monte Young's Theatre of Eternal Music, playing nonstop in a New York loft—perhaps as the last instance. Difference here has no being per se but exists everywhere, like the singular, at the limit between the common and the positively unique (like a virus); a difference without opposition, along a scale:

1) silence <> 2) note > 3) chord (upright) > Riff (temporalized)
different from   different within   different among
(apart)   (a part)   (departure)

19. In fact, one version of postminimal(ist) music is called totalism because of its rhythmic ferocity, sheer volume, and political confrontationalism. One example is the Ben Neill/David Wojnarowicz collaboration *ITSOFOMO (In the Shadow of Forward Motion)*.

20. Bernhard follows this convention in the typography of German-language literature, precisely to encourage an unbroken, minimal reading.

Chapter 5

1. See Shaviro *Passion and Excess* 150.

2. For a critique of Sontag's suicide metaphor, see D. A. Miller "Sontag's Urbanity."

3. See Keith Alcorn "AIDS in the Public Sphere" 204-05.

4. See Crimp "How to Have Promiscuity in an Epidemic," in _AIDS: Cultural Analysis/Cultural Activism_ 238-46. Crimp discusses at length Randy Shilts's unique archaeology of roughly the first decade into the AIDS crisis, called _And The Band Played On_, focusing on Shilts's drive to name the AIDS harbinger.

5. See Jan Zita Grover, "AIDS: Keywords," in _AIDS: Cultural Analysis/Cultural Activism_ 28-30.

6. My references to zombification derive from Wade Davis's _The Serpent and the Rainbow_.

7. Tim Dean and I, working independently at around the same time, arrived at the same conclusion. In Dean's words, "we are all PWAs (Persons With AIDS) insofar as AIDS is structured, radically and precisely, as the unconscious real of the social field of contemporary America" (84). This claim could, of course, be extended outside the boundaries of this country.

8. Ellis Hanson writes against "essentialist representations of gay men as vampiric: as sexually exotic, alien, unnatural, oral, anal, compulsive, violent, protean, polymorphic, polyvocal, polysemous, invisible, soulless, transient, superhumanly mobile, infectious, murderous, suicidal, and a threat to wife, children, home, and phallus" ("Undead" 325). I don't deny the oppressiveness of these representations and the need to read them (out) carefully, but I assert that by seizing and coopting them for our own devious purposes, we queers make virtues out of vices. Psychoanalysis has familiarized itself with uncanny figures, of course, in terms of their sources in the unconscious. Kristeva, for example, in her moments of radical passivity, grapples with the "abject" as a sort of undead being: "an Other who precedes and possesses me, and through such possession causes me to be" (_Powers of Horror_ 10). Abjection makes a claim on the self that is both horrifying and seductive, disruptive and necessary. It slices through the I even as it makes the latter, in a sense, possible.

9. See Delany 21-38.

10. I agree with Bart Beaty that _Longtime Companion_ "relentlessly distracts it audience from the pressing need for collective action on the political front." But he ironically claims too much authority for the film as a prime example of American realism's fundamental complicity with hegemony ("The Syndrome is the System" 121). _Parting Glances_ may not incite us to take to the streets, but even as a (mostly) realist fiction it certainly privileges a mischievous _street_ rather than a mainstream _straight_ sensibility. Simon Watney, in an effort to rescue _Longtime Companion_ from hostile critics, praises what he construes as the film's realism, its narration of a "_collective experience_" (italics Watney's). He claims that the fantasy ending "works precisely on the

level of its cathartic release of long-pent-up emotions," despite his earlier deploring the "morality play" of AIDS. I shall allow Beaty and Watney to scuffle over the value of this film's realism. I fail to understand how *Longtime Companion* seriously concerns a collective experience, however, when it focuses so consistently on the experience of the monogamous survivor, haunting various kinds of collective experiences with fears about individual pain and suffering somehow eluded by the stars. See "Short-Term Companions" 157, 163, 154, respectively.

Works Cited

Acker, Kathy. *Don Quixote*. New York: Grove, 1986.

ACT UP/New York Women and AIDS Book Group. *Women, AIDS and Activism*. Boston: South End, 1990.

Alcorn, Keith. "AIDS in the Public Sphere: How a Broadcasting System in Crisis Dealt with an Epidemic." *Taking Liberties: AIDS and Cultural Politics*. Ed. Erica Carter and Simon Watney. London: Serpent's Tail, 1989. 193–212.

Althusser, Louis. "On Ideology." Trans. Ben Brewster. *Critical Theory Since 1965*. Ed. Hazard Adams and Leroy Searle. Tallahassee: Florida State University Press, 1986. 239–50.

———. *For Marx*. Trans. Ben Brewster. New York: Pantheon, 1969.

Altieri, Charles. "Wordsworth and the Options for Contemporary American Poetry." *The Romantics and Us: Essays on Literature and Culture*. Ed. Gene W. Ruoff. New Brunswick, N.J.: Rutgers University Press, 1990. 184–212.

Altman, Dennis. *AIDS in the Mind of America: The Social, Political, and Psychological Impact of a New Epidemic*. Garden City, N.Y.: Anchor, 1987.

Anderson, Laurie. *Bright Red/Tightrope*. Warner Bros. 9 45534-2. 1994.

Arac, Jonathan. "Wordsworth's 'Nutting': Suspension and Decision." *Critical Genealogies: Historical Situations for Postmodern Literary Studies*. New York: Columbia University Press, 1987. 34–49.

Araki, Gregg. *The Living End*. Strand Releasing/Desperate Films, 1992.

Art Works for AIDS. *Art Works for AIDS*. Exhibition Catalog. Seattle, 1990.

Attali, Jacques. *Noise: The Political Economy of Music*. Trans. Brian Massumi. Minneapolis: University of Minnesota Press, 1985.

Barth, John. *Lost in the Funhouse*. New York: Anchor, 1988.

Barthes, Roland. *The Pleasure of the Text*. Trans. Richard Miller. New York: Hill and Wang, 1975.

Bartlett, Neil. *Who Was That Man? A Present for Mr. Oscar Wilde*. London: Serpent's Tail, 1988.

Bataille, Georges. *Visions of Excess: Selected Writings, 1927–1939*. Ed. and trans. Allan Stoekl. Minneapolis: University of Minnesota Press, 1985.

Baudrillard, Jean. *Simulations*. Trans. Paul Foss, Paul Patton, and Philip Beitchaman. New York: Semiotext(e), 1983.

Beaty, Bart. "The Syndrome is the System: A Political Reading of *Longtime Companion*." *Fluid Exchanges: Artists and Critics in the AIDS Crisis*. Ed. James Miller. Toronto: University of Toronto Press, 1992. 111–21.

Beckett, Samuel. *Waiting for Godot*. New York: Grove, 1954.

Berg, Charles Merrell. "Philip Glass on Composing for Film and Other Forms: The Case of *Koyaanisqatsi*." *Writings on Glass: Essays, Interviews, Criticism*. Ed. Richard Kostelanetz and Robert Fleming. New York: Schirmer Books, 1997. 131–51.

Bernhard, Thomas. *Wittgenstein's Nephew: A Friendship*. Trans. David McClintock. Chicago: University of Chicago Press, 1988.

———. *Wittgensteins Neffe: Eine Freundschaft*. Frankfurt am Main: Suhrkamp, 1982.

Bersani, Leo. "Is the Rectum a Grave?" *AIDS: Cultural Analysis, Cultural Activism*. 197–222.

Blackwood, Michael, director. *A Composer's Notes: Philip Glass and the Making of an Opera*. Michael Blackwood Productions, 1990.

Blanchot, Maurice. "The Essential Solitude." *The Space of Literature*. Trans. Ann Smock. Lincoln: University of Nebraska Press, 1982.

———. *The Gaze of Orpheus and Other Literary Essays*. Ed. P. Adams Sitney. Trans. Lydia Davis. Barrytown, NY: Station Hill, 1981.

———. "Sade." *Marquis de Sade*. 1966. 37–72.

Bloom, Harold. *A Map of Misreading*. New York: Oxford University Press, 1975.

———. *The Ringers in the Tower: Studies in Romantic Tradition*. Chicago: University of Chicago Press, 1971a.

———. *The Visionary Company: A Reading of English Romantic Poetry*. Ithaca: Cornell University Press, 1971b.

Bové, Paul. "The Ineluctability of Difference: Scientific Pluralism and the Critical Intelligence." *Postmodernism and Politics.* Ed. Jonathan Arac. Minneapolis: University of Minnesota Press, 1987. 3–25.

Bulfinch, Thomas. *Mythology.* New York: Modern Library, n.d.

Butler, Judith. "The Force of Fantasy: Feminism, Mapplethorpe, and Discursive Excess." *differences* 2 (1990a): 105–25.

———. *Gender Trouble: Feminism and the Subversion of Identity.* New York: Routledge, 1990b.

Caramello, Charles. *Silverless Mirrors: Self and Postmodern American Fiction.* Tallahassee: University Press of Florida, 1983.

Case, Sue-Ellen. "Tracking the Vampire." *differences* 2 (1991): 1–20.

Coleridge, Samuel Taylor. *Biographia Literaria or Biographical Sketches of My Literary Life and Opinions.* Ed. George Watson. London: Dent, 1971.

Cooke, Michael G. *Acts of Inclusion: Studies Bearing on an Elementary Theory of Romanticism.* New Haven: Yale University Press, 1979.

Crawford, Rachel. "The Structure of the Sororal in Wordsworth's 'Nutting'." *Studies in Romanticism* 31 (1992): 197–211.

Crimp, Douglas with Adam Rolston. *AIDS Demo Graphics.* Seattle: Bay Press, 1990.

Crimp, Douglas. "AIDS: Cultural Analysis/Cultural Activism." *AIDS: Cultural Analysis, Cultural Activism.* 3–16.

———. "How to Have Promiscuity in an Epidemic." *AIDS: Cultural Analysis, Cultural Activism.* 237–71.

———. "Mourning and Militancy." *October* 51 (1989): 3–18.

———. "Pictures." *Art After Modernism.* Ed. Brian Wallis. New York: New Museum of Contemporary Art, 1984. 175–87.

———. "Right On, Girlfriend!" *Social Text* 33 (1992): 2–18.

———. ed. *AIDS: Cultural Analysis, Cultural Activism.* Cambridge: MIT, 1988.

Crompton, Louis. *Byron and Greek Love: Homophobia in 19th-Century England.* Berkeley: University of California Press, 1985.

Davis, Wade. *The Serpent and the Rainbow.* New York: Warner, 1985.

De Man, Paul. "The Rhetoric of Temporality." *Critical Theory since 1965.* Ed. Hazard Adams and Leroy Searle. Tallahassee: Florida State University Press, 1986. 199–222.

Delany, Samuel. "Street Talk/Straight Talk." *differences* 3 (1991): 21–38.

Deleuze, Gilles. *Difference and Repetition*. Trans. Paul Patton. New York: Columbia University Press, 1994.

———. *The Fold: Leibniz and the Baroque*. Trans. Tom Conley. Minneapolis: University of Minnesota Press, 1993.

Deleuze, Gilles and Félix Guattari. *Anti-Oedipus: Capitalism and Schizophrenia*. Trans. Robert Hurley, Mark Seem, and Helen R. Lane. Minneapolis: U of Minnesota P, 1983.

———. "How Do You Make Yourself a Body Without Organs?" *A Thousand Plateaus*. 149–66.

———. *A Thousand Plateaus: Capitalism and Schizophrenia*. Trans. Brian Massumi. Minneapolis: University of Minnesota Press, 1987.

———. *What Is Philosophy?* Trans. Hugh Tomlinson and Graham Burchell. New York: Columbia University Press, 1994.

Deleuze, Gilles and Claire Parnet. *Dialogues*. Trans. Hugh Tomlinson and Barbara Habberjam. New York: Columbia University Press, 1987.

Derrida, Jacques. "Jacques Derrida in Discussion with Christopher Norris." *Deconstruction: Omnibus Volume*. Ed. Andreas Papadakis, Catherine Cooke, and Andrew Benjamin. New York: Rizzoli, 1989. 71–74.

———. "Structure, Sign and Play in the Discourse of the Human Sciences." *Critical Theory since 1965*. Ed. Hazard Adams and Leroy Searle. Tallahassee: Florida State UP, 1986. 83–94.

———. "White Mythology." *Margins of Philosophy*. Trans. Alan Bass. Chicago: University of Chicago Press, 1982. 207–71.

———. *Of Grammatology*. Trans. Gayatri Chakravorty Spivak. Baltimore: Johns Hopkins University Press, 1976.

Dowden, Stephen D. *Understanding Thomas Bernhard*. Columbia: University of South Carolina Press, 1991.

Drinka, George Frederick. *The Birth of Neurosis: Myth, Malady and the Victorians*. New York: Touchstone, 1984.

Dryden, John. *Dryden. A Selection*. Ed. John Conaghan. London: Methuen, 1978.

Duesberg, Peter H. "Human Immunodeficiency Virus and Acquired Immunodeficiency Syndrome: Correlation but Not Causation." *The AIDS Reader: Social, Political, and Ethical Issues*. Ed. Nancy F. McKenzie. New York: Meridian, 1991. 42–73.

Eagleton, Terry. *Literary Theory: An Introduction.* Minneapolis: University of Minnesota Press, 1983.

Fee, Elizabeth and Daniel M. Fox, eds. *AIDS: The Burdens of History.* Berkeley: University of California Press, 1988.

Ferguson, Frances. *Wordsworth: Language as Counter-Spirit.* New Haven: Yale University Press, 1977.

Ferry, David. *The Limits of Mortality: An Essay on Wordsworth's Major Poems.* Middletown, Conn.: Wesleyan University Press, 1959.

Fleischer, Leonore. *Mary Shelley's Frankenstein.* New York: Signet, 1994.

Foster, Hal. "Re: Post." *Art after Modernism.* 189–201.

Foucault, Michel. *The Archaeology of Knowledge and The Discourse on Language.* Trans. A. M. Sheridan Smith. New York: Pantheon, 1972.

———. *The Birth of the Clinic: An Archaeology of Medical Perception.* Trans. A. M. Sheridan Smith. New York: Vintage, 1994.

———. "The Discourse of History." *Foucault Live.* 11–33.

———. "The Discourse on Language." *The Archaeology of Knowledge and The Discourse on Language.* 1972. 215–237.

———. "Fantasia of the Library." *Language, Counter-Memory, Practice.* 87–109.

———. *Foucault Live (Interviews, 1966–84).* Ed. Sylvère Lotringer. Trans. John Johnston. New York: Semiotext(e), 1989.

———. *A Foucault Reader.* Ed. Paul Rabinow. New York: Pantheon, 1984.

———. "Friendship as a Way of Life." *Foucault Live.* 203–10.

———. "A Historian of Culture." *Foucault Live.* 73–88.

———. *The History of Sexuality.* Vol. 1. Trans. Robert Hurley. New York: Random House, 1980.

———. *The History of Sexuality.* Vol. 2. *The Use of Pleasure.* Trans. Robert Hurley. New York: Random House, 1986.

———. "Language to Infinity." *Language, Counter-Memory, Practice.* 53–67.

———. *Language, Counter-Memory, Practice: Selected Essays and Interviews.* Ed. Donald F. Bouchard. Ithaca: Cornell University Press, 1977.

———. "The Masked Philosopher." *Foucault Live.* 193–202.

———. *The Order of Things: An Archaeology of the Human Sciences.* New York: Vintage, 1973.

———. *Power/Knowledge: Selected Interviews and Other Writings 1972–1977.* Ed. Colin Gordon. Trans. Colin Gordon et al. New York: Pantheon, 1980.

———. "A Preface to Transgression." *Language, Counter-Memory, Practice.* 29–52.

———. "Sexual Choice, Sexual Act." *Foucault Live.* 211–31.

———. "What Is an Author?" *The Foucault Reader.* 101–20.

Frampton, Kenneth. *Modern Architecture: A Critical History.* New York: Oxford University Press, 1980.

Freud, Sigmund. *Civilization and Its Discontents.* Trans. James Strachey. New York: Norton, 1962.

———. *Five Lectures on Psycho-Analysis.* Trans. James Strachey. New York: Norton, 1978.

———. *Totem and Taboo.* Trans. James Strachey. New York: Norton, 1989.

Gallop, Jane. *Reading Lacan.* Ithaca: Cornell University Press, 1985.

Galperin, William H. *Revision and Authority in Wordsworth: The Interpretation of a Career.* Philadelphia: University of Pennsylvania Press, 1989.

Gilbert, Sandra M. and Susan Gubar. *The Madwoman in the Attic: The Woman Writer and the Nineteenth-Century Literary Imagination.* New Haven: Yale University Press, 1979.

Glass, Philip. *1000 Airplanes on the Roof.* Various Musicians. Virgin 7 91065–2, 1989.

———. *Akhnaten.* Conductor Dennis Russell Davies. The Stuttgart State Opera Orch. and Chorus. Columbia M2K 42457, 1987.

———. *Dancepieces.* Various Musicians. Columbia MK 39539, 1982, 1987.

———. *Einstein on the Beach.* The Philip Glass Ensemble. CBS M4K 38875, 1979.

———. *Glassworks.* Various Musicians. CBS MK 37265, 1982.

———. *Koyaanisqatsi.* Various Musicians. Antilles 7 90626–2, 1983.

———. *Music by Philip Glass.* Ed. Robert T. Jones. New York: Harper & Row, 1987.

————. *Music in Twelve Parts.* The Philip Glass Ensemble. Virgin 91311–2, 1990.

————. *The Photographer.* Various Musicians. CBS MK 37849, 1983.

————. *Powaqqatsi.* Various Musicians. Elektra Nonesuch 9 79192-2, 1988.

————. *Songs from Liquid Days.* Various Musicians. Columbia MK 39564, 1986.

Godwin, William. *Caleb Williams.* Ed. David McCracken. New York: Norton, 1977.

Graham, Kenneth W. "The Gothic Unity of Godwin's *Caleb Williams.*" *Papers on Language and Literature: A Journal for Scholars and Critics of Language and Literature* 20 (1984): 47–59.

Griffiths, Paul. *Modern Music: The Avant Garde Since 1945.* New York: George Brazillier, 1981.

Gropius, Walter. *The New Architecture and the Bauhaus.* Trans. P. Morton Shand. Cambridge: MIT Press, 1981.

Grover, Jan Zita. "AIDS: Keywords." *AIDS: Cultural Analysis, Cultural Activism.* 17–30.

Guillory, John. "The Americanization of Michel Foucault." *LGSN* 20 (July 1993): 35–37.

Habermas, Jürgen. "Modernity—An Incomplete Project." *The Anti-Aesthetic: Essays on Postmodern Culture.* Ed. Hal Foster. Port Townsend, Wash.: Bay Press, 1983. 3–15.

Hagstrum, Jean H. *The Romantic Body: Love and Sexuality in Keats, Wordsworth, and Blake.* Knoxville: University of Tennessee Press, 1985.

Halperin, David. "Bringing Out Michel Foucault." *Salmagundi* 97 (1993): 69–93.

Hanson, Ellis. "Undead." *Inside/Out: Lesbian Theories, Gay Theories.* Ed. Diana Fuss. New York: Routledge, 1991. 324–40.

Haraway, Donna. "The Biopolitics of Postmodern Bodies: Determinations of Self in Immune System Discourse." *differences* 1 (1989): 3–43.

Hardt, Michael. *Gilles Deleuze: An Apprenticeship in Philosophy.* Minneapolis: University of Minnesota Press, 1993.

Hartman, Geoffrey H. "The State of the Art of Criticism." *The Future of Literary Theory.* Ed. Ralph Cohen. New York: Routledge, 1989. 86–101.

———. *Wordsworth's Poetry, 1787-1814*. New Haven: Yale University Press, 1964.

Hazlitt, William. "My First Acquaintance with Poets." *Selected Writings*. Ed. Ronald Blythe. Harmondsworth: Penguin, 1985 (1970). 43–65.

Heller, Scott. "New Foucault Biography Creates Scholarly Stir." *Chronicle of Higher Education* (September 30, 1992): A8, A13.

Holmes, Richard. *Coleridge: Early Visions*. New York: Viking, 1990.

Homans, Margaret. *Bearing the Word: Language and Female Experience in Nineteenth Century Women's Writing*. Chicago: University of Chicago Press, 1986.

———. "Eliot, Wordsworth, and the Scenes of the Sisters' Instruction." *Critical Inquiry* 8 (1981): 223–41.

Hutcheon, Linda. *A Poetics of Postmodernism: History, Theory, Fiction*. New York: Routledge, 1988.

———. *The Politics of Postmodernism*. London: Routledge, 1989.

Irigaray, Luce. *This Sex Which Is Not One*. Trans. Carolyn Burke. Ithaca: Cornell University Press, 1985.

Jacobs, Jane. *The Death and Life of Great American Cities*. New York: Modern Library, 1993 (1961).

Jameson, Frederic. "Postmodernism and Consumer Society." *Postmodernism and Its Discontents*. Ed. E. Ann Kaplan. London: Verso, 1988. 13–29.

———. "Postmodernism, or The Cultural Logic of Late Capitalism." *New Left Review* 146 (1984): 53–92.

———. *The Political Unconscious: Narrative as a Socially Symbolic Act*. Ithaca, NY: Cornell University Press, 1981.

Jarman, Derek. *At Your Own Risk: A Saint's Testament*. Woodstock, N.Y.: Overlook Press, 1993.

Jencks, Charles. *Post-Modernism: The New Classicism in Art and Architecture*. New York: Rizzoli, 1987.

———. *What Is Post-Modernism?* New York: St. Martin's Press, 1986.

Johnson, Barbara. "My Monster/My Self." *Diacritics* 12 (1982): 2–10.

Kelly, Gary. *The English Jacobin Novel, 1780–1805*. Oxford: Oxford University Press, 1976.

Kimball, Roger. "The Perversions of M. Foucault." *The New Criterion* II, 7 (1993): 10–18.

Koestenbaum, Wayne. "The Marinere Hath His Will[iam]: Wordsworth's and Coleridge's Lyrical Ballads." *Double Talk: The Erotics of Male Literary Collaboration.* New York: Routledge, 1989. 71–111.

Kristeva, Julia. "Women's Time." *Critical Theory Since 1965.* Ed. Hazard Adams and Leroy Searle. Tallahassee: Florida State University Press, 1986. 471–484.

———. *Powers of Horror: An Essay on Abjection.* Trans. Leon S. Roudiez. New York: Columbia University University Press, 1982.

Laborde, Alice M. *L'Oeuvre de Madame de Genlis.* Paris: Editions A.-G. Nizet, 1966.

Lacan, Jacques. "The Agency of the Letter in the Unconscious or Reason Since Freud." *Écrits.* 146–78.

———. "Aggressivity in Psychoanalysis." *Écrits.* 8–29.

———. *Écrits.* Trans. Alan Sheridan. New York: Norton, 1977.

———. "The Function and Field of Speech and Language in Psychoanalysis." *Écrits.* 30–113.

Laqueur, Thomas. *Making Sex: Body and Gender from the Greeks to Freud.* Cambridge: Harvard University Press, 1990.

Levin, Todd. *De Luxe.* Deutsche Grammophon. 445 847-2. 1995.

———. *Ride the Planet.* Various Musicians. Point Music 434 872-2, 1992.

Logie, Jacques. *Waterloo: L'évitable défaite.* Paris: Duculot, 1989.

London, Bette. "Mary Shelley, *Frankenstein,* and the Spectacle of Masculinity." *PMLA* 108 (1993): 253–67.

Lopate, Phillip. "On Not Reading Thomas Bernhard." *Pequod* 33 (1992): 72–83.

Lyotard, Jean-François. *Libidinal Economy.* Trans. Iain Hamilton Grant. Bloomington: Indiana University Press, 1993.

———. *The Postmodern Condition.* Trans. Geoffrey Bennington and Brian Massumi. Minneapolis: University of Minnesota Press, 1984.

Magnuson, Paul. *Coleridge and Wordsworth: A Lyrical Dialogue.* Princeton: Princeton University Press, 1988.

Massumi, Brian. *A User's Guide to Capitalism and Schizophrenia: Deviations from Deleuze and Guattari.* Cambridge: MIT Press, 1992.

McHale, Brian. *Postmodernist Fiction.* New York: Methuen, 1987.

Mertens, Wim. *American Minimal Music: La Monte Young, Terry Riley, Steve Reich, Philip Glass.* Trans. J. Hautekiet. New York: Alexander Broude, Inc., 1983.

Miller, D. A. "Sontag's Urbanity." *October* 49 (1989): 91–101.

Miller, James. *The Passion of Michel Foucault.* New York: Simon & Schuster, 1993a.

———. "Policing Discourse: A Response to David Halperin." *Salmagundi* 97 (1993b): 94–99.

Modiano, Raimonda. "Blood Sacrifice, Gift Economy and the Edenic World: Wordsworth's 'Home at Grasmere'." Unpublished manuscript.

———. *Coleridge and the Concept of Nature.* Tallahassee: Florida State University Press, 1985.

———. "Coleridge and Wordsworth: The Ethics of Gift Exchange and Literary Ownership." *Coleridge's Theory of Imagination Today.* Ed. Christine Gallant. New York: AMS Press, 1989. 243–56.

Moon, Michael. "Flaming Closets." *October* 51 (1989): 19–54.

Morton, Donald. "Birth of the Cyberqueer." *PMLA* 110, 3 (1995): 379–81.

National Academy of Sciences (Eve K. Nichols). *Mobilizing against AIDS: The Unfinished Story of a Virus.* Cambridge: Harvard University Press, 1986.

Nietzsche, Friedrich. *Twilight of the Idols* and *The Anti-Christ.* Trans. R. J. Hollingdale. Harmondsworth: Penguin, 1968.

Nitchie, Elizabeth. *Mary Shelley: Author of Frankenstein.* New Brunswick, N.J.: Rutgers University Press, 1953.

Oates, Joyce Carol. "Frankenstein's Fallen Angel." Mary Wollstonecraft Shelley, *Frankenstein* (Berkeley edition). 1984. 243–54.

Owens, Craig. "The Allegorical Impulse: Toward a Theory of Postmodernism." Parts 1 and 2. *Beyond Recognition: Representation, Power, and Culture.* Ed. Scott Bryson et al. Berkeley: University of California Press, 1992. 52–87.

———. "*Einstein on the Beach*: The Primacy of Metaphor." Owens, *Beyond Recognition,* 3–15.

Patton, Cindy. *Inventing AIDS.* New York: Routledge, 1990.

———. "Public Enemy: Fundamentalist in Your Face." *The Village Voice Literary Supplement* (February 1993): 17–18.

Perkins, David. *Wordsworth and the Poetry of Sincerity.* Cambridge: Harvard University Press, 1964.

Philp, Mark. *Godwin's Political Justice*. London: Duckworth, 1986.

Pinch, Adela. "Female Chatter: Meter, Masochism, and the Lyrical Ballads." *English Literary History* 55 (1988): 835–52.

Pipkin, James W. "Wordsworth's 'Nutting' and Rites of Initiation." *Interpretations* 10 (1978): 11–19.

Poe, Edgar Allan. "The Philosophy of Composition." *Essays and Reviews*. New York: Library of America, 1984. 13–25.

Polin, Burton Ralph. "Philosophical and Literary Sources of *Frankenstein*." *Comparative Literature* 17 (1965): 97–108.

———. *Education and Enlightenment in the Works of William Godwin*. New York: Las Americas Publishing Company, 1962.

Poovey, Mary. *The Proper Lady and the Woman Writer: Ideology as Style in the Works of Mary Wollstonecraft, Mary Shelley, and Jane Austen*. Chicago: University of Chicago Press, 1984.

Pynchon, Thomas. *The Crying of Lot 49*. New York: Harper and Row, 1966.

Ragland-Sullivan, Ellie. "The Sexual Masquerade: A Lacanian Theory of Sexual Difference." *Lacan and the Subject of Language*. Ed. Ellie Ragland-Sullivan and Mark Bracher. New York: Routledge, 1991. 49–80.

Rajan, Tilottama. "Wollstonecraft and Godwin: Reading the Secrets of the Political Novel." *Studies in Romanticism* 27 (1988): 221–51.

Rajchman, John. *Truth and Eros: Foucault, Lacan, and the Question of Ethics*. New York: Routledge, 1991.

Random House Dictionary of the English Language. 2nd. ed. New York: Random House, 1987.

Reed, Mark L. *Wordsworth: The Chronology of the Early Years, 1770–1799*. Cambridge: Harvard University Press, 1967.

Reggio, Godfrey, director. *Koyaanisqatsi: Life Out of Balance*. Zoetrope Studios, 1983.

Reich, Steve. *Writings about Music*. Halifax: Press of the Nova Scotia College of Art and Design, 1974.

Reiman, Donald H. *Percy Bysshe Shelley*. 2nd. ed. New York: Twayne, 1990.

René, Norman, director. *Longtime Companion*. Companion Productions, 1990.

Rich, B. Ruby. "Top Girl." *The Village Voice* (October 1991): 29–33.

Rockwell, John. *All American Music: Composition in the Late Twentieth Century.* New York: Vintage, 1984.

Rothstein, Eric. *Systems of Order and Inquiry in Later Eighteenth-Century Fiction.* Berkeley: University of California Press, 1975.

Rousseau, Jean-Jacques. *Oeuvres Complètes.* Paris: Gallimard, 1961.

Sacher-Masoch, Leopold von. *Venus in Furs.* New York: Zone, 1989.

Sade, Marquis de. *Justine, Philosophy in the Bedroom, Eugénie de Franval, and Other Writings.* Trans. Richard Seaver and Austryn Wainhouse. New York: Grove, 1966.

Said, Edward W. *Beginnings: Intention and Method.* New York: Columbia University Press, 1985.

Scarry, Elaine. *The Body in Pain: The Making and Unmaking of the World.* New York: Oxford University Press, 1985.

Schaefer, John. *New Sounds: A Listener's Guide to New Music.* New York: Harper & Row, 1987.

Scheiber, Andrew J. "Falkland's Story: Caleb Williams' Other Voice." *Studies in the Novel* 17 (1985): 255–66.

Schrader, Paul, director. *Mishima: A Life in Four Chapters.* Zoetrope Studios, 1985.

Shaviro, Steven. "Masculinity, Spectacle, and the Body of *Querelle.*" *The Cinematic Body.* Minneapolis: University of Minnesota Press, 1993. 159–98.

———. *Passion and Excess: Blanchot, Bataille, and Literary Theory.* Tallahassee: Florida State University Press, 1990.

Shelley, Mary Wollstonecraft. *Frankenstein or The Modern Prometheus.* Ed. James Rieger. Chicago: University of Chicago Press, 1982.

———. *Frankenstein; or, The Modern Prometheus* ("The Pennyroyal *Frankenstein*"). Berkeley: University of California Press, 1984.

———. *Frankenstein; or, The Modern Prometheus.* Ed. Maurice Hindle. Harmondsworth: Penguin, 1985.

———. *The Last Man.* Ed. Hugh J. Luke, Jr. Lincoln: University of Nebraska Press, 1965.

———. *Mathilda.* Ed. Elizabeth Nitchie. Chapel Hill: University of North Carolina Press, 1959.

Shelley, Percy Bysshe. *Shelley's Prose or The Trumpet of a Prophecy.* Ed. David Lee Clark. New York: New Amsterdam, 1988.

————. *Shelley's Poetry and Prose.* Ed. Donald H. Reiman and Sharon B. Powers. New York: Norton, 1977.

Sherwood, Bill, director. *Parting Glances.* Rondo Productions, 1986.

Shilts, Randy. *And The Band Played On: Politics, People, and the AIDS Epidemic.* New York: St. Martin's, 1987.

Simms, Karl N. "Caleb Williams' Godwin: Things as They Are Written." *Studies in Romanticism* 26 (1987): 343–63.

Small, Christopher. *Mary Shelley's Frankenstein.* Pittsburgh: University of Pittsburgh Press, 1973.

Smith, Bruce R. *Homosexual Desire in Shakespeare's England: A Cultural Poetics.* Chicago: University of Chicago Press, 1991.

Smith, Elton Edward and Esther Greenwell Smith. *William Godwin.* New York: Twayne, 1965.

Smith, Paul. *Discerning the Subject.* Minneapolis: University of Minnesota Press, 1988.

Solomon-Godeau, Abigail. "Photography after Art Photography." *Art after Modernism.* 75–85.

Sontag, Susan. *AIDS and Its Metaphors.* New York: Farrar, Straus and Giroux, 1989.

Spark, Muriel. *Mary Shelley.* London: Constable, 1988.

Spivak, Gayatri Chakravorty. "Three Women's Texts and a Critique of Imperialism." *Critical Inquiry* 12 (1985): 243–61.

Stearns, David Patrick. "Pop Goes the Composer." *BBC Music Magazine* (February 1993): 10.

Stoekl, Allan. Introduction to Bataille ix–xxv.

Tamm, Eric. *Brian Eno: His Music and the Vertical Color of Sound.* Boston: Faber and Faber, 1989.

Tarasti, Eero. "Le minimalisme du point de vue sémiotique." *Degrés: Revue de Synthèse à Orientation Sémiologique* 53 (1988): 1–22.

Treichler, Paula. "AIDS, Gender, and Biomedical Discourse: Current Contests for Meaning." *AIDS: The Burdens of History.* 190–266.

Tysdahl, B. J. *William Godwin as Novelist.* London: Athlone, 1981.

Vickers, Nancy J. "Diana Described: Scattered Woman and Scattered Rhyme." *Writing and Sexual Difference.* Ed. Elizabeth Abel. Chicago: University of Chicago Press, 1982. 95–110.

Walling, William A. *Mary Shelley.* New York: Twayne, 1972.

Walton, James. "*Mad Feary Father*": *Caleb Williams* and the Novel Form." *Salzburg Studies in English Literature* 47 (1975): 1–61.

Warren, Leland E. "*Caleb Williams* and the 'Fall' into Writing." *Mosaic: A Journal for the Interdisciplinary Study of Literature* 20 (1987): 57–69.

Watney, Simon. "Short-Term Companions: AIDS as Popular Entertainment." *A Leap in the Dark: AIDS, Art and Contemporary Cultures.* Ed. Allan Klusacek and Ken Morrison. Montreal: Véhicule, 1992. 152–66.

———. *Policing Desire: Pornography, AIDS and the Media.* 2nd. ed. Minneapolis: University of Minnesota Press, 1989.

Webster, Sarah McKim. "Circumscription and the Female in the Early Romantics." *Philological Quarterly* 61 (1982): 51–68.

Wehrs, Donald R. "Rhetoric, History, Rebellion: *Caleb Williams* and the Subversion of Eighteenth-Century Fiction." *Studies in English Literature, 1500–1900* 28 (1988): 497–511.

Werckmeister, O.K. *Citadel Culture.* Chicago: The University of Chicago Press, 1989.

Wilde, Oscar. *The Picture of Dorian Gray.* Ed. Donald L. Lawler. New York: Norton, 1988.

Williams, Ioan, ed. *Novel and Romance, 1700–1800: A Documentary Record.* New York: Barnes & Noble, 1970.

Winters, Yvor. *The Function of Criticism: Problems and Exercises.* London: Routledge & Kegan Paul, 1962.

Wlecke, Albert O. *Wordsworth and the Sublime.* Berkeley: University of California Press, 1973.

Wojnarowicz, David. *Close to the Knives: A Memoir of Disintegration.* New York: Vintage, 1991.

Wolfe, Tom. *From Bauhaus to Our House.* New York: Farrar Straus Giroux, 1981.

Wordsworth, William. *The Oxford Authors William Wordsworth.* Ed. Stephen Gill. Oxford: Oxford University Press, 1984.

———. *The Prelude: 1799, 1805, 1850.* Ed. Jonathan Wordsworth, M.H. Abrams, and Stephen Gill. New York Norton, 1979.

———. *Poetical Works.* Ed. Thomas Hutchinson. Rev. Ernest de Selincourt. Oxford: Oxford University Press, 1969.

Wordsworth, William and Samuel Taylor Coleridge. *Lyrical Ballads.* Ed. Michael Mason. London: Longman, 1992.

Index

Abraham, Nicolas, 173n.26
Acker, Kathy, 139
AIDS, xv, xvii–xviii, xix, xxii,
    57, 73–74, 81–82, 84, 141–
    62 *passim*, 165, 177n.3,
    184–86nn.1–10
Alcorn, Keith, 184–85n.3
Althusser, Louis, 119–20, 137–38
Altieri, Charles, xix, 8
Anderson, Laurie, xi, xii, 119,
    183n.18
Arabian Nights, The, 128
Arac, Jonathan, 8, 19, 168n.4,
    172n.24
Araki, Gregg (*The Living End*),
    57–58, 144, 145, 157, 159–61
Aristotle, 174n.5
Ashe, Arthur, 73–74
Attali, Jacques, 121, 184n.18

Bach, P. D. Q., 122
Barnfield, Richard, 167–68n.3
Barth, John, xxii, 61, 100,
    182nn.15–16
    "Frame-Tale," 119, 126–30
    passim, 137
Barthes, Roland, 12, 47–48,
    68–69, 80, 94, 120, 124,
    138, 139
Bartlett, Neil, 178n.9
Bataille, Georges, xix, 12, 14,
    19, 63, 78, 95, 169n.8,
    170n.11
    The Accursed Share, 65

Bateson, Gregory, 180n.13
Baudrillard, Jean, 94, 96, 127,
    174n.8
Beaty, Bart, 185n.10
Beckett, Samuel, 77, 129,
    171n.14
Beethoven, Ludwig van
    (*Fidelio*), 55
Bentham, Jeremy, 9
Berg, Charles Merrill, 118
Bernhard, Thomas, xxii, 61,
    182n.17
    Wittgenstein's Nephew, 130–37
    passim, 184n.20
Bersani, Leo, 145
    "Is the Rectum a Grave?",
    81–83, 147–48, 149, 150
Bizet, Georges (*Carmen*),
    177n.3
Blake, William, 37
Blanchot, Maurice, xxii, 30,
    80, 91, 175n.16
    "The Essential Solitude," 46
    "Sade," 45–48
    "Two Versions of the Imagi-
    nary," 47
Bloom, Harold, 3, 7, 16, 30,
    56, 110, 111, 167n.2,
    168n.4
Bofill, Angelo, 111
Bondarchuk, Sergei (*Waterloo*),
    85–86
Boone, Bruce, 170n.11
Boswell, John, 81
Boulez, Pierre, xxi, 110, 121

201